RAVE REVIEWS FOR
YUL

"Poignant and colorful . . . This is no *Daddy Dearest*."
—Liz Smith, New York *Daily News*

"The imperious Yul Brynner, who is destined to be remembered as the King of Siam, was apparently also king of the bedrooms." —*Washington Post*

"A wonderful biography!" —Larry King, *USA Today*

"If Rock Brynner's story is universal, it is also unique, for Yul Brynner's only son had a father that was like no other . . . Rock Brynner emerges as both a sympathetic figure and a sensitive writer in a book that is considerably more ambitious and complex than most Hollywood biographies."
—*Chicago Sun-Times*

"With heartfelt emotion and with surprising skill, the younger Brynner unmasks his actor-father . . . This is a polished, affecting book by a talented writer." —*Booklist*

"You won't be able to put it down—it will tear your heart out."
—Liza Minnelli

Continued . . .

"And I thought I knew Yul very well. Now I know I didn't begin to know him until I read Rock's book. What a fascinating story!"
—Kirk Douglas

"Deep-cutting bio of Yul Brynner by his son, Rock, told lovingly throughout—until the son's brilliant post-mortem lays the king open for a tougher kind of love . . . Rock gets in the last word, with an analysis of Yul's character that in its devastating honesty is a tribute to the father and now frees Rock celebrate him."
—*Kirkus*

"A biography of great quality and compelling honesty, obviously written from the heart . . . I cannot think of any show business biography which comes nearer to illuminating the mystery of what makes a star, and which explores the raw nerve ends of a star's personality with such skill . . . Moving . . . passionate . . . authentic."
—Bryan Forbes, director

"Loving, honest . . . adventure-packed . . . What really elevates this book a cut above others in the tell-all genre are the poignant personal moments between father and son. Sometimes painful, sometimes funny and often bittersweet . . . these moments reveal a universal story of the complex, conflict-filled relationships that exist between all fathers and sons."
—*Atlanta Journal & Constitution*

YUL

THE MAN WHO WOULD BE KING

A Memoir of Father and Son

by

Rock Brynner

BERKLEY BOOKS, NEW YORK

This Berkley book contains the complete text of the original hardcover
edition. It has been completely reset in a typeface designed for easy
reading and was printed from new film.

YUL: THE MAN WHO WOULD BE KING

A Berkley Book / published by arrangement with
Simon & Schuster

PRINTING HISTORY
Simon & Schuster edition published 1989
Berkley edition / February 1991

ISBN: 0-425-12547-5

A BERKLEY BOOK ® TM 757,375
Berkley Books are published by The Berkley Publishing Group,
200 Madison Avenue, New York, New York 10016.
The name ''Berkley'' and the ''B'' logo
are trademarks belonging to Berkley Publishing Corporation.

PRINTED IN THE UNITED STATES OF AMERICA

10 9 8 7 6 5 4 3 2 1

Acknowledgments

My thanks to all the poets I've plundered, including the writers and photographers acknowledged below. The author and publisher have made every effort to acknowledge all source material appropriately and to secure permission from copyright holders where required. We are grateful for permission to use quotations from the following:

Chet Atkins, "I Still Can't Say Goodbye," © 1986 by Bob Lynn and James Moore. Used by permission of Captain Kidd Music. All rights reserved; Peter H. Brown and Jim Pinkston, *Oscar Dearest*, © 1987 Perennial Library. Used by permission of Harper & Row. All rights reserved; Hoagy Carmichael and Sidney Arodin, "Lazy River," © 1931. Used by permission of Peer International Organization. All rights reserved; e. e. cummings, "no man,if men are gods:but if gods must," reprinted from *Complete Poems 1913–1962* by permission of Granada Publishing, © 1944 the Trustees for the E. E. Cummings Trust. Copyright © 1961, 1963, 1968 by Marion Morehouse Cummings. All rights reserved; Ronald Harwood, *The Dresser*, © 1981. Used by permission from Amber Lane Press. All rights reserved; Blake Alphonso Higgs (Blind Blake), Hollis Music Inc., © 1941. Used by permission. All rights reserved; Marianne Moore, "Rescue with Yul Brynner," © 1966. Used by permission of Viking Penguin. All rights reserved; John Mortimer, *A Voyage Round My Father*, © 1971. Used by permission from Margaret Ramsay Ltd. All rights reserved; Randall Riese and Neal Hitchens, *The Unabridged Marilyn*, © 1987 by RGA Publishing Group, Congdon and Weed. Used by permission. All rights reserved; Jhan Robbins, *Yul Brynner—The Inscrutable King*, Dodd, Mead, 1987. Used by permission from Dodd, Mead. All rights reserved; Robbie Robertson, from "Broken Arrow," © 1988 MEDICINE HAT MUSIC. All Rights Controlled and Administered by EMI APRIL MUSIC INC. All rights reserved. International Copyright Secured. Used by permission.

For use of photographs, we are grateful to the following: no. 1, Betty Furness; final picture, Editta Sherman; nos. 13, 14, 16, 18, 22, 26, 30 and 35, UPI/Bettmann Newsphotos; no. 19, Eric Carpenter, *Life Magazine*, © 1958 Time Inc. Turner Entertainment Co.; no. 20, *Newsweek Magazine*, © 1958; no. 21, John Bryson; no. 25, Marv Newton, Garrett Howard Inc.; no. 27, Ruan O'Lochlainn; no. 28, Wide World; no. 29, Angelo Dundee; no. 31, Elisabeth Coleman; nos. 33 and 34, Henry Grossman; Inge Morath, for the two unnumbered photographs of Yul and Rock, playing darts and water-skiing. Nos. 2, 3, 4, 5, 6, 7, 8, 9, 10, 11, 12, 15, 17, 23, 24, 32, and the unnumbered photographs of Yul and Rock, excluding the two by Inge Morath listed above, are all from the Rock Brynner collection.

for the grandchildren of

Yul and Virginia

waiting to be born

Contents

Illustrations

no man,if men are gods;but if gods must
be men,the sometimes only man is this
(most common,for each anguish is his grief;
and,for his joy is more than joy,most rare)

a fiend,if fiends speak truth;if angels burn

by their own generous completely light,
an angel;or(as various worlds he'll spurn
rather than fail immeasurable fate)
coward,clown,traitor,idiot,dreamer,beast—

such was a poet and shall be and is

—who'll solve the depths of horror to defend
a sunbeam's architecture with his life:
and carve immortal jungles of despair
to hold a mountain's heartbeat in his hand

e.e. cummings

PART ONE

"Mr. Brynner is, quite simply, The King. Man and role have long since merged into a fixed image that is as much a part of our collective consciousness as the Statue of Liberty."

—Frank Rich, *New York Times*

Prologue

"Yul Brynner must be mad to imagine that he
could be Yul Brynner."
                                —Jean Cocteau

*Well, here it is, you old rogue elephant: the mystery of your
origins and the paradox of your career, revealed by your only
son. But this is not only your story, it is also the story of my
life with you, because I am the wax in which you left your
deepest impression.*

*When I was a little boy I spent many nights sitting in a dark,
hushed theater filled with grown-ups weeping as they watched
the death of the King, and I tried to imagine how your life
would really end. We used to laugh about the book I'd write
someday, recounting your adventures—this very book. Little
could we have guessed exactly how this story would conclude.*

*I held your hand as you died, Father: it was as close as I
will ever come to experiencing my own mortality. Since that
night you have challenged me, with all the terrible energy of
the dead, to make sense of your farflung odyssey, weaving
together the truths that only you and I knew about your life.
And so I climbed my mountain alone, and for a hundred nights
I shouted thoughts beyond the reaches of our souls, until my
lungs almost burst; but you were not there. Then I cursed you
long and loud, shouting, "Damn your dust, Yul Brynner. Do
you hear me? Damn your dust!" And a thousand nights I wept.*

That's OK, Dad. Everything is OK now.

* * *

3

It was in the unfolding of your life that I found the answers I have sought all along this crooked mile: in the story of your childhood there is much that explains my own. I have tried to experience your life as you did, year upon year, without knowing what would happen next. Gradually, events that once had seemed like a series of accidents began fusing together like parts of a plot, and as that plot unfolded, what emerged was a parable of power.

Yes, Father, you became King. Six days a week for almost fifteen years you demonstrated your command of the theater. Eight million loyal subjects came to your kingdom to pay homage. The final night of your reign came thirty-four years after the first: few real monarchs last so long. You were King all right, but at such a fearsome cost that no one could envy the Faustian deal you had made with yourself. Ultimately, the price of that ersatz royalty was everything else you held dear. Because all the power you had amassed could not control the terrible consequences of your own arrogance, and all the validation in the world was not enough to satisfy your hunger for praise. This, then, is the story of how a man became an artist, how the artist became King, and how the King became a slave to his own ego.

Old man, I loved you as only your son could. The whole world admired you, but I admired you more. "Yul Brynner's son": for years this mixed blessing was the central fact of my existence. Truly, I have been among the most fortunate people ever born; but I could not survive as an appendage of your persona, and therefore I was bound to disappoint you. For that you never really forgave me. Forgiveness was never exactly your forte. Suffering fools gladly was not your specialty, either, and much of my life I have been a fool—I freely confess that at the outset.

You regarded your only son as the extension of your own soul into the next generation: when I was a child, you loved me the same way you loved yourself. But when it came time to tear myself free from your kingdom, it seemed to you as if your own right arm was rebelling against your authority. I could not hope to survive without an identity; not sober, any-

way. Neither could I inherit your power, for we must each make our own.

What was the source of your power, and what was its impact on your life? Did your power bring you happiness, or take it away? This is all big game, even for a practiced hunter. But to examine your amazing life from my vantage-point I must aim high, knowing that if I miss I may scar myself for the rest of time. Of course, there is much in our lives and our friends' lives that I would not write about, out of a taste for discretion as much as a distaste for litigation. No doubt I am revealing much more than you would like: so be it. This book does not tell all: it says what needs to be said. Neither I nor anyone who is reading can judge your soul and all its epic contradictions, but I am compelled to assess your achievements and your failures, in order to get on with my own. You played the hand you were dealt, and it was not a very promising one. With single-mindedness bordering on monomania, as well as with the luck of the draw, you turned that hand into a winner. Like other mortals, when you bluffed, you usually paid a terrible price.

Must there always be a period of conflict between generations, expressed or repressed? Why do parents and children confront each other head-on over the very qualities they share? Our clashes lasted more than a decade before we reached an uneasy truce. Whatever subject we began with, we usually ended up arguing about your right, and the Divine Right of the chosen few, to overlook such fundamental principles of behavior as the Golden Rule. And at the center of all our duels was whether the hand you dealt me was mine to play, or yours.

Alas, Father, though you wished it so, there is no perfect arithmetic of the spirit, no zero-sum morality. Our transgressions cannot be ignored because of the magnitude of our virtues, and moral complexities cannot be willed into simplicities, even by the toughest gunslinger. In the sloppy, imperfect domain of human affairs, relativism prevails and paradoxes abound. Generosity is repaid with resentment, our loved ones always hurt us the most, and there are liars in public places. Throughout our lives we watch aghast as monsters mimic morality, while saints commit atrocities.

'Tis a puzzlement.

* * *

For some twenty years I was your son, your sidekick and your Sancho Panza; that means I learned a thing or two about mending windmills. Living at the edge of your volcano, physically and psychologically, I had to know what was on your mind. So I make no apology for asserting the thoughts and motives behind your adventures: you always made damn sure I knew what you were thinking. It was important to you that your son understood the decisions you made. Growing up with a father who boasted frankly that he had an ego as big as your average-sized aircraft-carrier, I learned a million things I probably would have never discovered otherwise. Most of those lessons have not been especially useful in the world of real people and real problems; still, they were lessons well-learned. As Mark Twain put it, "Anyone who's held a bull by the tail knows four or five things more than someone who hasn't."

If I seem to know your weaknesses especially well, it is because I share them all. Your talent is gone for ever, but most of your faults are alive and well, Father, right here with me. I did not inherit your power: just the arrogance that went with it. I've failed myself far more than you failed me.

So this narrative must serve as our legacy. For more than forty years the world has speculated about your origins. That is because you lied to every major publication in the world. The saga of our family was dramatic enough, set in the culture of Dr. Zhivago, to the music of Tchaikovsky, then flung to every corner of the globe. Now, for your grandchildren, and their grandchildren, the truth. Of course, they will know you from your films, but that was only a small part of the whole adventure. And besides, that was not you: it was the King of Siam, or Dimitri Karamazov, or Rameses, Pharaoh of all Egypt. Lest, in your absence, we lose sight of the distinction.

One day, Father, our eyes will meet again, wearing different faces. That day will come. And I will meet you by the witness-tree . . .

1

Oriental Enigma

"[To] gypsies, reality is often the exact opposite of appearance . . . When approached directly, they show a total disregard for consistency . . ."
—Jan Yoors, *The Gypsies*

Silence.

In that silence imagine all the magic of fire, its shafts rising to spike the black hood of night. You can see the great bonfire for a hundred miles—*shalmi versti*—dancing against the naked horizon as it lofts cinders like fireworks with every towering draft. Before you come close enough to feel its heat, you can hear the gypsies' guitars, and feel their power in the air.

Every summer the Tziganes gathered beside this river to hold court and settle feuds, to trade jewels, gold and horses, and to elect their leader, anointed as if royalty. All through the boastful night, alive with brandy and brawling, the men exchanged their yarns and challenges. Later, the women would welcome them to their tents with fiery whispers.

But, early on this summer night, the women gathered around the most beautiful girl in the *kumpania*. Her labor had already begun, so her sisters lashed her to a tree trunk, as is customary for delivering a first-born. Her name was Mara, and she kept her eyes fixed on the moon, round and full as her straining belly. At last, she cried out once, and her son was born directly upon the earth, before anyone had even touched him. Swiftly the cord was cut with a Cossack dagger, won in battle, and, as the manchild exhaled his first breath, the bonfire flickered and expired. An ember leaped past his shoulder, and burned the letters *YUL* into his skin; from the people, a cheer rose up

7

to the heavens. Then, baptizing the magical infant in the music of his people, a low, dark voice began to sing: "*Okonchen poots . . .*"

If Yul could have invented his own birth, it might have gone something like that. He would have created himself from thin air, had it only been possible. Through parthenogenesis or some mystical process, he would have had himself erupt from the molten core of the planet, with lava for afterbirth. Frankly, in the polite, repressed atmosphere of the 1950s when his stardom began, he might just as well have come from Mars. At a time when America was acting as if it was one big PTA meeting, Yul Brynner almost constituted a new species. Even his name was a mystery: one cannot confidently guess from which continent those three syllables emerged, for it is neither European nor Oriental. This enigmatic name was the providential first component in Yul's power of self-invention. Then the brightness of his stardom made an opaque riddle of his early life, and cast a shadow across our ancestors. This is also their story, as told by those who knew Yul's grandfather, Jules: it was with his adventurous departure from our Swiss ancestral village that the Brynner odyssey began.

Some time in the 1840s, Dr. Johann Bryner married a young girl named Verena Linck in their hamlet of Möriken-Wildegg, near Zurich. By the late 1840s their sixth child, Jules, had been born. While the family was Swiss-German, and well-educated, it was also poor: the practice of medicine was experimental at best, and the local doctor of a small village was not a wealthy man. According to remnants of family legend, it seems Johann and Verena were unable to afford their youngest son an education. But Jules was not eager for classroom learning, he hungered for adventure, and set out, determined to see the world beyond those landlocked, mountainous vistas. He never looked back, and never lived there again. An independent spirit, Jules was able to sever all emotional bonds to his family, and cut himself off completely from his past. He was fourteen years old.

In the nineteenth century pirates roamed the seas from the North African shoreline to the Orient. Their swift-sailing schooners with bellying canvas preyed upon the valuable cargoes of ships from the Orient: silk from China, spices from Japan, silver from Manchuria. It was in the galley of a pirate ship that Jules found work. The captain took the boy on and befriended him, promising to deliver him safely to Japan. Periodically, though, during the many months of travel, the pirates would lock young Jules in the galley without explanation. For hours he would sit with the cook, listening to the thunder of cannon above, and the murderous mayhem of search and plunder. Later, with the rest of the crew, he would swab the blood from the decks.

Jules was sixteen when the schooner arrived off the coast of Japan, near Yokohama. In America, the Civil War was just ending. Members of the small community of European merchants in and about Yokohama found Jules a job as clerk to an elderly English gentleman who ran his own export company, mostly from his desktop. In a few months Jules became indispensable and, within a year or two, he was accepted almost as a son. When the Englishman died, Jules became a wealthy and powerful fellow, responsible for a small shipping empire, with offices in ports throughout the Orient. He renamed it the Bryner Company. In only a decade the young adventurer had moved from a life of poverty in Möriken-Wildegg to prosperity in Japan. He married and had children. Jules Bryner had already lived a full life, but it was only beginning.

A few years later, Jules left Japan and abandoned his family there—again, without looking back. He travelled to nearby Vladivostok in the Russian Orient, to expand his enterprises. Vladivostok was a cultured if provincial outpost and Jules soon became a well-respected local figure. He remained there for the rest of his life. Ignoring his earlier marriage, Jules married Natalia Kurkutova, the daughter of a Mongolian prince. Few ever spoke well of her, it seems. Her brother, the Chief Justice of Vladivostok, was widely loved for his sensitivity and compassion: Natalia was not. Whatever qualities she possessed that attracted Jules, an affectionate and subservient nature was not among them. In their photographs, Jules appears more sensitive and refined than the stern, stocky Natalia, whose ancestors were said to be descended from Genghis Khan.

Natalia and Yuli Ivanovich (as Jules was now called) had six children. Their large house on Svetlanskaya Street came alive with the muted joy of children playing within earshot of a hostile matriarch and an often absent patriarch. Natalia seems to have preferred her sons to her daughters; her favorite was Boris, the most handsome.

When they graduated from *gymnasium,* Jules sent all three sons to university in St. Petersburg, now Leningrad: Switzerland was not even considered. There, Boris studied mineralogical engineering, with a view to taking charge of the silver mines that belonged to the family business on the island of Tetuhe, in Siberia. And it was there that he fell in love with Marousia Blagavidova, the daughter of a Russian doctor who also lived in Vladivostok. The Blagavidovs, though not wealthy folk like the Bryners, were members of the modern intelligentsia. Marousia's father Dimitri was the son of a Jew named Shary, who had taken the name Blagavidov upon his conversion to Orthodoxy.

Boris and Marousia were an attractive couple. Boris was self-centered, willful, with absolutely no ability to manage money, and a number of engineering schemes that sounded downright dreamy. One of his later inventions, however, proved very valuable to the Chinese: a sort of pressboard for light construction that could be made cheaply from vegetable fibers. Marousia, a pretty girl with a sweet soprano voice and a sophisticated sense of humor, had almost completed her studies at the Conservatory of St. Petersburg, when Boris insisted that he could not tolerate having a wife who was an actress. With lasting regret, Marousia renounced her acting career for the sake of marriage. They were married in 1914 in St. Petersburg, where their daughter was born two years later. They christened her Vera Bryner. Soon after, they returned to Vladivostok and settled in the Bryner compound of flats, where Marousia was subjected to her mother-in-law's wrath.

Boris's brother Felix caused their mother further distress by marrying Marousia's sister, Vera. But events sweeping across Russia soon dwarfed this unpleasantness. Felix accepted a commission as a white officer, to fight the Bolshevik revolution.

In fact, by 1917 Felix was keeping the peace in Petrograd when he tugged a hot-blooded speaker, Vladimir Ilyich Lenin, from a makeshift podium.

On July 11, 1920, in the presence of her sister, Marousia gave birth to a son. She and Boris Yulievich agreed to name the child Yul, after the family patriarch. Jules lived just long enough to see his grandson Yul christened in the Russian Orthodox church. Felix and his wife and their baby daughter Irena had also settled in Vladivostok, in close proximity to the explosive Natalia, who hated the two sisters who had married her sons with a furor that is hard to explain. The old matron spent all her days with her beloved parrot, who called her "Mama," and for months Natalia taught the parrot to shout "Blagavidova looks like a skinned ferret!" She even tried training the bird to fly into the flat of one of the sisters. Instead, to her dismay, the parrot settled for several days on a perch outside Natalia's window, screeching, "Mama looks like a skinned ferret!"

When I was growing up, my mother and I often walked across the campus of Columbia University to the playgrounds on Riverside Drive, and sometimes it dimly occurred to me how very different your childhood was from mine: so different, it seemed, that no comparisons could be drawn at all, and no lessons inferred. When I was seven, you described to me how a Cossack might ride all day, then cut a steak from his horse's flank for lunch—and ride on till sunset. I knew this was not approved practice at the Claremont Riding Academy near Central Park West.

But strange as you were, I belonged to that strangeness. In some very immediate way I was a part of that exotic background, just as it was part of me, and so I acquainted myself with my heritage the best I could, through the sound of all its languages—gypsy songs, Chinese proverbs, Russian names, French poetry, British vowels. But most of all, it was the songs of the Tziganes, which you sang at every party. I would awake at night to this most powerful, soulful sound—a sort of melodic grief, or tuneful wailing. I would burst in upon the grown-ups before the first song ended. Those songs represented all the ancestors I would ever know—because that is what they rep-resented to you.

   Yet, when it came to specifics about your early life, I had trouble piecing together the odds and ends that I picked up from different sources—especially from other members of the family, whose recollections were noticeably lacking in Siberian tiger hunts, gatherings of the Tziganes or circus acrobats. When I asked you to clarify these inconsistencies, sometimes you just gazed off toward the horizon and replied: "The facts of my life have nothing to do with the realities of my existence." Whatever that meant, I knew for certain that you meant it.

By 1921, famine had extended across Russia to Vladivostok: so did the daily threat to wealthy bourgeois families like the Bryners, whose politics were more anti-Bolshevik than pro-Tsarist. Among wealthy families, one heard stories of revo-lutionaries abducting children and smashing babies' heads against walls. The day came when the new proletarian gov-ernment obliged foreign families to choose between Soviet citizenship or exile. Passionately Russian in their outlook, the Bryners chose Soviet citizenship for the family, and laid aside their Swiss documents. During the 1930s, after all, much of the family's business was in Siberia, although the Bryner Com-pany had offices throughout northern China, in Harbin, Dairen, Peping, Tientsin and Shanghai. Yet for all the growing horror of the revolution, what happened next caused even greater turmoil within the family.

Yul was only four when his father Boris fell in love with Katya, an actress at the Moscow Arts Theater. Soon after Boris met Katya, he wrote to Marousia and explained bluntly that their marriage was over: he would devote his life to this en-chantress. Boris did not even bother to seek a divorce from his wife. Under emergency statutes of the provisional government, all Boris had to do was declare to the magistrate that, since his wife was nowhere to be found, she was dead or missing.

In anguish and shame, Marousia left the Bryner compound in Vladivostok with her children Vera and Yul, aged eight and four respectively. They settled with Vera, Felix and Irena in a small country house outside Vladivostok. Her love despoiled, her loyalty desecrated, the grief and chaos conjoined, Marousia never fully recovered from the abandonment. It was almost as if, when her husband had declared her dead, part of her had simply obeyed.

Russia had been savaged. On a trip to Petrograd, the family saw the devastation: in village after village, railway stations became the residence for thousands of luckier peasants. Boris decided to leave the Soviet Union for good, and settled in Harbin with Katya. Marousia took young Vera and Yul to Harbin as well, where they attended the best school in the region, run by the YMCA.

As a child, Yul was noted for his creativity, and his musical family heartily encouraged it. At Christmas and on other occasions it was customary for the children to dress up in costume and perform bits of poetry or song, and Yul threw himself enthusiastically into this play. Yul's first performance as an actor was as a squirrel in one of the family's Christmas pageants.

Even as a boy Yul was handsome, but it wasn't just his looks that attracted others. There was a compelling urgency to his needs and demands, and an obsessive tenacity of purpose. When he wanted something, he did not quit until he got it. Though life in Harbin had gradually acquired some degree of normality for Yul, at fourteen he was already quite beyond his mother's control.

Yul's sister Vera, at eighteen, was beautiful, passionate and spoiled. She was also a remarkable singer, as Marousia had been before Boris ended her career. In 1934, despite Boris's vagaries about financial support, Marousia risked what little stability they had in Harbin and set out for Paris where her daughter could pursue a career as a singer, Yul could have access to culture, and they could all escape the vicissitudes of war.

The white Russian community in Paris had grown dramatically since the Bolshevik revolution. Its influence reached far beyond the *quartier* where the Russian Orthodox church was located: especially in the evenings. At the theater Stanislavsky's influence was dominant, and there were Georges and Ludmilla

Pitoëff, who were often called the "Lunt and Fontanne of France," especially by each other. Igor Stravinsky had redefined the orchestra, Diaghilev had rewritten the rules of ballet, and Paris cheered Nijinsky, Anna Pavlova, and the young Serge Lifar. The leading star of opera in France was the great baritone Fyodor Chaliapin, especially in *Boris Godunov*. Russian restaurants and clubs, with their spiced vodkas and gypsy music, were the rage. This was the Paris awaiting Yul.

Yul and his sister came to know their way around the French capital with the help of the Russian community. Settling in rue Catulle-Mendès, Marousia got in touch with a family friend, whose son was secretary to the dancer Serge Lifar. Through Lifar, arrangements were made for Yul to go to one of the foremost private lycées in France, Moncelle, the Gallic equivalent of Eton or Harrow. Singing classes were arranged for Vera, who had a passionate though unrequited attraction to Lifar, who was bisexual. And Marousia settled in melancholy exile, forever awaiting money from Boris to pay the bills, and struggling to cope with daily problems in a foreign language. Boris hardly ever visited his children, and when he failed to send child support, she received help from Felix and his wife, who, by then, had brought Irena to settle in Switzerland, the land that Jules had abandoned seventy years earlier.

Fourteen-year-old Yul, now on the loose in Paris, had charm, guile and a powerful sense of entitlement to the fineries of life. Perhaps to compensate for the absence of their father, Marousia spoiled both her children, then tried too late to rein them in. Once she even took her son to consult a psychiatrist: the diagnosis was that he was willful, not disturbed. Yul was energetic, mischievous, clever and uninhibited, even before he met the gypsies. He had already concluded that he was unique enough to merit special privileges. After all the name of his grandfather, the family patriarch, had been handed down to him, as if it were a hereditary title, and he vowed someday to name his own son Yul.

Lycée Moncelle was the first environment Yul had encountered that tried to discipline him. The school failed, and everyone suffered in the attempt. Yul's exchanges with his teachers were more often physical than intellectual. He was brilliant but lazy, the extrovert in the back row—the teacher's perpetual bane. In the eighth grade, for example, he persuaded all the students to face the back of the class when the teacher entered the room.

He had only a rudimentary knowledge of French, at first. Apart from a scattering of Chinese dialects and some school-room English, he was fluent only in Russian. But it wasn't languages he was known for. Classmates at Moncelle remembered Yul's strength most of all, not only in playground fights, but in his many feats of endurance. Yul accepted any challenge or dare that involved stamina, pain and boasting rights. He quickly gained a reputation as one of the roughest kids in school, and he liked it that way. He was not a success in team sports, but excelled in gymnastics, swimming, skiing and *pelote* (Basque *jai alai*). Having learned some hatha yoga in the Orient, he could hold his breath underwater longer than anyone, including the seniors. In fact, it was generally agreed that Yul could whistle louder, climb higher, run faster and piss further than any kid there. But he did not spend much time on school grounds. He stayed at Moncelle for two school years, but he probably had less than six months in residence, and even then his attendance record was wretched. For a *real* education, he kept running away from Moncelle: to Paris.

Lifar's secretary took Yul and Vera to one of the restaurants where the Tziganes were the star attraction. From the first, Yul felt completely at ease with the Russian gypsies, and, as a teenager who was welcome backstage at a nightclub, his prospects in Paris improved. In short order he acquired a guitar, probably promising his mother he would take singing lessons. This he did and, though memorizing was never his forte, he learned the complete baritone part of *Don Giovanni*. But instead of playing classical guitar, he found a small gypsy seven-string, and began to learn the songs of the Tziganes. Because, as the gypsies insist: *The truth can only be spoken in Rom.*

Yul had the good fortune to fall in with a family called Dimitrievich. Of the four main tribes of European gypsies—the Lowara, the Tshurara, the Kalderasha and the Matchvaya—the Dimitrievich were of that branch of the Kalderasha who represented an important tradition in the decadent Tsarist years. It was at the Tzigane village of Mokroie, outside Moscow, that the royal family came to drink, gamble and wench. It was probably true that Ivan Dimitrievich, the gypsy patriarch, had performed for Rasputin, before moving his clan to Paris in the 1920s.

Ivan's three children, Aliosha, Valentina and Marukha, were just a little older than Yul, and it was Aliosha who taught him guitar. Marukha, the girl with the soft voice and sloe eyes, taught him everything else. Among the wandering Dimitrievich and their extended family, Yul discovered a sense of belonging, and a solemn set of rituals and traditions befitting a nomadic outcast. And he found a cabaret perspective of the world, a personal ethos that suited him perfectly.

Yul had a powerful build and robust shoulders, and that was fortunate, since he was carrying around a chip the size of a railway sleeper. Belligerent and headstrong, he had no respect whatsoever for institutions—government, church, school, family—none was reliable, all had failed him. His estranged father and grandfather had set examples for him, reinforcing the same lesson: that no human relationship is too strong to be broken, and that abandoning your family is often the manly thing to do. By the time he was sixteen, the most reliable institution Yul had ever known was a nightclub full of gypsies.

Steal only what you need for today. So went one of the rules of the road for surviving among the non-gypsies, the *gaje*. The Dimitrievich did not steal, of course: they were a family of *artistes*, nobility among the Tziganes. Valentina, Ivan's daughter, was already a huge woman when Yul met her in the 1930s. Her black hair was braided to her waist and she wore a profusion of gold jewelry. Valia summoned her voice from a place that was centuries old and hot as a volcano. It was a most life-affirming sound, for all its mournfulness.

Aliosha, while fanning his guitar in impromptu counter rhythms, sang with all the soulfulness of Muddy Waters. "A melodious complaint," as Yul called it. Aliosha was small and fierce, in a wiry sort of way, but like Valia, his voice seemed hurled out of a crater. Sometimes his strumming was so intense that, at night's end, his fingertips bled. It was Aliosha who taught Yul to play guitar, and to project his voice: *Not too loud, only to the horizon . . .*

They usually sang and conversed in Romany, for which no

conventional written language exists. In gypsy tradition, without written contracts or documentation, disputes were usually won by whoever had the power to prevail. Yul loved this ethos of persuasion above plausibility. On June 15, 1935, Yul gave his first professional performance at a large cabaret in a gypsy orchestra thirty guitars strong: he was not yet fifteen years old. Just before he went on to perform, Ivan gave Yul one piece of laconic advice: *When you play for a crowd, lead with your cock.*

The gypsies rely upon personal myth to sustain the past. Their family backgrounds might be recast at the drop of a hat or, their enemies might say, at the sound of a siren. Since most gypsies have no citizenship, they need "travelling papers" in order to exist in the bureaucratic world. To this end they registered births in village and city *mairies* throughout France. Since they often had children at a very young age, older relatives sometimes would take the babies to be registered. And, when a gypsy died, his papers were always passed along to others. So the documented history of a family often bore no resemblance to actual kinships. Just another way to tease the *gaje* . . .

Yul was informally adopted by the Dimitrievich family simply because they loved him. He lacked the bigotry they usually encountered in the bourgeoisie from Moscow or St. Petersburg, who were often their least generous customers in the clubs. And he had a powerful instinct for performing in the guitar orchestra, obeying naturally another maxim of the gypsy artist: *Be conspicuous, or you'll get lost in the crowd.*

Yul spent as much time as he could practicing with Aliosha, and as little as possible at school or at home. During the summer months, Marousia rented a small house in Normandy, not far from Deauville. There, Yul found the most conspicuous job available for a well-built teenager: he became a lifeguard. It was his first experience in a position of authority, and he liked it. From his lifeguard's bench he could scout the whole beach for girls. During that first summer, he had a brief affair with a French girl. When she became pregnant, Yul's family helped arrange for an abortion.

That summer, while standing under a cinema marquee in Deauville, Yul decided firmly that he would become a movie star before his thirtieth birthday. He was almost six feet tall, sixteen, notably handsome, and fashionably dressed. He noticed a fellow standing nearby, tapping an ivory-white meerschaum pipe against the heel of an elegant Italian moccasin. Somehow this struck Yul as the most stylish gesture he had ever seen, and he began saving his lifeguard's salary to buy a pipe like that and a pair of Italian moccasins. Then, suitably attired, the teenaged Yul proceeded to the same cinema, to relive that casual moment of elegance he had witnessed. He stood there dangling the pipe nonchalantly from his jaw for a while, before repeating the suave ritual, tapping the pipe on his heel. With the first tap, it shattered like crystal at his feet . . .

Returning to Paris, with fleeting visits to his school, Yul became more secretive with his family about the life he was leading around town. Few homes had telephones in Paris in the 1930s, and since there was no way for Marousia to check on him, he could claim anything he pleased. Most nights, in fact, he worked the Russian restaurants. But by now, he had discovered another world in which an adolescent could lose himself: the circus.

The *Cirque d'Hiver* was one of the oldest permanent circuses in the world, and from the first time Yul went there he felt at home. The flying acrobats appealed to his aggressive, physical nature, and from the moment he saw the trapeze artists, he wanted to be one of them. The great challenge for trapeze acrobats in the 1930s was the famous triple somersault: naturally, that became Yul's goal. He started his apprenticeship as a flying clown, and worked the trapeze with a husband and wife team. Yul made the audience laugh and cheer as a clown who tried to perform the triple, but failed comically. Soon he was informally part of the troupe, and a familiar figure at the nearby café where the circus artists congregated. When the sixteen-year-old finally brought his family to visit the circus, they were baffled at the way he was greeted by clowns, midgets and lion-tamers. They had never suspected he led this double life.

Yul was remembered at the circus for his romantic escapades during these two years—women of all ages succumbed to his teenage charms, and his conquests among the young ladies in the audience soon became part of his reputation at the circus, rife with rumors about this exotic young performer. One story had it that an irate husband was hunting him with a gun. Another story, entirely false, was that Yul had been questioned by the police about the murder of an irate husband. Not only women found Yul appealing: at some point Yul was also propositioned by the dancer Serge Lifar, who took him on board a privately-owned yacht. Yul had always boasted that he was willing to try *everything* once, but the preliminaries turned him off, and he could not go through with the experiment.

While practicing somersaults one afternoon, he bounced off the safety-net into a stack of scaffolding pipes. He suffered an indeterminate number of cracked ribs and broken bones, from his back to his legs. It was during his recovery that Yul encountered opium, first as remedy, then as diversion, and finally as addiction. That can happen to people who say they'll try anything once. He kept this secret from his gypsy friends, who loathed drugs. But among the French there had been a tradition of opium use, not only in popular remedies, but also smoked recreationally in a pipe, a custom the French learned in colonial Vietnam. Opium was available to anyone adventurous enough to go down to the dock and negotiate with the Vietnamese sailors, some of whom were actually paid in raw opium.

Yul smoked opium in the traditional manner: rolling the sticky ball of residue, which had been cooked in wine or port along with the dross, until it became a pellet. Then he speared that on the end of a long needle and, holding it over a flame, used the pipe to collect the smoke which boiled off the crackling lump of opium. He smoked up to three dozen pipes a day, until his clothing permanently carried that peculiar, unforgettable odor of opium. Picasso called it "the least stupid smell in the world."

One night after performing at a Russian cabaret, Yul was approached by an unusual, effete man who had been told that Yul might know where to find some opium. Since, by this time, he always carried a stash inside his guitar for emergencies, Yul shared it with the fellow, and then made a trip to the docks for another supply for both him and his new friend. That is how Yul Brynner met Jean Cocteau; and the first years of their friendship flourished mostly around small quantities of opium.

Cocteau was among the best known poets in France, famous
for his surrealistic movies as much as for his poems, plays and
novels. Born in 1889, he had done his best to meet Diaghilev's
challenge: ''Astonish me!'' Together with his friend Picasso,
Jean had designed sets and costumes for the ballets of Stravinsky, and outraged polite circles with novels suggesting in-
cest. He had been publicly pilloried by the Dadaists and rejected
by surrealists. For almost a decade he had been a habitual opium
smoker. In the early 1930s he had confined himself to a private
clinic to undergo withdrawal, which was little understood at
the time. He had even kept a notebook, *Opium—Journal of a
Cure,* describing both its ecstasy and the anguish of withdrawal.

Yul spent a fair amount of time in the orbit of Cocteau and
his friends. Together, they visited Colette. Yul listened to their
sophisticated, rapid-fire conversation. He watched in amazement as Cocteau sketched a portrait of Colette with one hand
and a portrait of Yul with the other, all the while sustaining a
hailstorm of witty repartee. Yul had first met Picasso with
Cocteau at *Le Boeuf sur le Toit,* where he also first became
friends with Salvador Dalí. Through Cocteau, Yul got to know
Marcel Marceau, Jean-Louis Barrault and Jean Marais, and a
world of intellectuals far removed from the circus or the nightclub.

The story gets a little hazy as Yul became genuinely hooked
on opium, but one thing became clear: it took more and more
trips to the docks just to avoid the suffering of withdrawal.
After several months of this, Yul realized that he was in over
his head, and that only his family could help him. He sought
out his aunt Vera, who now lived in Switzerland with young
Irena. He travelled to see them in 1937, and was hospitalized
after collapsing in their home. He spent a few weeks at an
expensive private sanitarium, then moved in with Vera and
Irena for further supervised care. To their acquaintances, the
family claimed Yul was suffering an endocrinal disturbance.
They said he was being treated with radiation. The stories he
babbled to Irena about drug dealers in France who wanted to
kill him were said to be ravings caused by this hormonal disturbance.

Yul spent a year in Lausanne with his aunt and cousin, though
his symptoms subsided within weeks. It was a calm, healthful

time, and his aunt Vera became a maternal ideal. At eighteen, he returned to Paris, and through his connections he became an apprentice at the Théâtre des Mathurins with Georges and Ludmilla Pitoëff, who ran a tiny repertory company, performing in both Russian and French. Yul swept floors, built sets and sewed costumes. It was his introduction to the theater, and he was instantly enthralled.

As Europe prepared for war, the family was once again in jeopardy. Yul's sister Vera married a Russian pianist and settled safely in New York, but Marousia decided to return to the Orient. So, in 1939, Yul travelled with his mother back to Dairen, in northern China, where his father Boris lived with his beloved Katya and their adopted daughter. This was Yul's first opportunity to know Boris and his stepmother Katya. They travelled together through China, and Katya enthralled Yul with stories of her studies at the Moscow Arts Theater with Michael Chekhov, Stanislavsky's co-director and the nephew of the great Anton Chekhov. In fact, while serving as apprentice with the Pitoëffs, Yul had tried to join Michael Chekhov in England, but without success. Now that war had begun, Yul learned from Katya that Chekhov had moved to America and had started an acting company near Danbury, Connecticut. By this time, Marousia was gravely ill with leukemia. Hoping to find medical treatment for her, and to enlist the help of his sister Vera, Yul prepared her for the long voyage to New York, and collected letters of recommendation to take to Chekhov. He was twenty-one years old with an aim straight and true, and a trajectory aimed higher than heaven.

If there was a single moment when Yul chose a career in the theater, this was it. He had dreamed of being a movie star: a big star, like Valentino. And his hunger for triumph was so fierce and tireless that anything less than stardom was unimaginable. He was a young man with great appetites, and a cabaret singer's view of the world. He had overcome many cultural disadvantages in his constant displacements, but he had also learned about a wide variety of cultures. Yul knew what he wanted, and that was really all he needed to know. He wanted power: the power to call the shots, the way the rich patrons he sang for in the clubs set everyone else's agenda, everywhere they went. That would take more than charisma. If he could only study with Michael Chekhov, he might master the craft of acting, and add the power of proficiency to his power of personality. America, after all, was where movie stars were made.

2

Actor's Apprentice

"Archetypes express the structure of the human psyche."

—Joseph Campbell

Yul's favorite story about actors went like this:

During the Depression a two-bit acting troupe had to reduce its payroll, so it fired the old man and the young boy in the company halfway through the tour. Since the company couldn't even pay their bus fare home, the stage-manager offered them half-pay to walk through the next town on the tour with sandwich-boards, advertising the production.

So it was that the old man and the young boy found themselves walking through a peaceful Southern town of a summer's eve covered in sweat, dust and sandwich-boards, with no place to sleep. As they walked through the town the boy noticed a family gathered on their front porch, sipping mint juleps as they waited for their supper.

"Look at that," said the boy. "Isn't that the life?"

"Oh, I suppose so," replied the old man. Then he smiled and winked. "But they can't act . . ."

Having left his mother in New York with a friend of the family, Yul arrived at Chekhov's school near Danbury, Connecticut in late 1941, and began studying immediately with "the Professor," as he called Chekhov, and with George Shdanoff, Chekhov's colleague and assistant.

For Yul, an actor was somebody with a calling, and someone without a calling was not really an actor at all. This was not

just a profession to him, or a shot at the brass ring, but a
consuming passion. While most families of the Bryners' social
class might have discouraged his interest in acting, in his father's home as well as Marousia's Yul had learned to regard
the artist as a dedicated craftsman with great social standing.

Michael Chekhov had begun his life in the theater in the
nineteenth century, and helped Konstantin Stanislavsky create
the Moscow Arts Theater; nonetheless, in important ways, he
disagreed with his colleague's Method. The difference between
their approaches to acting was more than an aesthetic debate,
for it concerned the very *stuff* of the human psyche. And the
rift between Stanislavsky's Method and Chekhov's approach
remains at the center of most arguments about the nature of
drama. As an actor, Michael Chekhov is best remembered for
his performance as the Freudian analyst in Alfred Hitchcock's
Spellbound (1945), but he had long had a distinguished career
on stage in Moscow, Berlin and on Broadway, where he and
his Moscow Arts Players appeared in *An Evening with Anton
Chekhov*, a great success in 1935. In Moscow, each of his
productions might have had as much as twelve months' rehearsal, so that the cast could study every facet of their characters. Such attention to the role is very different from what
we are accustomed to seeing on film or on television, for which
actors practice a sort of elevated make-believe. Pretending is
much the same thing as fibbing: there's no great trick to it,
you just act as if what you are doing is *natural*. Michael Chekhov was reaching for something of a different order.

According to Yul's mentor, to act was to express the emo-
tions and experiences of a particular character in a way that
might be universally shared. To express emotion, the actor
must experience it: make-believe would not do. But how did
an actor experience an emotion at will? How did he summon
up a *real* surge of fear? Stanislavsky's reply, in a word, was:
recall. Personal memory was the key to achieving that ''feeling
of truth'' on stage. This was the artistic criterion upon which
he might be said to have founded the Moscow Arts Theater in
1898.

But for Michael Chekhov, it was not enough to re-experience
memories on stage. ''I never stopped wondering,'' he later
wrote, ''what was so imaginative and creative about merely

copying life around us in every detail, photographically, as it were, and I regarded it as one of the beclouded facets of Stanislavsky's many-sided talent. Instinctively, intuitively, Stanislavsky tried to persuade his audience that they were not in a theater, that his performances were real life, that after the curtain went up, they were one with the characters on the stage.'' Chekhov felt this goal was neither possible nor desirable: it was not *creative*, it was imitative. He also disagreed fundamentally with Stanislavsky's techniques for achieving it.

> Stanislavsky's viewpoint was that when an actor gets a part he has to imagine that the character he will play is, figuratively speaking, seated within himself—absolutely and completely occupying the actor's inner self . . . My technique then, as now, was to imagine the character as being *outside* of me . . . it is like asking the character himself to show you how to do it . . . That was the gist of what we discussed— the supremacy of the character's ego (mine) against the actor's ego (Stanislavsky's)—and I must confess that neither of us convinced the other.

The heart of their dispute over technique was simple and important. Stanislavsky, as well as his disciples in America, believed the actor must perfect the power of memory. Chekhov considered memory reflective rather than creative, and called upon the actor to exercise and develop the *imagination* instead, to learn about the character. This emphasis upon the imagination was particularly appealing to Yul's psyche: inventing a character, then *willing* him into existence.

When Yul joined the company they were touring America with threadbare productions of Shakespeare, performing mostly at colleges. Since Yul spoke little English, and boasted that he could drive anything on the road, he was assigned to drive the company truck. After each performance, the set and costumes were loaded on to a creaky old van, and while the company slept at a local boarding-house, Yul drove on to the next town. After a few weeks, he was allowed to appear on stage in the role of Fabian in *Twelfth Night*. A few words of Shakespeare was all the English he could manage.

The 1941 tour was Yul's introduction to America. Driving

the truck around the outskirts of Baton Rouge, he was stopped by a sheriff and arrested for not having a Louisiana license. Since he couldn't speak enough English to explain himself, and since the white jail was full, they threw him into a cell with the "coloreds," until the company found him there. The experience left him with a lasting cynicism about American boasts of "equality" and "justice." *Twelfth Night* opened in New York on December 8, 1941, starring Beatrice Straight as Viola, and including "Youl Bryner" as Fabian.

For a year and a half Yul lived near Danbury, Connecticut, travelling regularly to New York to visit his mother and to raise money for her medical expenses. When he could not find work parking cars or waiting on tables, he worked as a bouncer or usher, and even as a nude model for photographers, just to help pay for Marousia's hospital bills. He got a taste of the prejudice that immigrants have always experienced on their way to becoming Americans, and it only strengthened his determination to achieve stardom quickly. He also auditioned at several of the city's best known nightclubs. Sometimes standing, sometimes sitting onstage, Yul would pull out the same little gypsy seven-string that had travelled with him from Paris to China to America, and sing "*Okonchen Poots*" and the other gypsy songs. Within a few months he had irregular work as the opening act at The Blue Angel, one of the hottest nightclubs in New York. Soon after that, he started finding work performing at private parties around the city. It was at just such a party in early 1942 that he fell in love with a young movie star named Virginia Gilmore. Yul was twenty-one years old.

Virginia Gilmore was born in El Monte, California in 1919 with the ungainly name of Sherman Poole. The Poole family had come from England and settled in Milton, Massachusetts in the 1630s. In the 1870s, at about the time Jules Bryner sailed to Japan on a pirate ship, Virginia's grandfather, a German immigrant in Missouri named Casebeer, set out for California with his wife. Along the way they had thirteen children. By the time their last daughter was born, "we were fresh out of names, so we called her Lady May, since she was born on May 1st." Virginia's grandmother described their trip in a book, *Descendants of John Kasebeer*, which is in the New York Public Library.

In about 1916, Lady May Casebeer married Albion Poole, who had tried his hand at a number of unsuccessful businesses before discovering aviation. From a landing strip in the San Gabriel Valley, he offered rides in his biplane for $5, and did a little crop-dusting on the side. When America entered the Great War, he kissed his wife goodbye and set off for Europe. He returned with a nickname, ''Bullets'' Poole, and a hatful of hair-raising war stories about dog-fights over the Ardennes. Well, it turned out he'd never left America. ''Bullets'' had spent a couple of years shacked up with a girlfriend on the East Coast. Flying his biplane back to California, he suffered serious burns when the engine leaked oil into his face as he landed. By the time his daughter Virginia was born, ''Bullets'' was generally known as a mean-spirited drunk.

Lady May, who took a drink now and again herself, divorced ''Bullets'' and married a fellow named Gilmore, who made a good husband and a caring stepfather for little Virginia. They settled in San Mateo, where she graduated from high school in 1937, despite the fact that she failed her final exam in Economics. Virginia blamed that on a friend of Fritz Lang's.

Lang, the renowned director, had fled Berlin in the mid-1930s along with much of the German intelligentsia. Shortly before she turned eighteen, Virginia had become Lang's protégée and girlfriend, and visited his house every chance she could. One afternoon she was cramming for her Economics exam in Lang's living-room when a small, peculiar German friend of Fritz's offered to help. For the rest of the evening he tutored her in economic theory. The fellow was Bertolt Brecht.

At Lang's suggestion, even before she was out of high school Virginia auditioned to become a Goldwyn girl. For the first year that only meant the studio paid for her dance lessons and orthodontics. She was a teenager when Renoir gave her the starring role in *Swamp Water*. After that, her career advanced swiftly. The studio thought her stepfather's name would look better on a marquee than ''Poole,'' so she became Virginia Gilmore. After her legs were insured by Goldwyn Studios for a million dollars, she was called ''Gams Gilmore.'' She was known to enjoy highfallutin' literature, at a time when ingénues

were not generally recognized for their cognitive faculties. Her
poetry, coached by Lang, was remarkable, at least for a teenage
Goldwyn girl. Samuel Goldwyn himself described her as "an
honest-to-God American beauty with brains who even writes
poems."

She also appeared in *Winter Carnival, Berlin Correspondent*
and *Laddie*, as well as some twenty or more "B" pictures—
enough to earn her the title "Queen of the 'Bs'" by 1941.
But she also appeared in a handful of important Hollywood
films. She costarred with Robert Young in *Western Union*,
with Caesar Romero in *Tall, Dark and Handsome*, and with
Gary Cooper in *Pride of the Yankees*, during which Virginia
also became friends with Babe Ruth, who appeared in the
movie.

She had a small room in Hollywood, but while working in
New York she swapped her place for a flat over a dry-cleaner's
on East 38th Street, and commuted back and forth to LA.
Ingénues were already doing that in 1942.

Virginia met Yul at a New York party given by Margaret
Lindley, who was nominally Yul's agent, and who hoped that
an American girlfriend might help improve his English. They
spent the whole evening together. Virginia remembered that
the glow of his eyes was more eloquent than his halting Eliz-
abethan English. Yul's black, wavy hair was already thinning,
which helped make him look older than twenty-one. She was
a year older. Though well-muscled, he was underweight, evinc-
ing just the right amount of tender concern. She also noticed
that he was trembling visibly.

As they sat talking, Yul was especially taken by Virginia's
girlishness. She may have been more knowledgeable about
Broadway and Hollywood; still, he was more worldly. She
recounted to Yul how, at her first lunch with a Hollywood
agent, she had tried to appear sophisticated by ordering fish
for her main course, and so she ordered Baked Alaska. Later
Yul brought out his seven-string and began singing gypsy
songs—not too loud, just to the horizon. There and then she
fell in love with him, once and for all.

After the party was over, Virginia invited him to her *pied à
terre* for a nightcap. As they walked to her flat, Yul kissed
her. They climbed the two stories over the dry-cleaner's with

some anticipation. Soon she slipped into the other room to change while he waited for her in bed, smelling the naphthalene from downstairs and trembling feverishly. She emerged in a pale lace and satin negligée, eyes wide with innocence and curiosity. By the time she reached the bed, Yul was shaking like a leaf. Then suddenly her eyes narrowed and she barked, "Hey, that headboard's silk! Get your greasy hair off it or my roommate will kill me!"

That was when he began to vomit.

Yul explained clumsily that when he had come from the Orient several months before he had brought a small quantity of opium with him, hidden inside his seven-string guitar. Smoking just a little each day he had made it last, but now he was sick from withdrawal.

"Opium!" she exploded with derision. "Oh you . . . you . . . *actors*!"

He retched again pitifully. He had eaten nothing since leaving Chekhov's two days earlier, and he'd had several drinks at his agent's party. With what little strength he had left, he jotted down the address where he was staying, and dragged himself out of the door.

The next night she appeared by surprise at the address Yul had given her. They made love and, before dawn, declared eternal devotion to one another.

He never did smoke opium again.

I was still a boy when my father told me about the night he met my mother. Almost a lifetime later my mother described that night to me as well, and used exactly the same words to describe it.

Yul was even more forthright on the subject of his early experiences with opium, although his memory was somewhat unreliable on that phase of his life. When we lived on Central Park West, among the well-chosen objects strewn casually on the living-room coffee-table was the opium pipe Yul had once used, complete with its leather case: the odor still clung to it, at once repugnant and appealing. Cocteau once described the smell as "something between a circus and a sea-port," and Picasso called it "the least stupid smell in the world." During

*the early years of the cold war, this was definitely an exotic
item to find in an American living-room. Much later, Yul described his period of opium use as a promised land to which
he would never return, but never forget. For a number of years
he speculated that after retiring, he might take up the pipe
again, but I suspect he was just trying to find a way to make
retirement sound more interesting.*

Since club dates were scarce, Yul was still taking odd jobs
everywhere he could to help with Marousia's bills at New York
Presbyterian Hospital—he sold ice cream, parked cars, ran
errands. At the same time, while he studied with Chekhov, he
thought about how he could make some contribution to the war
effort. He offered his services to the Office of War Information,
OWI, which put him to work broadcasting daily news bulletins
to the French Resistance. For several hours a day, several days
a week he translated the news bulletins into French and then
delivered the radio broadcasts: his facility with languages as
well as his knowledge of European and oriental cultures kept
him busy in several different departments there. It was at OWI
in 1943 that Yul came to know many of the real pioneers of
broadcasting who had worked with NBC and CBS, the fledgling
networks of both radio and the brand new "picture radio." He
took the gypsy advice and made himself conspicuous: on the
radio he forecast a blizzard in July, for example. He quickly
became known around broadcast circles for his pranks, his
voracious appetite and the speed with which he usually gorged
a huge dinner during the fifteen-minute interval between news
reports.

Later that year Yul's mother succumbed to leukemia. He
had grown cool toward Marousia after his visit with Boris and
Katya, almost as if he had finally chosen allegiance to his father.
But in the last year of her life Yul showed Marousia great
dedication. She wrote of his care and attention in one of the
last letters to her family in China, concerned that Yul was
spending too much time looking after her. Yul and his sister
Vera had Marousia cremated without ceremony.

Virginia returned to Hollywood to finish her contractual obligations. Goldwyn had farmed her out to Twentieth Century-

Fox, as abusive an employer as any during the days of contract players. The studio executives made their contempt for actors clear by boasting that they were "stables of stars." The studio could, and did, dictate what its star "assets" did with their private lives, where they did it and with whom. In those days the casting couch was not just a metaphor, but the very spot where directors and producers often chose women for their movies: who, after all, would blow the whistle on them? Nothing outraged Yul's sense of justice more than a studio that used its power like a bully. Virginia and Yul both blamed Fox for extending their separation; meanwhile she was using all her contacts to find work on the New York stage. They pined for each other, coast to coast, until Yul couldn't stand it any more, and proposed over the telephone to marry Virginia.

Yul made his first trip to Hollywood by rail—he loved the power of locomotives—and by the time he reached Los Angeles, the Louella Parsons column had already announced that "Virginia Gilmore and some gypsy she met in New York will be married on September 6th . . ." They were married at the Los Angeles County Courthouse, and to the last minute Fox executives threatened that she'd never work again if she married him. Yul vowed never to forget those threats, much less forgive them.

By the end of the year they returned to New York, where Virginia stepped into her first Broadway role in *Those Endearing Young Charms* (1943). Then there was a long thin stretch when unemployment insurance ran out and the newlyweds were plain broke and hungry. When money did come in, they binged. Yul always maintained a cavalier attitude toward money, even before he had any with which to be cavalier. "I have no respect for money at all," he often repeated to his wife. "I piss on it."

The following year Virginia achieved bona fide stardom on stage when Moss Hart cast her in the title role of *Dear Ruth*, a wartime comedy by Norman Krasna that ran for almost seven hundred performances. That meant enough money to pay the rent, though it left precious little for pissing on.

* * *

Yul was now a featured performer at the Blue Angel, a night-club that blended elegance with the avant-garde, specializing in sophisticated acts from Europe. He sang mostly gypsy songs, two shows a night, but as he became more comfortable with English he performed a few of Josh White's folk songs, and even a few comical numbers he learned from Bil Baird, the marionetteer. That meant a small but steady income while his wife was onstage, and left him free to look for work during the day. Prospects were more promising now that he was a naturalized American citizen, but there were still long dry stretches between jobs. When there was no work, he built furniture, butcher block coffee-tables with a Danish look. He sold these to friends.

The Brynners (Yul had added the second "n" to reflect the correct pronunciation) were very sociable, and accepted into Manhattan's young intellectual crowd—more avant-garde than mainstream. Because Virginia was a celebrity, they were often introduced as "the Gilmores." Though Virginia was starring on Broadway, earning a few hundred dollars a week, she read tirelessly, keen to pursue higher spiritual and cultural studies. Yul worked to improve his English and absorb American culture. Along with serious literature, which he read to compensate for a truncated academic career, he read detective novels in bulk, to become acquainted with the language of the streets. And, of course, he went to the movies. Although he hotly resented the occasions when he was addressed as "Mr. Gilmore," he also felt a vicarious sense of belonging to the world of Hollywood. After all, his bride had co-starred with Gary Cooper, and he had met most of the stars himself at the studio commissary after his marriage. Yul was not especially impressed with them, but felt that at least he'd found a worthy class of peers. Twenty-four and married, he did not have much of a job, or speak a great deal of English, but his self-assurance was prodigious.

Someone at the Office of War Information mentioned to Yul that CBS Television was holding auditions for an on-camera job, hosting a new variety show called *Mr. Jones and his Neighbors*. His accent would be no obstacle, since the job mainly involved wearing a series of silly hats. The pay was twenty-five dollars a week. There were only a few thousand TV sets in the New York region in the early 1940s, and there were broadcasts only on Tuesday and Friday afternoons from two to four. The whole venture was still highly experimental, and it was not clear that commercial television would survive. It was six years before the first transcontinental broadcast in America, and television was too uncertain a medium even to sell advertising yet, so there were no commercial breaks. Not many people saw Yul's first broadcast performance as Mr. Jones. In any case, it was canceled after the first week. There was one positive note: he had not been *fired*. He had made it into CBS's labor pool.

When he heard the network was looking for television directors, Yul promptly applied. It never occurred to him that he couldn't do it: he had watched Michael Chekhov direct for years. He knew that his limited English was a handicap he could overcome: the urgency with which he expressed himself seemed to make itself understood. So he made himself conspicuous, and immediately landed a temporary job directing ''fill'' material. That led to a couple of other small jobs. So now he belonged, at least tentatively, to the small pool of twenty or thirty TV directors with *experience*—the pioneers of television broadcasting.

In 1945, the producer Michael Myerberg began preparing the Broadway production of a new musical based upon a classical Chinese play, *Lute Song*. With a young actress named Mary Martin as its star, the production looked promising indeed. Myerberg was looking for a male lead with an ''oriental quality.'' He had already hired a very prestigious set designer, Robert Edmund Jones. The director was a promising young fellow who had been Orson Welles's colleague with the Mercury Players, John Houseman.

The musical was a curious blend of styles. A fifth of the text was sung, in arias rather than choruses. The libretto had a pristine simplicity to it, but the set and costumes were heavily stylized. The story told of a young villager, recently married, who goes to take his examinations in the capital city. There, wisdom is judged by the number of volumes a scholar has read: since the young scholar has read six thousand volumes, he is chosen as chief magistrate, but he learns that with that title he is obliged to marry the daughter of a prince. His grieving first wife survives famine, enters a nunnery and, in the end, is reunited with her husband by the kindness of his second wife.

The production premiered out of town in December 1945, and opened at the Plymouth Theater on Broadway on February 6, 1946. Despite all the work, it never achieved a balance in its dialogue, song and look. "Mr. Jones' " settings, costumes and lighting are the heroes of the evening," wrote Lewis Nichols in his *New York Times* review. "Miss Martin has a difficult part, and on the whole she does it well . . . Yul Brynner is the luckless husband and gives a satisfactory performance." Faint praise, indeed, considering that he won the Donaldson Award, as the most promising new Broadway star of 1946. Despite mixed reviews, the play kept running. Many were enchanted by its delicate magic, but at the box office it had no legs.

Still, Yul Brynner had made it to Broadway. Was it some *hereditary* gift of Yul's that brought such achievement so young? Like his grandfather Jules, Yul had travelled halfway around the world and, against all odds, established himself as a Broadway star at twenty-five. Was that charisma? Was it power? A fierce purposefulness pervaded the atmosphere wherever Yul went, and he set the agenda for anybody else who happened to be in the vicinity. His intensity would not and did not yield to compromise or social convention. The mundane world of turns and twists and laundry lists tended to melt to insignificance in the presence of Yul's lofty ambition.

Virginia and Yul had everything except money: their combined salaries on Broadway were no match for their extravagance. Yul was partial to giving out engraved silver cigarette cases, which became, for a time, the minimum unit of his generosity; definitely an extravagant gesture in postwar America. Yul also hired a personal dresser to deal with his costumes and, eventually, with his extensive personal wardrobe. His dresser, Don Lawson, was a gentle, loyal and joyous soul who had been a tap-dancer himself. He had some bills to pay, so he took the job, knowing that Yul's own paycheck was small and not very sure. He remained at Yul's side for more than twenty years, a comical and endearing sidekick. Don was not only Yul's dresser, for a long time he was "Mr. B's" closest friend and companion, even while it did not always look or sound like a friendship of equals.

Virginia left the production *Dear Ruth* before the show closed. Elia Kazan had cast her as the female lead in a new play, *Truckline Café*. Her co-star was an exciting young actor fresh from Nebraska named Marlon Brando. Critics and audiences alike soon decided that the play was not as good as its cast. During the second half of 1946 Virginia and Yul were mostly separated—he toured, she did not. Of course, stories got back to her of Yul's romantic . . . generosity. According to more than one report Virginia received, with the exception of her friend Mary Martin, Yul had made love with every woman in the cast of *Lute Song*. Virginia was told that the list included a pretty chorus girl in the show named Nancy Davis, who had not yet met the love of her life, Ronald Reagan. In spite of all the gossip, Virginia stayed behind in New York that spring when *Lute Song* left Broadway and went on the road. Because by then she had learned she was expecting a child in December.

Dolly Haas took over for Mary Martin on the road. She and her husband Al Hirschfeld, the theater caricaturist, were close friends of Yul and Virginia. Dolly had done broadcasts for the OWI, too; and she was also expecting a baby. As the tour meandered uncertainly toward the west, paychecks were small, few and far between, until they played Chicago. There, Claudia Cassidy gave *Lute Song* its first rave review, and the play could have brought in audiences for months, but the Shubert Theater was booked solid, and wouldn't let them stay. They drifted from Des Moines to Colorado Springs, waiting for another theater. Finally they went on to the Curran in San Francisco, with every intention of returning to Chicago.

Yul's first professional biography, as it appeared in the program, was as much a work of fantasy as the play:

Yul Brynner is partly Mongolian and first saw "Pi-Pa-Ki" in Peking with Mei Lan-Fang playing the role which Dolly Haas animates tonight. He served his theatrical apprenticeship in Prague, Riga and Warsaw, was thereafter with Georges and Ludmilla Pitoëff for six years at their Théâtre des Mathurins in Paris, appearing in plays of Pirandello, Ibsen, Claudel, and Chekhov. Brynner came to this country five years ago. His only other Broadway appearance was in the Chekhov Theater Group's production of "Twelfth Night" in the role of Orsino.

Just teasing the *gaje* . . .

Virginia went in to labor in New York two days before Christmas, 1946. She left word for Yul at the theater in San Francisco to send money right away: they were still constantly broke, and living over the dry-cleaner's on East 38th Street. Twelve hours later, their son was born. Virginia was unable to reach Yul to tell him, for he was on his way to join her. In the meantime, Vera scraped together enough money to get Virginia and the baby out of the hospital and back to the little flat. When Yul arrived from California he persuaded Virginia to name the baby after him, insisting that this custom dated back to Jules, their Swiss patriarch. "In our family, Yul is not just a name," he insisted, "it is a title." So, to everyone's eventual chagrin, they named their son Yul Brynner.

Yul rejoined *Lute Song* in Los Angeles without Virginia and the baby. It was his first time on the loose in Hollywood, and being a family man was the furthest thing from his mind. He and Virginia had both been unfaithful before during months of separation, and it was not in Yul's character to overlook opportunities.

Joan Crawford made herself one of those opportunities. She came to see *Lute Song* soon after it opened in the spring of 1947. After the curtain came down, she visited Yul backstage and, without any preambulatory chitchat, invited him to her house for a nightcap. She offered to send her driver after he'd showered. When the chauffeur dropped him at the elegant Beverly Hills house, the front door was ajar. Yul rang the bell, and Crawford summoned him to her boudoir.

Intrigued, he followed her well-known voice to the bedroom. She was awaiting him on her *chaise-longue*, scantily clad, expecting to be serviced promptly and efficiently, with no sloppy sentimentalism. He obliged, but it was among the least erotic half-hours of his life, and he left feeling offended by the whole exercise. Ardent as Yul was, to him romance meant chivalry, seduction and conquest, not hit-and-run humping.

Judy Garland came to see *Lute Song* the night the play closed in Los Angeles. Her husband, Vincente Minnelli, was not with her. This was less than a decade after *The Wizard of Oz*: her daughter Liza was only a year old. That night, when he met her after the show, Yul fell in love with Judy, and they began their short, secret romance. This really was a romance, but the obstacles were insurmountable: to begin with, they were both married. Since their respective spouses were out of town, their immediate problem was that Yul had to leave for Chicago. After several weeks in LA word had come that the Studebaker Theater in Chicago was available. The producer, still trying to capitalize on Claudia Cassidy's review, announced their final show on the Coast.

Judy tried to free time to visit him, but MGM would not rearrange her shooting schedule. They concocted another plan to arrange a tryst. Using her considerable clout, Judy persuaded MGM to fly Yul back out to LA, ostensibly for the purpose of shooting a screen test. Reluctantly, the studio agreed to test Yul for the lead role in a film about the life of Rudolph Valentino, of all people. Sure enough, within a week Yul was on a plane to Hollywood. And while it only served as a pretext for a few nights of passion, somewhere at MGM there exists a canister of film with a 26-year-old Yul Brynner cloaked as Rudolph Valentino in *The Sheik*.

That week, Judy and Yul ended their brief affair. After all, they had families to attend to.

If money had been a problem before, with a baby it was a real anxiety for Virginia, if not for Yul. While he was earning a steady paycheck with *Lute Song*, it was not enough to fund his extravagant style—that much was ominous. In fact, he was still handing out engraved cigarette cases while family and friends chipped in to help pay the hospital bill for his son's birth. Virginia urged Yul to find steady work, so they could raise the baby in a place that didn't smell like a dry-cleaner's. Perhaps, she suggested, CBS could use a floor manager.

Yul made it exquisitely clear to one and all that he was not temperamentally suited to be a floor manager. Since there was no other work, he accepted producer Myerberg's offer to play *Lute Song* in London. After a few months in that role, the play closed and he was offered the romantic lead in *Dark Eyes* which ran for almost a year at London's Strand Theatre. Virginia and the baby crossed the Atlantic by ship to join him. They lived well, considering they were in postwar Britain, but they spent every shilling Yul earned, and when *Dark Eyes* closed, Yul was completely broke. His wife and child went home by airplane. Hoping to follow with a little folding cash, Yul sat down to a poker game, and ended up losing his plane ticket home. At least, that's what he reported to Virginia. The next morning he was on his way to Paris.

Much had changed in the eight years since he had left his beloved Paris. The German occupation had left its mark: clubs and restaurants were empty or closed, and the Dimitrieviches were nowhere to be found. At first Yul was told they had been taken off to concentration camps, where some 400,000 European gypsies had died. Later, he learned the family had escaped to Argentina. Through the manager of Maxim's, Yul found work performing at a club, and returned to New York only a few months later. There had never been any doubt in his mind that he would return to New York: his infant son had become a powerful magnet. He let everyone know that having a son was important to him: it gave him hope that at last someone might share his precise perspective of the world.

In 1948 Yul and Virginia tried pooling their talents at CBS, and proposed themselves as co-hosts for the first husband and wife talk show in television history, *Mr. and Mrs*. They were hired and put on the air live every afternoon for thirteen weeks. Later Yul described it for the *Saturday Evening Post*:

Hilarious . . . Virginia and I were the producers, writers, directors and performers, although we occasionally had guests if we could hoodwink some unsuspecting celebrity. We paid our guests' taxi fare. The budget didn't allow more than that. But we got some startling offbeat effects. The idea was that when we went on the air, we'd chat with our guests for ten or twelve minutes, then the floor manager would snap his fingers and yell, "You're on!" Virginia would turn to me and say with a surprised air, "We're on," and I'd say, round-eyed, "We are, are we?": then, theoretically, we were on the air for the first time, although we had already started our conversations with our guests. Once we staged a meeting between Salvador Dalí and Al Capp. The conversation was so censorable I'm amazed we were allowed to stay on the air, but in the end they did something very charming. They both did a drawing on the same sheet of paper. It was during Al's Shmoo period, and he did a drawing of a Shmoo. While he was drawing it, Dalí drew a window in its stomach, showing a desert horizon and skeletons in the distance throwing long shadows.

Often their year-old son Rocky stayed all day with them at the television studio. That's right, little Yul had become Rocky, after Rocky Graziano. They figured it was a good, street-tough name for a Manhattan brat.

At the start of the final broadcast Yul opened a bottle of champagne and poured them each a glass: Virginia went to take a sip, only to spit it out in a vesuvian spray. She also spat out a frisky goldfish Yul had put in her glass.

After weeks of job-hunting, Yul capitulated and sought steady work at CBS. They hired him as a director, which was hardly steady work in those days, even for someone who respected authority, which Yul clearly did not. But for three years Yul directed a wide variety of television shows for CBS. This, despite the fact that he was fired more than once for insubordination of one kind or another. Then, because of the shortage of trained TV directors, he would be grudgingly re-hired and assigned to some demeaning chore. As soon as he'd

directed something again and decided he was indispensable to
CBS, his creativity on camera would emerge again, and management would feel compelled to fire him once more. His stunts
were usually experimental in nature. Once, for example, when
he was assigned to direct a bald singer, as filler material between scheduled programs, he noticed that the fellow was tapping his foot. Yul split the screen horizontally, took the camera
shot of the foot tapping, and placed it so that it looked as if
the foot were tapping the top of the singer's bald head. He was
fired immediately. Rehired a week later, he was assigned to
direct a filler of a little-known black piano-player with a toothy
grin. Again Yul split the screen, and showed only half of the
top of the pianist's face, and below it the fingers dancing back
and forth across the keyboard, as if the fellow were playing
the ivories of his own smile.

Because of its novelty, and its dramatic possibilities, tele-
vision attracted some of the best young talent from the theater:
Yul's two closest friends at CBS were directors Marty Ritt and
Sidney Lumet. They took turns directing shows on *Studio One*,
Danger and *Omnibus*; Yul's assistant was a kid named Johnny
Frankenheimer. With other broadcasting pioneers of the time—
Edward R. Murrow, Walter Cronkite, Paddy Chayevsky and
Budd Schulberg—they were inventing the fundamental vocab-
ulary of broadcast news, drama and sports.

CBS provided a steady income, but the salary was still no
match for Yul's spending. The baby was a financial burden,
and the couple were just no damn good with money. It was
little wonder, really, that when their checks bounced, they
began to have their noisiest fights. Oh yes, they argued aloud—
but only when the baby was out of earshot.

Neighbors recalled that while they shouted and screamed
quite a lot, most of the time their behavior in public together,
after five years of marriage, was very passionate, even em-
barrassing; sometimes, the passion seemed to follow directly
upon the arguments. They usually argued about money, and
occasionally about politics. Although they were both to the
political left of mainstream America, Yul retained a certain
cynicism about social reform. After a few years, when they
had begun having brief affairs which they hid from everybody
except each other, they finally had something *real* to argue

about. Perhaps fling is a better word than affair for most of their romances. As for Yul's encounter with Tallulah Bankhead, it was no fling—it was more like a collision.

Yul had often been attracted to older women: nevertheless, he was not especially attracted to Tallulah Bankhead. They had met when Tallulah was in her late forties, at an Actor's Fund benefit luncheon, back when *Lute Song* was still on Broadway. Tallulah was sitting, hung over, between Yul and a bubbly young understudy who had just been catapulted to stardom in a hit musical. Tallulah nursed her third Bloody Mary as the ingénue prattled on about seeing her name in lights.

"And do you know what, Miss Bankhead?" intoned the bubbly ingénue, leaning forward with a stage whisper, "I'm still a virgin! I still have my cherry."

Tallulah slammed down her highball glass and glared at the kid. "Baby," she replied, "doesn't it get in your way when you fuck?"

After the luncheon Yul helped Tallulah out to the street and offered to drop her at her hotel; but in the cab the aging Southern belle began demanding that Yul escort her to her room. The more he refused, the more defensive she became about her body. Finally, trying to convince him, she tore open her blouse to show him how youthful her breasts were. Unfortunately for everybody, she did it just as the hotel doorman opened the cab door.

Not long after the *Mr. and Mrs.* show folded, Yul was offered another talk show, working on both sides of the camera. But this time it would go out on the air live from the fanciest club New York had to offer, The Stork Club. During Yul's broadcast one day, Tallulah stumbled drunkenly in to the club, having heard that Yul was there. Failing to note the cameras, the crew, or Virginia, Tallulah advanced swiftly toward Yul, unbuttoned her blouse, dropped her coat and announced to the world, in her deepest baritone, "Look, Yul, look—isn't that better? I had my tits lifted!"

At least, that's the story Yul told Virginia.

In late 1948 Yul's father arrived in New York with Katya. It was only a short visit—Boris's health was not good, and he

was anxious to see his grown children. Yul was largely preoccupied at CBS, so Boris spent most of his time with Virginia
and his grandson Rocky. Although it was becoming obvious
that Boris would probably not live long enough to visit again,
Yul's attitude toward his father remained ambivalent. For years
he had despised Boris for abandoning the family: then, he had
grown close to Boris and Katya, and turned palpably cooler
toward his own mother—perhaps because of stories he heard.
In fact, Yul grew emotionally distant from both his parents at
the end of their lives. He was glad that Boris could visit to see
his own son, Yul Jr., the great-grandson of Jules; but Yul was
completely involved in all things American—Dodger games,
Coney Island, and new recordings of Charlie Parker—and he
did not much care to reflect upon his childhood in Vladivostok.
Boris returned to the Orient, where he died the following year.
A few years later, Katya succumbed to cancer in London.

After almost a decade living and working prominently in
New York, the Brynners had become very much a part of the
city's creative social world, on the fringes of the Power Elite.
Their friends included most of the hard-working theater crowd,
actors, writers, artists and directors. Bil and Cora Baird, the
marionetteers, were close friends, as was Julio deDiego, the
painter married to Gypsy Rose Lee; and film composer Alex
North and his wife Sherle; Sidney Lumet, who was dating the
actress Rita Gam; Marty and Adele Ritt; and a young agent
who introduced him to Gucci shoes, and signed Yul as one of
his first clients. His name was Ted Ashley.

When Virginia was cast in the lead of a play called *The
Gray-Eyed People*, she hired a young black nanny, Hazel, to
help her with the baby in Philadelphia. The Brynners' hotel
refused to allow Hazel to use the front entrance because of her
race. Although the show was opening that same night, Virginia
insisted on changing hotels. From then on, Hazel remained
with the Brynners loyally for several years, even after Yul
accused her of stealing a wad of money, when in fact he had
merely forgotten where he had hidden it.

With the kind of single-minded determination that he was becoming known for, Yul had kept fresh in his mind the vow he

had taken in Deauville, to become a movie star by the age of thirty. In his twenty-ninth year he was offered the role of a suave villain in a small "B" movie called *Port of New York*. Scott Brady was the star, playing a narcotics officer; Yul played the cruel and exotic killer who specialized, of all things, in smuggling opium.

The film had all the artistry of an industrial commercial. It looked as if the Port Authority had final cut. Yul took his paycheck and laughed off the whole adventure. Given the end result, that was about all he could do. He also stole the film. *Port of New York* is one of those movies in which you're forced to root for the villain just because he's so much more interesting than the hero. Yul's character is faintly reptilian, almost lizard-like. In a soft voice, with an indeterminate, Continental accent, wavy black hair, and a taste for suede gloves, his character stands out like a sinister fugitive from Rick's Café who has stumbled into some Air Force training film.

So it was that, by the end of the 1940s, Yul reached the target he had aimed at since adolescence. It was not much of a movie, to be sure. Nonetheless, he had made it to the silver screen. And he was right on schedule.

3

Broadway King

"I am King as I was born to be, Siam to be ruled
in my way. Not English way, not French way, not
Chinese way . . . *My* way."
—Oscar Hammerstein, *The King and I*

When *South Pacific* opened at the Majestic Theater in April
1949 starring Mary Martin and Ezio Pinza, it became the third
triumphant musical by Rodgers and Hammerstein in that decade. In 1943 they had redefined the American musical with
Oklahoma! Two things in particular signalled its revolutionary
impact. First, more than any operetta or vaudeville musical,
the songs were part of the plot; even the ballet of Laurey's
dream advanced the story line. That ballet was avant-garde in
other respects: Agnes DeMille's choreography fused classical
ballet with the Freudian unconscious, both of which she pop-
ularized in this dream sequence. The other revolutionary aspect
of *Oklahoma!*, in the midst of its untrammeled celebration of
all things American, was that the play had no villain: Jud is
portrayed as a twisted, unhappy figure, a "bullet-colored,
growly man," but not an instrument of Satan—a fact empha-
sized in Curly's dirge "Pore Jud Is Daid," which never suggests that Jud is bound for hell, only that "his fingernails have
never b'en so clean."

Rodgers and Hammerstein then adapted *Liliom*, Ferenc Mol-
nár's lyric fantasy. It became *Carousel,* with John Raitt as the
irresistible Billy Bigelow—barker and braggadocio—and
opened in April 1945 to universal acclaim. Then came *South
Pacific*, which contrasted the fates of two sets of lovers torn
apart by institutionalized racism, the same that was quietly

45

tearing apart America. With the song "You've Got To Be Taught," the creators brought that national disgrace to the forefront of American popular culture.

Rodgers and Hammerstein began looking for their next vehicle. Margaret Landon's chronicle of an English schoolmistress in Siam had been filmed in 1946: *Anna and the King of Siam,* starring Irene Dunne and Rex Harrison, Linda Darnell and Lee J. Cobb, is still an interesting film, with good performances. Hammerstein chose to use a great deal of the book unchanged. It seemed a curious choice for a musical, but they went ahead anyway. The result was *The King and I.*

In the Sunday *New York Times* four days before the opening, Rodgers and Hammerstein wrote a piece describing the play, and their reasons for undertaking it:

Our basic problem was how far could we capture this remote reality and still give our production the lift and glow that all musical plays must have. Obviously *The King and I* is not an example of stark realism in the theater, or a documentary work on the orient in the middle of the nineteenth century. We have not been slavishly literal in following the book, nor completely conscientious historically. But in spite of whatever factual compromises we have seen fit to make, we have tried very hard, within our own romantic medium, to present the King and Anna as the genuine and fascinating man and woman we believe they were.

The strength of their story lies in the violent changes they wrought in each other. Yet their life together bears unmistakable implications of deep mutual attraction—a man and woman relationship so strong and real and well founded that it seems in some ways more than a love affair, more than a marriage . . .

The intangibility of their strange union was a challenge to us as librettist and composer. In dealing with them musically we could not write songs which said "I love you" or even "I love him" or "I love her." We were dealing with two characters who could indulge themselves only in oblique expressions of their feelings for each other, since they themselves did not realize exactly what those feelings were . . .

We knew, and everyone else knew, that Miss [Gertrude] Lawrence was one of our most versatile actresses. In addition, with faith in their past performances, we rounded up Yul Brynner to play the King, John van Druten to direct, Jerome Robbins to create the choreography, Irene Sharaff to design the costumes and Jo Mielziner to do the sets.

Gertrude Lawrence had been born in nineteenth-century London. She had first starred on Broadway twenty-five years before, in 1926, when she had introduced the song "Someone to Watch Over Me" in George Gershwin's *Oh Kay!* But it was with Noël Coward in *Private Lives* that she found the right material, and a co-star who was at least her match for wit and panache. Through the 1940s Gertie, as she was known, rarely took an intermission from the stage, on one side or the other of the Atlantic. In 1936, she and Noël had performed *Tonight at 8:30,* a set of Coward one-act plays. She returned to Broadway in 1939, starring in *Lady in the Dark,* written by Moss Hart, with lyrics by Ira Gershwin, music by Kurt Weill, and costarring Danny Kaye and Victor Mature. In 1945, she revived *Pygmalion,* playing Eliza Doolittle, to Shaw's delight.

In his biography of Rodgers and Hammerstein, Frederick Nolan described the sequence of events this way:

The film was a big hit (even though Fox had wanted James Mason or Robert Montgomery as the King), and after seeing it, musical comedy star Gertrude Lawrence became convinced that she and only she should play Anna on the stage, and that she should do so in a show written for her by Rodgers and Hammerstein. They were still unconvinced . . . her vocal range was, to say the least of it, limited, and she had a distressing tendency to sing flat. They had never set out to write a show with a specific star in mind . . . they asked Fox to screen the movie for them. They emerged determined to do the show no matter what.

It was Mary Martin who recommended Yul for the new musical. Richard and Oscar had not seen *Lute Song.* Yul was reluctant, and Virginia was downright unhappy that Yul would even consider giving up steady work for another acting job that would put him on a nighttime schedule and, eventually, come to an end. Yul countered that she was jealous—afraid to see Mr. Gilmore become famous in his own right. Virginia insisted she was just concerned about their family life. But Mary Martin persuaded Virginia that it was an irresistible match of actor and character, and besides, Yul agreed that he would continue directing at CBS *while* starring on Broadway.

Richard Rodgers described Yul's audition:

> They told us the name of the first man and out he came with a bald head and sat cross-legged on the stage. He had a guitar, and he hit this guitar one whack and gave out with this unearthly yell and sang some heathenish sort of thing, and Oscar and I looked at each other and said, ''Well, that's it!''

They had offered the role to Rex Harrison, but he was unavailable, preparing for a production of T. S. Eliot's *The Cocktail Party*. They then considered Alfred Drake who, thanks to *Oklahoma!*, had become too big a star to consider the small salary offered. Gertie, it seems, was already taking 10 percent of the gross and a further 5 percent of the net. She liked Yul, whom she had met years before at The Stork Club. He and his young agent Ted Ashley agreed that this show would affirm his stardom once and for all. The budget for the entire production was an unimaginable $250,000, and the actual cost exceeded the budget by a further $100,000. Consider then, that choreographer Jerome Robbins was paid $350 a week. Yul received somewhat less.

What was *The King and I* all about? Rodgers and Hammerstein made it clear that it was an oblique love story; but also that the story was neither biographical nor historical. For example, Hammerstein decided that the King must die at the end of the play, years before the real King did. Historical circumstance had little to do with the dramatic themes that gave the story its structure. At first glance, it seems that the play is about the triumph of democratic thinking over royal rule. A Welsh widow is invited to be schoolteacher to the royal children of the polygamous King of Siam—and she stays to transform the kingdom into a modern, democratic state. It is not exactly monarchy she seeks to eliminate, for she is herself a loyal subject to Queen Victoria. Mrs. Anna is defending the equal dignity of all people: if reason and compassion are to prevail in government, the King will have to give up his willful, arbitrary rule. The King has already foreseen the end of autocracy in his soliloquy, early in Act One, " 'Tis a Puzzlement.''

But then, is this musical really just about a schoolmarm who teaches etiquette to a bare-chested monarch?

Before he began rehearsing with Yul, it may not have been clear to Hammerstein that the primary conflict of the play was within the soul of the king: a Manichean struggle between reason and passion, instead of good and evil. The King, as Yul conceived him, represents the soul of an angel struggling to escape from the body of a beast. Though in their struggle for predominance Mrs. Anna wins every battle, she loses her heart to the King—along with every woman in the audience, and every man who identified with the King.

Everything Yul had learned in his thirty years, everything that had made his own life unique, was fused in this performance: all the mystery of the Orient from his childhood, his experience as a gypsy singer, his acrobat's physique, and the emphasis on physical characterization which Chekhov had taught him. Instead of reproducing a nineteenth-century oriental monarch, he completely re-invented the King. Gradually, Yul took command of the overall production: not because his assertive nature demanded it, not because he alone could coax Gertie to rehearse, not because there was a power vacuum—though all that was true. He took command of the production because only Yul could imagine the King, without whom there was no play. This was a role in which he could "lead with his cock.''

I spent much of my childhood on the backstage side of Siam, in the basements and dressing-rooms of the St. James Theater, filled with the King's wives and children, the dancers and the orchestra musicians in black tie, and stagehands shooting craps and betting the ponies. After the show I would always sit in my father's tiny dressing-room and meet the dignitaries who came to see him. In particular, I remember one guest, an

ancient old man who came backstage after a matinee. As I
shook hands with him, my father told me never to forget it. It
seems this old codger had served in the Civil War. But what
was even more remarkable was that, when he was a boy, he
had shaken hands with another ancient old man, who had
served under General Washington in the Revolution.

"Remember this, laddie, for the book you may write some-
day," my father said. "You once shook hands with a man who
shook hands with a Revolutionary soldier."

"Oh Dad, I'll never remember that."

Nolan, the biographer of Rodgers and Hammerstein, writes:

> Yul Brynner proceeded to make the part of the King—and
> indeed, much of the play—his own. The director of *The
> King and I* was John Van Druten, but Van Druten wasn't
> tough enough to handle Gertrude Lawrence, who was in-
> secure and temperamental. Brynner had directed on Broad-
> way [*sic*] and in television . . . When he spoke, Lawrence
> listened. Rodgers confesses that they would have been in a
> lot of trouble had Brynner not been around.

Performances began at the Shubert Theater in New Haven on
February 26, 1951, with Gertie singing so far off key as to
make the audiences consistently uncomfortable. The show ran
for well over three hours, and it included such long since
vanished numbers as "Waiting," "Who Would Refuse?" and
"Now You Leave." According to Nolan, Leland Hayward,
who had invested $15,000 with his wife Nancy, shocked Rodg-
ers by suggesting that they close out of town. While Gertie
concentrated on her singing, Yul worked on his accent. A blend
of French and Russian, it was already strange enough offstage.
When he tinged his accelerated singsong with an oriental twang,
the result was often incomprehensible.

The King was a creature of Yul's imagination: short in stature
and barefoot, he had nonetheless to dominate the St. James
Theater and environs totally—and sing loud enough to reach
the horizon. The character of the King—his willfulness, his
innocence, his noble ambitions—was there in the script: but

the stature, power and urgency of the King all came from Yul. The animal magnetism of the King's fierce prowl grew directly out of Chekhov's exercises. Yul imagined the movement of a wolf, a bull, a stallion, even a panther: not by analyzing, but by *imagining*. On a cold March night in New York, his imagination filled the stage with tropical warmth. He was barechested and barefoot throughout most of the play, but never failed to make the audience feel warm. When the King erupted with anger in the second act, the climate in the theater became volcanic. And the moment the King first saw Mrs. Anna as a woman, his eyes could have ignited a forest.

No single element defined the style of the production better than the King's make-up, which Yul designed himself. Everyone else onstage was in ''life-like'' make-up: only the King wore a fierce mask of paint. Kabuki-like, inspired by the classic masks of Siam, his make-up set the character apart, and the King took on an entirely different dimension of reality than the other characters on stage. The face alone took Yul more than an hour to paint each night: and then there was his body, which he sponged liberally with dark walnut make-up, the same shade, in fact, that Lena Horne used: Light Egyptian.

Oh yes, the bald head. His black wavy hair was almost gone now, and only a bit more than a fringe was growing. He had already clipped his hair close to the skull for the audition. Designer Irene Sharaff encouraged him to use electric barbershop clippers, which resulted in a nearly shaved head. She pointed out that as a matter of history, the King had spent time in a Buddhist monastery. With that bit of information, Yul was easily persuaded. Virginia's enthusiasm lagged a tad behind.

Dick and Oscar were still looking for a way to give the whole show ''lift,'' and Gertie suggested she sing with the children. When Mary Martin visited them out of town, she reminded them of the schottische ''Suddenly Lucky,'' which they had dropped from *South Pacific*. Within days, Oscar had transformed the song into ''Getting to Know You.''

The most innovative element of the production was the Siamese ballet version of *Uncle Tom's Cabin,* created by Jerome Robbins at the peak of his inspiration. The choreographer remained at that professional peak throughout the 1950s, as he turned out success after success: *Peter Pan, West Side Story,*

Gypsy. The ballet in *The King and I* continued the tradition of a play within a play, but in all other respects it was unprecedented. The fusion of Rodgers' music, Hammerstein's narrative, Sharaff's costumes and Robbins' choreography produced a unique moment of theater and dance.

Nevertheless, it was when Gertie began sailing through the air during "Shall We Dance?" that the production really got off the ground. And it took a lot of practice: dancing was emphatically *not* one of Yul's natural graces, or of Gertie's. But once they had rehearsed enough to avoid tripping over Mrs. Anna's voluminous skirts and falling on their faces, the play was made. The power of the King sweeping Mrs. Anna literally off her feet satisfies the audience's craving for some romantic union between the two.

From "Shall We Dance?" the play moves swiftly to its conclusion, as secret agents drag in the fugitive concubine of the King, who dares to love another man. Mrs. Anna pleads for the girl as the King roars to the gods: "Am I to be cuckold in my own palace?" Tearing off his shirt, he prepares to bullwhip the girl. It is a moment of monumental power on the live stage. Something real actually happens as the King confronts his own violence, something within him breaks. Poised to strike the girl, he flings the bullwhip past her and bolts from the hall in humiliation. Perhaps it is his very will to live that is broken because, when next we see him, he is on his deathbed. The sequence was a problem for Yul—the death scene followed directly upon "Shall We Dance?" and the whipping scene, and he could barely regain his breath for the controlled whispering that was demanded of him minutes later. After a week of performances, Yul decided to have Don Lawson, his loyal valet, stand by with an oxygen tank. Yul would lie down on a gurney in the wings and breathe oxygen, deliberately slowing his pulse and respiration, as he had learned in hatha yoga. It worked.

March 1951. It was Truman's America, all forty-eight states of it. Orchestra seats were $5. Phone calls cost a nickel. Advance sales for *The King and I* were good, but 1951 was the year television erupted across America with national broadcasting—the number of TV sets in America multiplied tenfold that year, and the sale of movie tickets was plummeting. No one knew how Broadway as a whole would fare, but all the indicators suggested success: *South Pacific* was still the biggest hit in town, and even before *The King and I* opened, Frank Sinatra was in a studio recording three songs from the show: "We Kiss in a Shadow," "I Whistle a Happy Tune," and "Hello, Young Lovers."

As always, Yul suffered intense stage fright before every performance. Starting with the first dress rehearsal in New Haven, he became accustomed to vomiting about an hour before curtain, and he trembled perceptibly on his way to the stage. But once the curtain went up, his fierce concentration and imagination took command: he wore the character like skin.

It was as if Yul had been born to represent authoritarian paternalism. The King was tyrant, father-figure, and prolific sire to a nation of children. He was an innocent, struggling with the paradoxes of life, reluctantly accepting the invaluable help of an educated woman. To women he represented an appealing image of the dominant man, a willful little boy at heart, who is utterly dependent upon Anna's knowledge. To men he represented masculinity itself, full of swagger and masterful power. And he was as mysterious and exotic a figure as they had ever been in the same room with.

The play was a triumph from opening night. But Brooks Atkinson, the leading critic of the *New York Times,* stuck his neck out in the first paragraph of the review: "As a matter of record, it must be reported that *The King and I* is no match for *South Pacific,* which is an inspired musical drama." A few weeks later, in the Sunday edition, Atkinson ate crow.

Like *South Pacific, The King and I* is a skillfully written musical drama with a well-designed libretto, a rich score, a memorable performance and a magnificent production . . . Mr. Rodgers and Mr. Hammerstein have got way beyond the mechanical formulae on which musical shows are founded and are saying something fundamental about human beings. Again, like *South Pacific, The King and I* is literature, and since the literature is expressed largely in music, it is tremendously moving . . . Always a charming woman,

> Gertrude Lawrence plays the part of Anna with force and intelligence . . . Yul Brynner's vehement, restless, keen-minded King is a terse and vivid characterization with a blazing spirit and stylized ruthlessness of manners and make-up.

In his opening night review, Atkinson's mention of Yul said only that he played the role with "a kind of fierce austerity," and he added, "Mr. Brynner is no great shakes as a singer, but he makes his way safely through a couple of meditative songs." At least according to one biography of Yul, Otis L. Gurney Jr. in the *Herald Tribune* was more effusive: "Musicals and leading men will never be the same after last night . . . Brynner set an example that will be hard to follow . . . Probably the best show of the decade."

Outside the St. James Theater every night large crowds collected—so large, in fact, that mounted police escorted Gertie, and later Yul, as they left the theater. This was not uncommon in the early 1950s, except that the crowds usually slacked off after a couple of weeks. For *The King and I* the cops on horseback were still needed when the play closed on Broadway two years later. One of the police was Chris Forster, a young sergeant on his way to detective, with whom Yul soon became fast friends.

Yul's success was galling to Virginia. She was grateful for the financial stability, but she realized that her career had been eclipsed and that, with the responsibilities of motherhood, it probably could never be revived. The Brynners were finally able to move out of the room over the dry-cleaner's to a large, bright flat overlooking Central Park. Admittedly, it was on 104th Street, but after seven years of naphthalene it *seemed* like home, and they delighted in decorating it—in their different ways. For all her devotion to Rocky, Virginia was not ready to retire at thirty-one: she kept trying to find film and stage work. And she began drinking a little too much wine alone at home in the evening, when her husband was at the theater and her little boy was asleep. Finally, Virginia did just what Marousia had done a generation earlier: with lasting regret, she renounced her acting career.

While playing eight shows a week, Yul actually continued to direct at CBS during the day. He directed some episodes of *You Are There,* a documentary-style dramatic show introduced by Walter Cronkite; he even starred in one episode as François Villon. He appeared twice on the Ed Sullivan show, and directed a few more episodes of *Studio One.* On *Omnibus* in March 1953 he directed a dramatization of Hemingway's *Capital of the World,* starring a teenage Anne Bancroft who was unable to relax in front of the television camera, Yul said, until he persuaded her to remove her bra. This was an original technique of Yul's—one he did not learn from Michael Chekhov. Bancroft's costar was a 13-year-old Italian kid from the Bronx, playing an aspiring young matador. Yul liked the kid so much he hired him to play Prince Chulalongkorn in *The King and I.* Eventually he became like another son to Yul and Virginia, and a big brother to Rocky: the kid's name was Sal Mineo.

With the play's success, Yul began meeting all the stars and personalities who visited New York, many of whom were curious enough to come backstage to shake his hand: dignitaries from Albert Schweitzer to Eleanor Roosevelt, and entertainers like Frank Sinatra and Joe E. Lewis. Real monarchs of the world, including Queen Juliana of the Netherlands, were only too happy to welcome Yul's elevation to their ranks, even if it was all in jest. In the circumstances, they were well aware that it was Yul's power that had drawn them there. Adults, General MacArthur included, became intimidated backstage. Naturally, children always felt comfortable with the King, because of the love he showed for the children onstage.

In 1952, as *The King and I* began its second year, Michael Chekhov wrote a book entitled *To the Actor,* in which he encapsulated what he had learned in more than half a century in the theater. The book was dedicated to his longtime assistant and collaborator, George Shdanoff, who had been Yul's coach. Chekhov asked Yul to write the preface.

New York, July 23, 1952
Dear Mr. Chekhov, my dear Professor:

It started in the late twenties when I saw you in a repertory
of plays that you did in Paris: *Inspector General, Eric the
Fourteenth, Twelfth Night, Hamlet*, etc. I came out with the
deep conviction that through you and through you only I
could find what I was working for—a concrete and tangible
way to reach a mastery of the elusive thing that one calls
the technique of acting...

I tried to join your group when you first started the Chekhov Theater at Dartington Hall in England. Then I heard that
you had moved to America with most of your group to
continue your work in Connecticut, and it took me several
years, through all the world events to finally come to America
with the sole purpose of at last working with you...

... When you are a pianist you have an outside instrument
that you learn to master through finger work and arduous
exercises and with it, you as a creative artist can perform
and express your art. As an actor, you the artist have to
perform on the most difficult instrument to master, that is,
your own self—your physical and emotional being...

Yours,
Yul Brynner

By this time, Michael Chekhov had settled in California, working as a coach and teacher of a number of established Hollywood stars. Gregory Peck was one, and a promising newcomer,
a young blonde named Marilyn Monroe, was another. Marilyn
was devoted to Chekhov. In his workshop she played Cordelia
to Chekhov's King Lear. She once gave him a portrait of
Abraham Lincoln with this message: "Lincoln was the man I
admired most all through school. Now that man is you."

She studied *To the Actor* religiously, and relied upon Chekhov's technique in all her early roles. When she missed lessons,
she was racked by remorse. One note she wrote to him said:
"Dear Mr. Chekhov, please don't give up on me yet—I know
(painfully so) that I try your patience. I need the work and your
friendship desperately. I shall call you soon. Love, Marilyn
Monroe."

Not long after, Michael Chekhov died. Marilyn contributed generously to a fund for Chekhov's widow, and even left a bequest for her in her will. In the meantime, Marilyn hoped to find someone else who could teach her Chekhov's technique, and remembered that Chekhov had asked Yul to write his preface. It was also about then, while working with director Billy Wilder on *The Seven Year Itch*, that she first expressed an ambition to play Grushenka in a dramatization of *The Brothers Karamazov*, which Chekhov had told her was the greatest work of literature. This idea was widely mocked in the Hollywood press: Billy Wilder reportedly replied that he'd be happy to direct Marilyn Monroe in ''a whole series of Karamazov sequels, such as *The Brothers Karamazov Meet Abbott and Costello*.'' The studio that had her under contract, Yul's old nemesis, Twentieth Century-Fox, actually announced it had no intention of permitting her to play the role, although at that time no one was even working on the project.

Gertrude Lawrence's closest friend was, of course, Noël Coward, who came to see *The King and I* soon after it opened. So did Coward's longtime friend, Marlene Dietrich, who prevailed upon Noël to introduce her to Yul. That first evening their romance began, and it continued off and on throughout most of the 1950s. This was quite unlike any other affair he'd had— Marlene was like no other lover. For the first time, Yul found himself making love to a woman whom he had admired since his childhood. Marlene Dietrich and Yul Brynner: in some ways it was so right, these two exotic nightclub entertainers, that they could *almost* overlook the fact that Marlene was twenty years older than Yul; at least, Marlene could. She was also the most determined, passionate and possessive lover he had ever known, not in the least concerned about discretion since, after all, she was not married. It would have suited her fine if Yul's marriage to Virginia had collapsed. She even grew fond of Rocky during the hours she spent with the little boy backstage. And he was crazy about her, too.

But the fact remained that she was almost twice Yul's age. It was up to Yul to enforce discretion, not only with Marlene, but with the other women who regularly offered themselves to him after the play. As his fame grew, so did his reputation for romance, until it became too risky for him to continue slipping into hotel rooms. Finally, as a solution, Yul rented a studio flat secretly, just for his romantic trysts, and especially for the nights he spent with Marlene, before slipping home at dawn. His dresser kept the place tidy and supplied with fresh clothing. Whatever she may have guessed, Virginia never knew about the flat.

Most nights after the curtain came down Yul set out on the town, looking for excitement. Ten years earlier he had been a powerless foreigner broke in the streets of New York, an object of his *own* contempt. Now he was the toast of the town, the King of New York, and he reveled in his triumph. After a midnight supper he might spend a couple of hours winding down at Eddie Condon's, with old friends or new. Or Sugar Ray Robinson might pick him up in his heliotrope Cadillac and, with five-year-old Rocky asleep on the back seat, run up to Ray's club in Harlem for nightcaps. Or he might go down to Chinatown with Danny Kaye; or up to the Carlisle to pick up Marlene for a night in his *pied à terre,* before returning to his unhappy wife at dawn. Fortunately, he could thrive on less than five hours' sleep each night.

Yul loved being a star. By the time he was thirty-one, his most farfetched fantasies of power and fame had all come true. He was the leading man of American theater. That is exactly what he remained for the next three years, and 1,246 performances. He had made the play his own, and everyone knew it. Ordinarily, Gertie might have been a little irked at this shift of focus, but two things prevented that. First, she herself passionately adored Yul. Second, she was dying. By the end of 1951, she was diagnosed as having leukemia. Keeping the gravity of her illness secret, she took an extended vacation after New Year's Eve, during which time Celeste Holm played the part. Gertie returned to the stage in mid-March.

The last performance that Gertie and Yul gave was just three weeks before her death in September 1952. Until then they performed Yul's deathbed scene every night knowing full well that she was the one who was dying. Yul's adoration for Gertie, while never romantic, made this the toughest test of thick skin he'd ever had to pass. It was she more than anyone else who had helped him achieve stardom.

In the summers the Brynners rented a house in Norwalk, Connecticut, at a spot called Wilson's Point. It was only twenty-five miles away from the house near Danbury where Yul had studied acting with Chekhov a decade before. Weekdays, Yul often stayed in the city, but because of his passion for sea bass fishing, he often drove back to Connecticut at about three in the morning. After a cup of coffee, he went out on the Long Island Sound with his son and a crusty old local, to try out a new spoon-lure that sea bass just couldn't resist. In the late morning he would nap before heading back to the city in his new 1952 Cadillac, to face two hours of make-up and costume, followed by three hours of performance. Yul's exuberance was something no one else could keep up with, even Don, his best pal and closest confidant. It was there, off the shore of Norwalk, that the Brynners' lifelong love of waterskiing began. When Virginia's birthday came that year, Yul gave her a speedboat, christened with her nickname, *Gin*. Yul and Don took Rocky along to pick up the speedboat on the East River, and cruised up the coast past Norwalk, to the house.

Between new Cadillacs every year, the new flat, the summerhouse, the speedboat, and hand-tailored suits, Yul's spending continued to outstrip his earnings. This was true even after Gertie's death, when he received top billing and a dramatic pay increase. In fact, he and Gin were on something of a financial binge: the bedroom in their new flat over Central Park had a working fireplace, wall-to-wall lambskin carpeting, and a kingsize bed suspended from the ceiling by brass elephant chains from India. Their bedside lights were small crystal chandeliers, and one wall was antique mirror. The living-room had a grand piano, striped satin furniture, a television built-in to the bookcase, and a stereo hi-fi with a Rube Goldberg record-changer that physically flipped the record to play both sides. Yul loved gimmicks like that.

He just wasn't worried about the debts; especially after a

small stranger barged his way backstage during the intermission. Later Yul described what happened:

> I was spending hours creating an illusion of character, and everything I worked for would be destroyed for anyone who came backstage to see me in the middle of the performance. I couldn't talk to a visitor in the character of the King, because Rodgers and Hammerstein had written no dressing-room dialogue for me to use on visitors. However, one evening when the curtain came down after the first act, someone said, "A man who claims to be Cecil B. De Mille wants to see you." I couldn't refuse to see a man of his stature—a man who has created far more illusion than I ever dreamed of. So I said, "If his illusion about me as the King is destroyed, that's his problem. Show him in." When he was ushered in he said, "How would you like to play in a picture which your grandchildren will be able to see?" I said, "I'd like it very much . . ." He told me about Rameses, and in a few minutes he gave me such highlights of Rameses' character and such glimpses of the immensity and richness of the material that before he left I accepted the part and we shook hands. From then on, it didn't matter what the business people did about the contract.

De Mille, of course, was the man who had directed the first feature-length motion picture of all time, *The Squaw Man*. He was one of the men who had virtually invented Hollywood, having built the first movie studio and then created Paramount Pictures. De Mille was offering Yul the role of the Pharaoh in a remake of his silent, 1923 black-and-white masterpiece, *The Ten Commandments*. Filming was still more than a year away.

At this point, Yul had a number of options. Several film scripts had been offered to him, and tentative negotiations were beginning for the film of *The King and I* (which Twentieth Century-Fox, ironically, had owned since the Rex Harrison version). Or he could stay on Broadway. Instead, he made a tougher choice: he would take the play on the road for a year, then play the Pharaoh, and then film *The King and I*. He reasoned that by visiting their towns, he would earn loyalty from his fans that would last his whole career. He weighed that against the fact that his family had just settled into a home, that his son was in the second grade, and that the disruption to their lives would be total. But, as Yul told Gin, ''This is my job, and I don't walk out on it because the going is a little rough.'' Her reply was, rough on who? Admittedly, their marriage was shaky after a decade filled with infidelities, and the last few years had become especially uneven. In the growing salvos of hurt and disregard, Virginia had retaliated for Yul's flagrances in a quick affair with Marc Blitzstein, best known for his adaptation of Brecht's *Threepenny Opera*. The fact was, though, that she and Yul were still very much in love. And besides, there was the kid . . .

The King and I set out across America in 1953, and with it went dozens of families—the King's wives and children, dancers, key members of the orchestra, backstage crew, et cetera. To carry sets, curtains, and props, plus hundreds of costumes not to mention the entire troupe, the company leased its own railwaycars. A tutor, Ernest Painter, went along, to teach the children travelling in the company, and a de luxe carriage was added for the Brynners to travel in. And so the small, wandering kingdom of Siam set forth, lurching across the country: Washington, Philadelphia, Cincinnati, Cleveland, Detroit, Milwaukee, St. Louis, New Orleans, Atlanta, Kansas City, Fort Worth, Chicago, Denver, Salt Lake City, Portland, San Francisco, Los Angeles . . .

Compared to most this was a comfortable tour. The stops were for two weeks, some for a month, Los Angeles for three months, Chicago for six. But comfort on the road is relative at best. In 1955, Virginia wrote a lengthy, painful magazine article about the tour. Those who remembered Virginia Gilmore as a vivacious, intellectual blonde movie star with great legs must have found this portrait of her life on the road sadly lacking in glamour.

Hotels that sounded fine and conveniently located turn out to be firetraps, miles from the theater. Restaurants become such a perilous gamble that if kitchen facilities are not available, out comes the illegal hot plate, which must be hidden from the cynical-eyed maid after each meal. By the time you have located a convenient shopping center in one town, you are ready to leave for the next engagement. Laundry accumulates in perplexing quantities and can't be sent out because you are leaving shortly; consequently, the bathroom becomes a damp, hazardous crypt, strung with wash that refuses to dry. Finally, when the day's work is over and you have the leisure to sit quietly with your husband, he is not there. He has gone to work, and you find yourself alone in a strange city. Since you are never in one place long enough to make friends or find any continuity to living, loneliness and a sense of isolation from the rest of the world become your bitter enemies, which have to be fought continually and with any weapon at hand . . . the wife is left to face a series of empty hotel rooms in a string of unfamiliar cities. She is alone, often after a physically tiring day, absent from her friends and the familiar belongings of home. Unless she takes great care, she soon builds up a desperate state of mind about what to do in the evenings.

Yul told everyone how proud he was of his wife's talent as a writer. He often added that he hoped his son would write someday, too.

4

My Dad

"A hostess who entertained the Brynners for a weekend . . . was impressed by Yul's relationship with
his son, then about six. 'The little boy was a car-
bon copy of his father, same chunky build, same
intense, dark eyes. They played together with
a special understanding, a wonderful, intimate rapport.' "

—*Cosmopolitan* magazine

"Dad, who is it you pray to every night?"

"Who? Who?"

"Who is that god that you call to? You know? Booder?"

"I don't understand, laddie."

*"But Dad, every night you call out to him for help. You
know. Just before Intermission?"* The smell of real leather in
our new Cadillac was starting to suffocate me.

*"Ah-ha! Buddha! He was prince, son of the most powerful
king of the East."*

"So then, Prince Booder was just like me!" That made him
smile. I loved to make Dad smile.

*"The kingdom where Buddha grew up was a perfect place—
without sorrow, without hunger, without disease. The young
prince never even knew these things existed: as a student he
knew only an ideal universe."* My Clark bar had melted on
the car seat. I wiped it with a little sarsaparilla.

*"But one day when he was a young man, he sat on the wall
that surrounded the kingdom, looked out and saw a leper beg-
ging in the road. He jumped down to the beggar, asked him
to wait, and brought him food to eat, servants to bathe him,*

and silk robes to dress him. After that, he ran to his father to ask how there could be such grief in the world, but even the powerful king had no answer. And so the young Prince Buddha set out from his father's kingdom, carrying only a wooden bowl to beg with . . ."

"Whatever became of the prince?" My accent was more British than American. When I was six, I had fallen helplessly in love with Gertrude Lawrence.

"The rest you must find out for yourself, laddie. You must discover the prince's philosophy."

"What's phisolophy?*"*

"Well, the prince became very wise . . . et cetera, et cetera, et cetera."

That always made me giggle.

When I was a boy, my father loved me the way he loved himself. I was not only the extension of his own soul into the next generation, I was also his best hope for immortality: through me, his descendants could be expected to remember him until the very end of time—if only I could survive childhood.

For it was a rare point of agreement between my parents that, aside from being An Angel and A Genius, their son was also The Clumsiest Child on Earth. I was almost ten before I discovered that accident prone was two separate words. In my defense I would note that throughout my childhood I had been resettled in unfamiliar surroundings several times each year; that I was an unusually curious and precocious child; and that occasional lapses in coordination owed much to my left-handedness, which we diagnosed quite late.

Only occasionally did my accidents require major medical attention. At three, I snorted a bolt that I had unscrewed from our record-player, which had to be removed from my sinus by a surgeon. At four, I took a dramatic dive headfirst from one end of the bathtub right into the other end, resulting in a concussion. At five, I fell and poked my buckteeth all the way through my lower lip. When I was six years old, it was a very good year: aside from a few wasp stings at Richard Rodgers's Connecticut home, I escaped 1953 largely unscathed. But I paid for it in 1954, when I stepped on a beehive in the Bahamas and was stung, almost fatally, some two hundred times. In my eighth year, while weight-lifting, I dropped fifty pounds on my right foot. Et cetera.

My mother raised me by the book, and that book was Spock. His masterwork, published the year I was born, was responsible for much of my upbringing and some of my confusion. For example, Dr. Spock recommended that parents did not press a child to become right-handed by forcing items into the right hand. Rather, they were advised to offer them in the middle, and let the kid choose which hand to grasp it with. Well, my mother always went out of her way to be fair, and later admitted having virtually forced articles into my *left* hand.

I also ran the gamut of trivial childhood diseases, and it was often my father who took care of me. At one point, after *Lute Song* had closed, we moved temporarily to a farm that belonged to Jack Kirkland, who years before produced a brief run of *The Moon Vine* in which Yul appeared. Jack's daughter Gelsey later recalled how Yul had cared for me night and day when I was stricken with severe dysentery. Late one night, he built such a huge fire to warm our room that the chimney itself ignited, and the Kirkland farm nearly burned down.

That was not characteristic of Yul: he was an extremely handy and practical man, both eager and capable of dealing with household problems. Not only was he an able carpenter, but he also had a knack for designing, assembling, constructing, finishing and refining—in short, a love for crafts of all sorts. It was in the exercise of such pursuits that he honed the meticulousness that he applied to all other spheres of his life. That is why they began as hobbies, and then became something quite different. Yul told one reporter, "The word hobby implies a man who has time on his hands and instead of sitting around playing cards or getting drunk, he tries to occupy his mind . . . My hobbies have nothing to do with tension. I'm neither over-wrought nor do I need therapy."

After *The King and I* opened he put this skill to work building a train-set in the dining-room of our large new apartment. He negotiated the space with my mother in advance, and she agreed that half the room could be for the trains. But when she arrived after the carpenters had finished, she found Yul had ordered a four-foot-high table wall-to-wall across the entire dining-room. She hadn't expected him to take the *lower* half of the room. This train set became a vast, complex network with dozens of switches representing, roughly, the movement of grain supplies across North America, with parks, trees, villages, a round-house, and every bell and whistle any boy could wish for: even Yul. Sometimes he got back late from the theater and began installing additional track, and I would find him there at dawn. Then we would have breakfast together.

Yul delighted in burning the candle at both ends. No matter how much of a night-life he was living, he maintained our ritual of early breakfast. When I awoke, I would pad out to the kitchen or dining-room to join him, and there he would stand in a silk kimono, grilling a couple of steaks on the very latest kitchen appliance—he loved modern appliances of all kinds. The steaks were for him, of course. I just had cereal. We read the paper together (even before I could really read), watched Dave Garroway, and savored the morning as the familiar wake-up smells of coffee, cigarettes and grilled sirloin made the day begin. All this transpired without a word between us. The rest of the day might have been filled with conversation, but breakfast was a sacred, silent ritual, a building block in the larger lesson Yul was trying to teach his son: the value of rituals. As his world continued to change radically, he used daily rituals to place himself in time: like the cycles of a gyroscope, rituals gave his life stability.

Because I was an only child spending most of my time with adults, I concentrated on intellectual pursuits. Given my near-fatal combination of curiosity and clumsiness, this was encouraged by everyone. I especially enjoyed reading books and playing chess. This pleased both my parents—something I was always eager to do. Although Yul did not consider himself an intellectual, it pleased him to believe his son was. By the time I was seven years old, I was a member of the Manhattan Chess Club, and my sights were set on Bobby Fischer, three years older than I. On the chessboard, at least, I could be graceful.

Like his other hobbies, Yul's photography swiftly became a second profession. He had worked with cameras as a television director, and he was eager to learn the aesthetics, as well as the technical foundations of black and white photography. Before we went on tour, Yul took portraits of each member of the cast to offer as Christmas presents. By the time we settled outside Chicago in 1955, Yul was hungry to learn more, so he set up a darkroom in the little house we rented in Evanston, and became a straight-A student of photography at Northwestern University. And he was still playing eight shows a week.

He also hungered for knowledge. He was usually in the company of college graduates, and while he was considerably more cultured and worldly than almost anyone he knew, he was driven to intellectual challenges. While attending Northwestern he also took a Master's level seminar in philosophy with Dr. Paul Schilpp, whose farm we visited at weekends. Some time later a reporter contacted Schilpp and asked his opinion of Yul Brynner. Schilpp said:

Mr. Brynner was a student in my ethics class as well as in my philosophy-in-religion class in the winter of 1955 here at Northwestern . . . He was playing at that time [in *The King and I*]. But . . . I know that he not only did all the required reading for classes, but a great deal more. It is my deliberate judgment that he is one of the most brilliant students I ever had.

The reporter went on:

If Northwestern philosophy students were surprised to have as an early morning classmate a Mongolian athlete with the make-up of a Siamese king barely wiped from his face, other students were astonished, too. Brynner also took and passed brilliantly courses in photographic laboratory techniques and, on top of that, taught a professional class in acting. He never missed a performance of *The King and I,* matinee or evening.

The *Saturday Evening Post* was more breathless:

For those who regard him as a living doll—and many do— it may be a comedown to report that he is more of a living philosopher. He thinks deep thoughts without effort, and although they're offbeat, they make clear, hard sense. When I first met Brynner he said, "I've noticed that most interviewers are afraid to report a man's philosophy. It's the most direct approach to his character. It motivates his whole way of life, his actions. All my life, I've had a certain understanding. It's this: in the realist sense you live your life alone; in essence you are born, live and die alone. If you can learn to live with yourself, the relations you acquire with other people, be they close or casual, are gravy.

"I grew up with another conception too," he went on. "Death is an integral part of everyday life. You know when your birth was, but your death is not predicted. What makes you think it will be ten years from now? What makes you think it won't be tonight? But if I knew I was going to die tonight, with what care I would live this day! How much more clearly I'd hear the songs sung around me. How much deeper would I look into the faces of my friends. That is what I mean when I say, if you could really know your life for even one minute, in that minute you could have it all."

The *Post* interviewer said to Yul, "I've heard you think the words 'He has arrived' ought to be used only on people's tombstones?"

"I'll answer that question this way . . . One day a philosophy professor asked me if I'd mind if his class asked me a few questions. 'Why not?' I said. So one young man asked, 'Mr. Brynner, can you explain the terrible compulsion which drives you, a man who has already arrived, into attending a university in your spare hours? You're doing eight performances a week and commuting, yet in the few hours which remain to you, you study and seek new goals. What's eating you?' I said, 'Only when I am dead and buried will the time come when I would like to have it said of me, "He has arrived." If you are stupid enough to think you have arrived before that, you are dead already. From then on there can be only stagnation. You're merely animated meat.' "

He smiled, and his deep voice lifted for a moment. "What drives me is not compulsion," he said. "It's more because of something someone once said of me: "'Yul has an extra quart of champagne in his blood.'"

This bore absolutely no resemblance to most celebrity interviews of the 1950s. I knew just how different my dad was from everyone else, and I reveled in his uniqueness which, he insisted, was our uniqueness. I must have read that particular magazine article a dozen times, and every word of my father's philosophy, which he had often repeated to me, burned like an ember in my heart. In essence, the core of my dad's philosophy was: man is born alone, man lives alone and man dies alone, and anything else we experience is only a fleeting relief from that universal truth. At the time, I had to wonder if that truth could ever become more powerful than the bond between us.

I was five years years old when I first saw my father on his deathbed, in the final scene of *The King and I*. My mother prepared me the best she could, and I fully understood that this was just acting, of course. But she could not have prepared me for the impact of hearing two thousand people sniffle and weep. It was in those strange circumstances that I first grappled with the notion of death and dying, watching my father die before my eyes, night after night.

I was at the theater at every opportunity, even before we went on the road. Most of my friends were in the play, including that cool kid from the Bronx, Sal Mineo, who played Crown Prince, and made it clear he'd always be my big brother. Sal was not exactly an ideal role model—Hollywood had already typecast him as a juvenile delinquent. In *The King and I*, the character of the Prince centers entirely on his resemblance to the King. I tried to copy that resemblance in real life. Like every seven-year-old boy, I wanted to be just like my father. In my case, regrettably, that meant being a clumsy seven-year-old who behaved as imperiously as Yul Brynner, and affected a Gertrude Lawrence accent. It did not go over well in American schools, let me tell you. The regal stance was just not calculated to win friends. But it was the only persona in my repertory. And besides, it was my dad's.

* * *

Omnibus, the CBS television show hosted by Alistair Cooke, was presenting Leopold Stokowski conducting an all children's symphony orchestra in a performance of Haydn's Toy Symphony. Dad arranged for me to play the cuckoo, which has a damn solo every four bars or so. Stokowski was enraged to learn that the children were so young they couldn't even read music. He was even more enraged when the smart-aleck six-year-old cuckoo-player informed him that the instrument he'd been given was of the wrong pitch, and might he please be given the correct instrument? The maestro stormed out of the rehearsal. The orchestra director double-checked and, sure enough, the pipsqueak playing the cuckoo was right. The whole story of how the little kid had humiliated the seventy-year-old conductor was in the papers the next day. Dad loved it.

My first fights were in and around the New Lincoln School on Manhattan's 110th Street, and they were relatively bloodless affairs, since only a few of the kids knew my father was a famous tough guy. Living on 104th Street, I had already learned how a kid could break off a car antenna and make a zip gun, if he needed to. But I was too clumsy to do it myself.

After the second time I came home bloodied, Yul sent me for private boxing lessons with a toothless old trainer at the New York Athletic Club. After the third time, my mother asked Chris Forster, the mounted policeman whom Yul had befriended, to pick me up after school in his police car for a few days. That took care of the playground fights. Sometimes, after school, Chris would take me on his rounds of Harlem before dropping me off at the theater: I would look at the streets swarming with poor kids playing and fighting and hustling, and like the spoiled Prince Buddha, I wondered how there could be such grief in the world. Most nights I watched the start of the play from the wings, and fell asleep in Dad's dressing-room. Of course I often stayed home with my mother, but Yul liked having me with him, and he usually got his way.

Matinee days I always had early dinner between shows with Dad—either dim sum at the House of Chan, or more often a meal at the "21" Club, where Walter, the maître d'hôtel, was gracious enough to send out for a hot dog if I insisted. Since everyone was eager to acknowledge that Yul was King, they were just as quick to call me the Prince, and treat me accordingly. And I milked it for all it was worth. Whenever I did something especially clumsy, I acted especially imperious.

Here was a kid with a sense of entitlement. I was on a first-name basis with the salesmen at F.A.O. Schwarz, as well as with every sports figure I ever admired. Since Yul wanted me there, I was accustomed to being the only child at a table full of adults. And, because Yul was so proud of his son's accomplishments, however clumsy he was, I was all too often the center of attention. Parlor tricks became something of a specialty, and I began to enjoy the attention. One way to get it was by being a child prodigy.

The best trick I had for winning the attention of adults was to play two games of chess simultaneously—in my head. I enthralled Gloria Vanderbilt's houseguests several weekends running. I would sit in a dark study at her Southampton home without a chessboard, while my two opponents sat, with chessboards, in two other rooms. They would send me bits of paper with their moves on them. I always acquitted myself admirably: even against the best players, I never once lost *both* games.

And there was a reason why. By the last weekend, one of Gloria's regular guests noticed that I always played white against one player and black against the other. Then he observed that I *always* won against one player and lost against the other—except once, when both games were a draw. The gig was up: that's when they figured out my scam. I wasn't playing at all: I was just transmitting the other two players' moves to each other.

Yul had never been prouder. His son had found his own way of teasing the *gaje* . . .

We were driving through Laurel Canyon during our first stay in Los Angeles in 1954. I had been staring for a long time at his Italian moccasin pressing on the accelerator pedal, racking my brains trying to think what it reminded me of. At last I remembered: Dad's Gucci shoe looked just like the face of Ollie the Dragon, from Kukla, Fran and Ollie.

I noticed a sign by the road that read:

Fire Hazard
No Smoking in Cars
$500 FINE

"Look at the sign, Dad. Better put out your cigarette!"

My father ran his thumb across the hundreds in his money-clip.

"That's OK, laddie," he said, flicking his cigarette ash, and taking a long, deep drag.

We began water-skiing in Norwalk, Connecticut in 1953. With Don Lawson driving the boat, my mom and dad would take turns skiing out into the Long Island Sound; first on two skis, then slalom, then on trick skis. Personally, I was only six, and not quite ready yet. In a few months Dad was ready to try jumping: that was the latest thing in Cypress Gardens, Florida, the capital of this new sport. Within a year, Dad had jumped seventy-five feet—nearly the world record.

One of Yul's more memorable demonstrations of self-sufficiency occurred one idyllic morning when he'd come home from the theater with Don, and we'd gone straight on to the boat to ski on the Sound. We had come a long way out from port, to be clear of traffic. Dad was in the water, and Don tossed him the tow-handle: it struck his head, putting a two-inch gash in that famous pate.

Dad was disgusted that our day had been ruined. It wasn't a serious wound, even though it bled profusely; still, we would have to cruise in to Westport to find a doctor or an emergency room. Unless . . . In our toolkit Yul found a set of small fish-hooks, and thin nylon line. As Don held the mirror and I watched, Yul used one hook to thread two stitches through the flaps of bleeding flesh and tie them shut. A half-hour later he was skiing again.

All through childhood, I took such feats for granted. I thought everybody's father did that kind of thing: I thought that was just the kind of thing *fathers* do.

We literally water-skied across America with *The King and I*: Dad stayed up one night after the show and built a coffin-shaped travelling case for our skis. He had also become a master of rope splicing, for making tow handles. Et cetera. The man was tireless.

I first water-skied next to my dad in 1954, near Dallas. It was the happiest day of my short life. From then on, we skied together every chance we could get. Gradually I grew stronger and less clumsy, at least over water. In fact, Peter Fonda admitted that he intensely envied my gracefulness on the diving-board.

There was a song that Yul and I always sang together as we skimmed across the water:

Up a lazy river, by the old mill run,
That lazy, lazy river in the noonday sun;
Linger in the shade of a kind old tree,
Throw away your troubles, dream a dream with me . . .

We skied on the Mississippi, Lake Pontchartrain and Puget Sound. We skied on Lake Michigan, Saltan Sea and the Columbia River. We skied the Pacific Ocean from San Francisco to Puerto Marquès, and the Atlantic from Montauk to Key West. Most of the time Yul was playing eight shows a week.

I was eight when Dad took me to my first bullfight. We chartered a small plane in Los Angeles and flew down to Mexico for two days. I had already studied all about the corrida, and I was learning the various passes with the cape. As the first bull entered the ring, Dad pulled out his camera and focused on the bull. Years later, Yul described what happened next, and how he became a professional photographer. "I saw a bullfighter misreading his bull . . . This bull was blind in one eye. He wasn't hooking in the direction the bullfighter expected him to hook. I focused my camera, took a meter reading, set the exposure and watched the action through the camera. In thirty-six shots I covered the steps that led up to the matador's goring. He was hooked in the stomach, swung around and thrown, and I photographed him as he was carried out. Then I went into the infirmary where they laid him down. That night he died. A newspaper representative who saw me taking those pictures offered me two hundred dollars for my film before I developed it . . . It paid for half the cost of my equipment and it qualified any expenses I incurred as a tax exemption . . . I've sold practically everything I've photographed since then.''

The following year, while we were living in Mexico, we again went to the arena every week, and soon I was studying bullfighting with a young pro, the same kid who was giving me diving lessons, fifty feet over La Quebrada. It's amazing, really, that I survived childhood.

"You don't have to wave at the waiter like that to get his attention, lad," Dad told me over dinner at Romanoff's. "Watch." He merely arched his eyebrow, and the waiter appeared instantly. Then it was my turn. I spent the rest of the meal trying to catch the waiter's eye. I'll bet everyone else there felt sorry Yul's kid had such a terrible twitch.

My mother watched with growing alarm as her young American son developed a marked tendency to transform himself into a strutting, shrimp-size despot with a phony English accent. Of course, she was pleased that her husband and son were so close. And yet she was concerned that her son's life was so different from all his friends'. But Virginia was struggling just to keep her own keel even, as her mood swings from melancholic apathy to tipsy euphoria grew more pronounced by the year. With just a half-glass of white wine, her speech became slightly slurred, and her personality shifted from something like Jean Arthur's to something more like Ethel Merman's. It could be overlooked by company, but Yul was slowly growing to despise her lapses into excessive behavior. And so was I.

Yet of all my memories of my father and mother together, there remains one that remains pristine. It was at the start of a vacation in the Bahamas in 1954. The night we arrived, I was alone in our hotel suite, having trouble falling asleep. Swept away by the whole tropical atmosphere, I followed the sound of music to our balcony. The singer, I knew from our record collection, was Chicago's Blind Blake, with ''His Royal Bahamians.''

Was love, love, love alone,
That make the King to leave his throne . . .

Leaning against the railing, looking down at the outdoor night-club of the hotel, I could see my father and mother dancing. The dance floor was scattered with elegantly dressed couples swaying to the Caribbean rhythm, and the moment reminded me of some tropical nightclub I had seen in an old movie. It may have been the intoxication of gardenias that made it so dreamlike, or the colors that were as vivid as hibiscus. But the sight of my parents dancing beneath the moon beside the ocean remains the most painfully sweet image I have of them together.

5

Hollywood King

Yul arrived in Cairo for the shooting of *The Ten Commandments* within twenty-four hours of his last performance of *The King and I* in Chicago. Mom and I went back to New York, temporarily. He had to shoot only a few days of locations in Egypt—most of Rameses' scenes were interiors and they would be shot on lavish sets in Hollywood later in that sweltering summer of 1955. By the time he arrived in Egypt, the company had been in the Middle East preparing to shoot for more than a year.

As he was driven from the Cairo airport to the location where reproductions of the giant walls of ancient Egypt had been built for the great exodus scene, his car passed through a broad corridor lined by rows of twenty-foot sphinxes, two dozen altogether, each of which wore Yul's face—as Rameses II. Mom swore he was never quite the same after that.

The Ten Commandments earned its title as the biggest motion picture ever made; nothing so ambitious had ever been undertaken. De Mille even used a special kind of movie camera and film, called Vista Vision, just for this juggernaut. He had begun the project in 1952, and before he was done *The Ten Commandments* had taken De Mille four years to make and cost thirteen million dollars, most of which, Yul always liked to point out, could actually be seen on the screen; *Cleopatra* cost more because of inflation and ill-fortune.

Probably Yul's favorite single anecdote about the film had to do with the extraordinary demands that De Mille made upon his propman, Bob Goodstein. Think back to the exodus scene, with its thousands of extras of all ages—a sea of humanity— all in costume, with carts, wagons, pigs, cows, goats, tools, weapons. Consider that job for just a moment: prop man on *The Ten Commandments*.

Goodstein got a call from De Mille on Friday night before the Monday shooting of the big scene. The director had suddenly decided to start the entire exodus sequence with the release of five thousand white pigeons from the top of the fifty-foot gates of ancient Egypt. Goodstein had forty-eight hours, or some similarly absurd time, in which to round up the white pigeons. Coping with the uncertainties of Egyptian radio-telephone in the mid-1950s, Goodstein located all the white pigeons in cities all across Europe. Within hours, pigeons began arriving by air freight and even by chartered plane. By midday on Monday, the propman had in his possession the five thousand captive pigeons Mr. De Mille had demanded.

But then began the long wait before they would actually shoot the scene. Monday passed, then Tuesday, each day hotter than the day before. Finally, on Thursday morning, everything was in place for the great exodus. Even as he set the pigeon-cages in position, Goodstein had a premonition that all would not go well.

And lo, as the ceremonial trumpets called forth the multitudes of Israel, white pigeons at the foot of the great wall were released, and white pigeons from the top of the wall were launched into the air. Somewhere, I am told, there is actual film footage of what followed: thousands of overheated birds *waddled* out of the great gates, and thousands more plummeted to their deaths from the fifty-foot walls. In Vista Vision.

De Mille was second only to Michael Chekhov in his influence on Yul's life, although their friendship was quite unlikely, on the face of things. De Mille was not generally known to form close friendships with actors, but he clearly felt a paternal streak toward Yul, and he made that plain to everyone, including me, whom he treated like a grandson. Yul, in turn, had unqualified admiration for everything De Mille did and said. In one interview Yul allowed that "the reason why I felt so close to Mr. De Mille was that he thought like me, on a grand scale." And De Mille was quoted as saying, "Yul Brynner is the most powerful personality I've ever seen on the screen: a cross between Douglas Fairbanks, Sr., Apollo, and a little bit of Hercules." De Mille was an effortless authoritarian without a scrap of irresolution in him. He recognized, above all, the importance of his position—the leadership represented by his every gesture—to a cast of thousands and crew of hundreds. You might well say that, as producer and director, De Mille led with his cock.

For example, De Mille cultivated the curious habit of suddenly sitting down, without warning, wherever he was on the set. He had one assistant whose job it was to make sure there was always a stool under him in time to prevent Mr. Cecil B. De Mille from falling flat on his arse. According to De Mille, this helped keep everyone on the set more alert. It was just the kind of gesture Yul loved.

Sam Cavanaugh, a cameraman on *The Ten Commandments,* described the relationship between the two men. "I knew from experience that [De Mille] wouldn't tolerate the slightest interference. Why, he'd stomp off the set if anyone dared to raise their voice. But it was very different in the case of Brynner. It was as if De Mille was paying close attention to a very intelligent, favorite child . . . The old man took [Yul's] advice without a murmur. Later the script called for a mob to try and tell Pharaoh its troubles—almost one at a time. Yul thought it would be more striking if they all babbled simultaneously. De Mille agreed and reshaped the entire scene."

Since the death of Boris in 1949, Yul's feelings toward his own father had become more and more ambivalent. Frequently, Yul denied that Boris was his father at all—he rather liked being thought of as a bastard, because it made his background more mysterious and independent, and repaid Boris for having abandoned the family; but, of course, that story reflected on Marousia, and thus enraged Yul's sister Vera. As Yul came to favor Boris over Marousia, his impressions changed. "Boris was a great man," said Yul, a few years later, "but I had to mature to realize it." To me, Yul spoke mostly of his bitterness toward Boris, and told me that once his father failed to show up for a long-anticipated reunion, when Yul was twelve. "I promised myself that someday I would kill my father," Yul told me, on more than one occasion. An odd thing to say to one's son. But anyway, compared to Boris, De Mille was a flawless father figure—or perhaps grandfather figure, since Yul had long served as his *own* role model, his own father figure, his own hero.

As a director himself, Yul was delighted to spend hours at De Mille's side, picking up tricks the old man had learned during almost half a century as a director. Yul was much more informed about directing than many Hollywood directors, having worked in television and studied photography at Northwestern University. From De Mille, he learned how to look like a movie star on the screen. While Chekhov had taught Yul about acting for a camera, there was still much he could gain from De Mille's vast experience. After all, the only film Yul had appeared in before *The Ten Commandments* was *Port of New York,* just six years earlier. Most of all, Yul learned how to use key lighting for given camera angles; how to prepare scenes for editing, between close-ups and long shots, say, in a single scene; and how to reduce the scale of the performance to suit the close scrutiny of the huge Vista Vision screen. After 1,246 straight live performances onstage, a movement as subtle as the arching of his eyebrow had to be toned down for the movies.

Apart from De Mille himself—and, possibly, God—the star of *The Ten Commandments* was, of course, Charlton Heston. He had also worked in television and on stage before film, and had just starred in another big budget Paramount film under De Mille's aegis, *The Greatest Show on Earth*. Heston was among the second generation of top Hollywood stars of the talkies. The first generation had been dominated by Clark Gable, Gary Cooper, Henry Fonda, John Wayne, Jimmy Cagney, Spencer Tracy, James Stewart and Cary Grant (who were still giving some of the best performances of their careers in the 1950s). But a new generation of leading men had appeared in the post-war era and the early Fifties. As a group, what distinguished the second generation was that, by and large, they had broader chests and shoulders. That was because the Hays office, which dictated screen morality, had begun allowing men to take their shirts off. The most prominent of this group were Burt Lancaster, Kirk Douglas, Anthony Quinn and Charlton Heston. Robert Mitchum was, of course, the bad 'un of the bunch. Yul Brynner was the new one.

It was immediately apparent that broad shoulders were almost the only characteristic that Yul shared with these gentlemen: he neither looked nor sounded like them, and didn't try to. Yul often joked that he was "just your average, clean-cut Mongolian kid." And he meant *clean*-cut. His looks, his manner and his accent made him ill-suited for most American roles. Yul's success seemed more to resemble the earlier phenomenon of Rudolph Valentino than the success of his contemporaries. In any event, Yul felt that he belonged in a different realm of leading men altogether, and so his competitive drive was never fully engaged against his peers. With time, he came to feel varying degrees of genuine affection and grudging respect for each of these men; when he was younger he was not always so generous. But whenever any competition arose—no matter when, where, or with whom—Yul was *compelled* to win. As a younger man he applied his aggressive energy to compete against himself or against nature, not against mere mortals. He preferred to remain aloof, unless he was personally challenged. When challenged, it was simple: he did not sleep until he had crushed his opposition. That was my dad.

Because of the oddness of Yul's background, and the extent of his early stardom, he had already decided that exceptional rules applied to him—and that meant almost no rules at all. The quality of his stardom was different from that of other stars: Yul Brynner was just a whole different species from Gregory Peck, Ray Milland, William Holden or Glenn Ford. His exotic masculinity tapped different chords, promising the danger and excitement of all that was uncommon. In that respect, the romantic persona of Yul Brynner embodied the quintessential foreigner of indefinite origins. Of course many stars were popular with the ladies—Clark Gable, Spencer Tracy and Henry Fonda, for example—but the image that Yul projected was that of earthbound avatar, not well-bred gentleman. Maybe that is what Hedda Hopper meant in her column when she wrote: "What totally bald actor regards himself as being too good for his peers?"

His role as Pharaoh demanded more physical stamina than he had anticipated. Most of his work in Egypt turned out to be action footage—especially chariot work. He agreed with De Mille that the audience should see that he really was in the front chariot, leading a hundred mounted soldiers on chariot in hot pursuit of Moses. But the chariots were all precarious affairs at best, especially Yul's, which was laden with Pharonic paraphernalia. To top things off, as it were, Yul's costume included a blue metallic helmet that stood almost eighteen inches above his brow. It magnified and stored the blistering heat, and weighed almost twenty pounds. One bad bounce on the chariot could break his neck, or throw him out into the path of hundreds of stuntmen driving chariots close behind. This scene and the subsequent pursuit were most of what Yul had to shoot in Egypt.

Returning to Hollywood to shoot the remainder of his scenes Yul, for the first time, was working among a group of stars who also had reputations for being as temperamental as himself. Yul, well aware of being a newcomer, was grace and elegance to all. When Yul engaged all his charm, he could become a sort of irresistible object, especially to women. But men usually admired Yul, too, and were not uncomfortable showing it: Yul seemed so exotic he stood apart from the natural rivalry for roles. No director ever had to pick between Fred MacMurray, Jack Lemmon and Yul Brynner. Like De Mille, the studios picked Yul Brynner to play roles that were Larger Than Life, more powerful than ordinary mortals, and he did nothing to disabuse them of this perception. Since anger is the emotion that expresses power most effectively, it was largely for his Old Testament temper that the studio executives hired him in the first place. Almost to a man, they lived to rue the day.

Yul's capacity for anger, onstage and in life, was already legendary. During his years as an immigrant, speaking little or no English, he had accumulated his fair share of scores to settle with those who belittled or abused or otherwise crossed him. It was easy for him to extend that resentment beyond the individuals to the *types of individual* who had wronged him. Yul had as acute a sense of aggrieved injustice as any human being might hope to cultivate, and having achieved the social and professional position from which to wreak vengeance on the targets of this well-fermented resentment, his viciousness was often that of the cruelest man. His capacity for bitter fury was, of course, perfect as the basis for the character of Rameses II, Pharaoh of All Egypt; at home, it was less welcome. While it was never directed at either my mother or myself, Yul's anger, when unleashed at anyone or anything, was pervasive and intimidating enough to spoil an evening or two. Financially, he had been well-rewarded for his temper: for four years, at exactly 10:43 P.M., during Act Three, Yul had unleashed his own physical embodiment of the wrath of God, to the point of requiring oxygen. Since his daily schedule was so highly regimented, it is fair to guess that for many months Yul was a little touchy, let us say, from about 10:35 every evening.

His most righteous fury, inflicted with all the power he could marshal, was usually reserved for larger prey: most often for movie studios. Since the days when Virginia had been a contract player for Twentieth Century-Fox a decade earlier, the studio had made a perfect target for his rage: he remembered how they had threatened to destroy her career when she married Yul. Now, new executives at Fox *had* to negotiate with him for the film of *The King and I,* and in the intervening years his loathing for the institution and all its "uncreative parasites" had grown only more bitter.

One Fox executive at the time, Harvey Grant, was quoted as saying:

My hair or what's left of it started falling out after our first meeting. I'm certain Brynner wanted to sign, but out of sheer orneriness he made things difficult. He put up every obstacle you can think of. First he wanted script approval. When that was allowed he insisted on cast approval. Every day there'd be something else. Once we were very close to calling it all off—and for the oddest reason. I had noticed a newspaper article that listed his height as a "shade under six feet."

Innocently, I said that it must have been an error because I was six feet and was about three inches taller than he . . . You'd think I'd said his mother was a whore the way he reacted.

By this time Yul had even had a graphic artist remake the studio's famous logo to read: **16TH CENTURY FUCKS**. He had several boxes of matchbooks made up with this logo and distributed through the studio commissary. He and Sinatra discussed changing the billboard-size logo near the studio entrance also, but never got around to it. This was all before the first day of shooting on *The King and I*.

At last, the Brynners could afford their first mortgage. Gin had already found a house to buy in West Los Angeles, and so in August we gave up our New York flat and, while Yul was shooting in Egypt, my mother and I gathered all our belongings and traveled to California. It was a very modest house in Brentwood, where Sunset crosses Sepulveda—a tiny two-bedroom home in an unfashionable area on half an acre, without a swimming pool. It had one great advantage, though: it really was a great neighborhood for a kid, full of bicycles, paper routes, Halloween traditions and, most of all, other kids who might just teach *this* kid some norms of behavior.

The decor of the house was somewhat unusual, considering its modest exterior. The dining-room table was the face of a huge clock from the Gare de Lyon in Paris, mounted on the wood stove of a French caboose. At the head of the table sat a throne, its back perhaps six feet tall, from which hung the silver-handled bullwhip De Mille had given Yul. The master bedroom again featured the bed suspended on elephant chains over a white fur carpet, and lit by crystal bedside chandeliers.

In the garage Yul built an extensive wood shop and, in the backyard, a trampoline awaited us when we arrived. This was part of Yul's campaign against my clumsiness, and an opportunity to teach me the circus acrobatics that he had performed as a young man. Soon after, Yul had a professional darkroom built in the basement. We planted a garden of fine herbs for Gin, and made arrangements for water-skiing. I was enrolled in a public school, and got a summer job at the Westwood Book Store.

Yul's relationship with most of the Hollywood establishment of the 1950s was cool at first, then hostile, and finally combative. Apart from De Mille and one or two old friends of Gin's, the Brynners did not generally mix with people from the film community; many of their friends were from nearby UCLA, where Gin had attended lectures as a Goldwyn girl fifteen years earlier.

The King and I may have been Yul's greatest triumph on the screen, but it was also his disenchantment with Hollywood. From the beginning, his relationship with Fox was confrontational; his rapport with the film's producer, Charles Brackett, and with veteran director Walter Lang, was no better. From the studio's point of view, Yul was one more uppity New York actor who had not yet been disciplined by the contract system. The truth was that the studio could—and did—punish its players by burdening their contracts with penalties, keeping them out of work, and otherwise controlling their lives. "He would try to goad me," Brackett said in an interview. "Threaten to walk off the set if his ideas weren't instantly adopted. In story conferences he'd always have the last word. The moment he'd squat on the floor like a baseball catcher I could be certain I was in for a lecture."

In a cover story on Yul, *Newsweek* went further:

Brynner's off-camera personality strikes some acquaintances as an extension of the half-brutal, half-pathetic roles he has played onscreen. He has a tendency to chop people down in ruthless, volatile tirades. "He is so full of hate for incompetence," says a friend, "that he often becomes downright violent . . ." During *The King and I* filming, it is said, he became exasperated with producer Charlie Brackett and told him: "You don't know it, but you died several years ago."

An executive at Twentieth Century Fox, which Brynner often refers to as Nineteenth Century Fox, recalls: "At a party one night, Yul drank a lot and had nothing to say unless the conversation was on a subject he hated. Then he ranted like a boor. He was pleasant enough to me until he learned I was with the studio. Immediately his lynching spirit came out. I've never received such a going-over. In his opinion, all studio officials are untalented dunces.''

Why the bias against bigwigs? According to director [Richard] Brooks, ''Yul is suspicious of studio people, but he doesn't take on the little fellows, just the big ones. He becomes violent about the mendacity of what he calls the parasites of the business. He feels that producers, agents, studio personnel are making no contributions, and whenever one of them is caught in a deceit, he gloats, justified that they were really as bad as he knew or hoped they would be.''

Yul saw things somewhat differently, of course. Having created the role of the King and performed it for four years, he knew every subtle nuance of the play. Now these pompous, parasitical studio heads wanted to change the script so that the King was wounded struggling with a fuckin' white elephant! The bastards were even too stupid to understand what everyone else across America understood: that the King had died of humiliation and a broken heart. These no-talent motherfuckers made him so pissin' mad he'd ram their teeth down their throats. Then he'd kick 'em in the stomach, just for mumbling.

Dad's vocabulary had grown considerably with his stardom.

Deborah Kerr was the ideal choice for the role of Mrs. Anna, since she was already an authentic English star with a screen image suitable for a Victorian schoolmarm. To the latent sexuality of the musical she might perhaps bring a suggestion of the passion she had shared with Burt Lancaster in *From Here to Eternity*. It had brought her an Oscar nomination three years earlier. Deborah could not sing at all, however, and since Mrs. Anna performed fully two-thirds of the musical numbers (dubbed by Marni Nixon), that was quite some handicap. Later, when they were already committed to using an experimental new Cinemascope camera, they discovered the thing was so noisy that virtually every scene of the film would have to be dubbed anyway.

But the greater problem that the film faced was trying to achieve some kind of stylistic integrity. A whole movie set of

Bangkok had been built to scale on the back lot of the Fox studio: but that would make Yul's highly stylized mask of make-up look wildly excessive, especially in close-ups, a problem that didn't exist on stage. So the face that Yul had worn as King for four years was replaced with conventional, "invisible" film make-up. But only under protest.

The director Walter Lang, interviewed about Yul, was quoted as saying, "If you didn't agree with him you could expect to be called a bloody fool or lots worse. He would claim that he was really the picture's director, that I wasn't needed. That without him calling the shots the movie would wind up being second-rate." According to Yul, the movie did wind up second-rate, though few agreed with him. And later, *Newsweek* wrote: ". . . he drove director Walter Lang into wild rages of frustration by interfering with the direction. But when Lang received an Oscar nomination for the movie, the cast credited Brynner with the direction, and co-star Kerr sent Brynner a wire congratulating him on Lang's nomination."

Deborah Kerr was described as rapturous about Yul's contributions to the film.

> His imaginative suggestions and instructions were responsible for turning *The King and I* into a great movie. If not for him it would have wound up being just another pleasant Hollywood musical. He had a wonderful way of handling actors—got things out of them they never realized they possessed. Nothing escapes him—he was interested in the most minor scene. I will always be grateful to him for making me look better than I really am.

And the reviews unanimously echoed the *New York Herald Tribune*'s:

> It is Brynner who gives the movie its animal spark. He is every inch an oriental King, from the eloquent fingers that punctuate his commands to the sinewy legs and barefooted stance. He stalks about the palace like an impatient leopard. His eyes glower with imperial rage, they widen with boyish curiosity, they dance with amusement at his own simple jokes, and on his death couch they are heavy with resignation

and accumulated wisdom. This is a rare bit of acting—
Brynner is the King, and you don't forget it for a second.

The few surviving members of Yul's immediate family were in
America by now, and witnessed the impact of his stardom. For
those who had known him since his childhood, it came as a confirmation of his exceptional nature, which none had ever
doubted. His sister, Vera, was also meeting with great success,
appearing as the alternate lead in the premier production of
Giancarlo Menotti's opera *The Consul*, as well as starring in the
first color broadcast of an opera on live television, *Carmen*, on
NBC. My aunt Vera was the gentlest, most feminine figure I had
ever known, along with my mother. She was a perfumed cloud
of furs where I could bury my face. Yul's own aunt Vera, Marousia's sister, had settled with her daughter Irena in San Francisco after the death of her husband, Felix, in the Orient. Though
largely blind from cataracts, Yul's aunt Vera could enjoy Yul's
national triumph on behalf of her late sister. His aunt had known
of his ambition for stardom since he was sixteen.

"Dad, what's a sex symbol? Is that, like, Marilyn Monroe?"
   "Why do you ask that, laddie?"
   "Well, a kid on the bus says you're a sex symbol."
   *"Well, we've discussed all that before, Rock. You're already
nine years old, for Chrissakes!"*
   "Well, what I mean is: aren't you a sex symbol, Dad?"
   *"That's what they say. I don't especially mind that—and
neither should you. If a husband and wife go home and make
love because they've seen my performance, that's fine by me.
But if some kid on the bus is saying that that's all I am—"*
   *"Well, should I ram his teeth down his throat, Dad? And
kick him in the stomach, just for mumbling?"*
   "No, laddie, of course not."
   "Oh."

Virginia's mother, Lady May, was still alive near San Francisco, and occasionally my mother, with nothing but free time,

went to visit her reluctantly, often with me in tow, kicking and screaming. On one occasion about this time my mother and I were just leaving to visit Lady May when I developed a sudden, intense fever and was sent to bed. A few hours after dark, as I heard Dad's car drive in, I rushed to the front door to greet him.

Marilyn Monroe stood before me, smiling as she bent to kiss me on the cheek. "You must be Rocky," she volunteered. "Your father talks about you all the time. About how smart you are. My name is Marilyn."

"Duh—" I replied. She wore black pedal pushers, a white blouse and an emerald scarf, and she smelled like my aunt's perfume. My head was swimming. Marilyn Monroe! Wait till I tell the kids. Wow! And to think, Mom just missed her!

Dad was surprised to see me there, until he read the note from Mom. "She says you're supposed to be in bed, laddie." He wasn't angry. "Why don't you sit with us for a few minutes?"

I tried, I swear to almighty God I *tried* not to stare at her tits. I had already stared at them enough when Dad took me to see *Bus Stop*.

"Your dad tells me you love to water-ski?" she asked, as Dad brought her a drink.

"Mmm," I answered firmly, locking my eyes on her forehead.

"We're going to see if Marilyn can visit in Mexico while Richard Brooks and I are writing the script for *Brothers Karamazov*," said Dad.

All in a great rush I pictured Mexico, water-skiing and low-cut bathing suits. No longer swimming, my head was sinking.

"Off to bed with you, laddie." I kissed my dad, I kissed Marilyn Monroe, then I went to bed, where I set some kind of record for saying "wow."

A little while later, I heard the strum of my father's guitar as he began to sing "*Okonchen poots*"; before the song was over I was asleep. In the morning, as I made my own breakfast and rushed to catch the school bus, I saw that the corridor to the master bedroom was locked. On the living-room carpet lay the emerald scarf in a silken heap. I saw it again the next day in Dad's dressing room at Fox, where both Marilyn and Yul were working on films.

"That's the scarf—"

Dad looked me square in the eye. "That will be *our* secret, laddie."

I nodded, and we both grinned. I never brought it up again. I was the only one who knew that these two famous sex symbols had spent the night together. It was an awesome responsibility for a nine-year-old to keep that fact a secret from the world. But keeping the secret from my mother was the greater burden.

Though filmed after *The Ten Commandments*, *The King and I* was released first, and the American public at large came to know Yul Brynner. A slew of interviews and articles in national magazines described Yul in prose ranging from perplexed to positively purple. Each article contained the mandatory quota of bald jokes, the impact of his sex appeal on women, and included an incredulous description of Yul's appetite.

An article in *Redbook* began this way:

At precisely five o'clock every morning, in a small redwood house in Los Angeles, a bald-headed man in his thirties wakes up with the tormenting conviction that he is starving to death. This is the fabulous Yul Brynner . . . who is being widely hailed as the most exciting male on the screen since Rudolph Valentino.

At five o'clock Brynner stalks his kitchen and begins his day. His breakfast consists of a large steak, sometimes two, washed down with coffee. Before nine o'clock, tigerish hunger smites him again and he tides himself over until 12 o'clock lunch with a few large meat sandwiches. For lunch he has chops, steak, turkey, or roast beef, and this may get him by until two o'clock when he sends out for sandwiches and cake. In the afternoon he refreshes himself several times with snacks. At dinner Yul eats large helpings of roast beef, with bread, potatoes and dessert. He has a snack before bedtime and goes to sleep at once. He would take a nap after lunch, he says, but can barely doze off before hunger disturbs him.

This preoccupation with eating does not affect Brynner's remarkably photogenic physique. He stands just under six feet, weighs 180, and is muscled like an athlete.

Et cetera.

That much of the article was true. But when they began assembling the facts of Yul's background, discrepancies appeared. In fact, they abounded. That was inevitable, really, since Yul had begun a policy of public disinformation about his origins ten years earlier, during *Lute Song*. When I asked him about it, he explained that the press didn't get the story of his background straight even if he gave it to them straight. Since all records of his childhood were behind the Iron Curtain, the facts were unverifiable. Also, when he had first arrived in New York trying to get work, he had added five years to his age, while his sister had subtracted five from hers.

Now that Marousia and Boris were dead, only Vera could speak in English about his childhood with any authority, and remind Yul how Boris had abandoned their mother. But having seen his father's happiness with Katya, Yul had begun to think that perhaps Boris had done the *smart* thing when he had left Marousia. After all, as long as Yul could remember, his mother had been an unhappy woman. Perhaps, he concluded, leaving behind an unhappy marriage was the manly thing to do. The more unhappy Yul's own marriage became, the more sensible his father's decision seemed. That put his own family history in a different light: Yul and his sister had always regarded Boris as disloyal. But since Yul didn't see it that way any more, he became even more creative with his biographical variations to the press. So, according to *Redbook*:

Yul Brynner is, by his own account, part Mongolian, part Romanian gypsy and part several other warm-blooded nationalities, depending on his mood. Several years ago he was part Russian, and was born in Russia, but he changed his mind about that. He prefers now to be born on the island of Sakhalin, off the east coast of Siberia. His age varies. When

I talked to him at Paramount, where he played the brutal and interesting Pharaoh, he was 34.

But *Collier's* version went this way:

Brynner was born in Sakhalin, a large island off the coast of Siberia. (The year of his birth is given in the World Almanac as 1915, but on his passport as 1920). His father was a Mongolian who had been born in Switzerland, attained Swiss citizenship and studied mining engineering at the University of St. Petersburg; in Switzerland Brynner *père* adopted the name of Brynner, a fairly common Swiss one, substituting it for his real Mongolian name, Taidje Khan. Yul's mother was a Romanian gypsy, who died at his birth. Yul spent his first eight years in China, where his father owned silver and lead mines and an import-export business. Toward the close of his eighth year his maternal grandmother took him to live in Europe; she died not long after their arrival. Yul refuses to discuss the next five years of his life: "Some people who were supposed to do right by me let me down, and I want to forget about it."

And to the *Saturday Evening Post* he offered a whole array of options:

"In one story I was born in Sakhalin, an island lying off the coast of Siberia. In another my father was a Mongolian who chanced to be born in Switzerland, thus qualifying him for Swiss citizenship. There is still another story that my father borrowed the Swiss name Bryner, and substituted it for his real name, Taidje Khan, and that I added another "n" to it. Some of the stories have it that my name at birth was Taidje Khan, too, although they do not make it clear whether I am supposed to be Taidje Khan, Jr., or my father's name was really something else. Still another story runs that my mother was a Romanian gypsy, and in my eighth year my mother's mother took me with her to live in Europe and not long after our arrival there she died. Why don't you use one of those versions?"

Looking me squarely in the eye—and when Brynner looks

you squarely in the eye, there is a noticeable impact, you can almost hear a click—he said, "If you took the trouble to trace those stories, you'd find that none of them was really told by me. They came out of conversations someone is supposed to have had with me, but when writers come to me to verify them, I tell each of them, 'Yes, that's true . . .' Because no matter what story I tell them, writers invent things about me, and once they've invented them they believe them. They tell these tales at a dinner party, and they become part of the Brynner story. I don't want to embarrass anyone, so who am I to take the trouble to deny all this fiction? In fact, I enjoy it . . . They may not get the story they came for, but they'll get a story that's not dull . . .

"There is some confusion as to when I was born, but the correct date is the 7th of July, 1920. The place was the little town of St. Elizabeth . . ."

Just teasing the *gaje* . . .

At home, things were not good, not good at all. Virginia was regularly drunk in the late afternoon, making for sad, angry dinners. And Yul was rarely there. Virginia was still struggling to be a conscientious and dedicated mom, and my confidante. Usually, her beauty and humor made me proud of her when she chauffeured me around my friends' homes, the way mothers in Los Angeles are expected to do. But I was beginning to make a life of my own there; Virginia was having a tougher time trying to do the same. The public school I was attending, Kenter Canyon, was way behind the Lincoln Public School I'd left in Evanston. Before that, I'd had my own tutor. I frequently had fights, both at school and on the long school bus ride: my English accent and standoffishness were both more conspicuous than they had been back east.

The special opportunities my father wanted for his son were enough to make my life fundamentally different from other kids'—a fact that pleased Yul. That year, for example, I read Nevil Shute's *On the Beach,* and since Yul was unable to answer my questions about nuclear war, he made some phone calls and arranged for us to meet with an Air Force General attached to the Strategic Air Command—if I remember rightly, his name was General Shreiver. Though mildly surprised to be interrogated about nuclear strategy by a nine-year-old, the general did his best to allay my concerns. Perhaps he too was curious to meet Yul Brynner. If I was under the illusion that my father really was as powerful as a monarch, it was partly because the whole world helped mislead me: all across democratic America people assured me that Yul was King—and therefore I had to conclude that I was Prince. How could I argue with the whole world?

In an effort to lend my life normality, my parents pulled me out of the LA school and sent me to stay with a family we had met in Evanston, and I finished the school year there. Then my mother picked me up and we travelled to France to join Yul for the summer. He was shooting *Anastasia,* with Ingrid Bergman. My tutor Ernest Painter came along, as much to keep me company perhaps, as to teach me French, and we rented a house in Saint-Jean-de-Luz, Pays Basque, within driving distance of Hemingway's retreat in Pamplona. The house had belonged to Lael and Charles Wertenbaker: both Yul and Virginia had read and admired Lael's recent book *Death of a Man,* which recounted the stages of her husband's terminal cancer, and how he had chosen to end his own life.

Yul met us at the Savoy, a far cry from the bed-and-breakfast where we had lived during the London run of *Lute Song* in 1948. A few days later we went on to Paris, where filming had begun some weeks earlier. *Anastasia* was a perfect choice for Yul in all respects. Set in Paris, the story cast Yul as a Russian con artist trying to collect the fortune of the Tsars by training an imposter to pose as heiress to the imperial throne. The director, Anatole Litvak, was an old Hollywood pro, and himself a soulful Russian: when Tola and Yul discussed the script, the conversation flowed without interruption from Russian to French to English.

I was a great admirer of Ingrid Bergman, but I did not get to know her in the least: she seemed ill at ease with me. At first I thought she was uncomfortable with children, as some adults are. But when I was alone with Yul and Ingrid, I realized what was behind her discomfort, and my father introduced me to our next secret, making no effort to conceal their affair from me. It was not just my imagination that he and Ingrid lapsed into soft-spoken French whenever my mother left the room. I had never heard him use that particular tone of voice with anyone except my mother. I did not ask him about it; I did not have to. I had seen enough Broadway shows to recognize a romantic atmosphere. And try as I might, I could not pretend to myself that this wasn't important—even if they could.

We spent most of that summer in Saint-Jean-de-Luz, waiting for Dad to visit at weekends, which he did only rarely that summer. He had even bought a Mercedes convertible to be able to drive the five hundred or so kilometers to see us. We did not see much of him. But Irwin Shaw and his family lived there, and together we went to the running of the bulls at Pamplona, played *pelota*, and debated the subject of euthanasia and our landlady Lael Wertenbaker's book. Charles Wertenbaker had been a *Time* magazine correspondent in Europe during and after the Second World War; instead of submitting to the dubious medical protocol for cancer, he had spent months of peaceful reflection with morphine. When the pain became insurmountable, he slashed his wrists with a razor that his wife had prepared for him.

"I would rather choose the moment," Wertenbaker explained, "than have the moment choose me."

"Was that really the same as suicide, Dad?"

"Of course not, laddie." We went on coiling the tow ropes in silence.

"Is that how you'd like to die, Dad?" I shivered, remembering watching my father on his deathbed night after night, in The King and I.

"In that situation, yes." Another long silence. "Nothing could be worse than a lingering death, bedridden and kept alive by doctors: it's probably the only thing in the world I'm really afraid of. The way to win the big battles in life is to make sure you never pick a fight that can't be won. Your mother and I agreed years ago that we'd never let each other suffer that way. Personally, I would take care of business well before that. We only get one life and one death, and I want to ex-

perience it fully. I want to feel *my bones being crushed, and taste the blood in my mouth . . .''*

A storm was moving in from Biarritz to the north as we drove back to the Wertenbakers'. I made damn sure Dad didn't see me cry.

But I could not hide my tears when my parents announced that they were sending me to a boarding school fifty miles from Los Angeles. I *should* be in the very best school in the region, explained Dad. I needed more contact with kids, explained Mom. I would be able to come home every second weekend, they explained—and Bucky, my dog, and the new friends I had made in our neighborhood would all be there when I got home. But the betrayal was deep, and my mother seemed the most responsible. I was inconsolable. My friend and tutor was leaving us after three years, and my father was exiling me from our breakfasts and water-skiing and acrobatics. They were sending me to an institution, and I was just nine years old.

It was the best thing that had ever happened to me.

It seemed as if all Yul's dreams were coming true: he had returned to Paris a movie star, spending the summer there, in love with Ingrid Bergman, shooting *Anastasia*; it was almost mystically perfect—so long as he overlooked his marriage. And as for Ingrid, in one interview she declared that Yul had emancipated her.

To complete his dream, Yul had made his character in *Anastasia* a gypsy nightclub owner—and so, of course, the Dimitrievich family had to sing in the film, and the song "*Okonchen poots*" was featured prominently. It was as if all the accidental elements of his life had fused. Now he strolled through Paris with his son, pointing out the landmarks of his adolescence. We visited the nightclubs, but I was unable to meet the Dimitrievich family, whom I had heard about for as long as I'd listened to Yul sing. Still, at the circus I met people Yul had worked with twenty years earlier, and at the Théâter des Mathurins, where he hired his old boss George Pitoëff for a small role in *Anastasia*. He introduced me to Cocteau and Picasso and Dalí, and we spent evenings at Harry's or Rosebud or the Ritz with Hemingway, and James Jones and Jimmy Baldwin. Cocteau pronounced himself my godfather—certainly a strange match for my godmother, Mary Martin—and he offered me a piece of advice that remains virtually untranslatable from French. "Il faut toujours savoir jusqu'à où l'on peut aller trop loin" (roughly, "One must always know how much too far one can go"). Cocteau also adapted his famous *bon mot* about Victor Hugo to apply to my father: "Yul Brynner must be made to imagine that he could be Yul Brynner." That delighted Dad no end; so naturally it delighted me.

On stage we saw Edith Piaf, Yves Montand and Marcel Marceau, who had known Yul in the 1930s. That was a lot more exciting for a nine-year-old than Versailles or the Louvre, where my mother had always insisted on taking me.

"Dad, do you think you belong in America, or do you belong in Europe?"

"Our lives will always be different, Rock: we will never really belong anywhere. You too were born to travel, from the first month of your life: like me, like Aliosha, like every gypsy. We are not the same as settled folk, and the rules of our road must be different: though the scenery around us is never the same, our values must be unchanging. The only constants in our life are blue skies over green fields, the colors of the gypsy flag. And the knowledge that we are born alone, we live alone, and we die alone . . ."

PART TWO

"I saw a hat in a Salvation Army store,
Just like the one my father wore;
I tried it on, and cracked the brim—
Still trying to be just like him . . ."
                          —Chet Atkins

6

American Superstar

"Brynner admits to close friends that his urge to gild his life story began after a conversation with Jean Cocteau, who once told him: When you become a star, be sure that in your public relations you never let people think that you go to the bathroom."

—*Newsweek*

By the end of 1956, *The King and I, The Ten Commandments* and *Anastasia* were all record-breaking classics and movie audiences across the country had finally seen the shaven-headed phenomenon for themselves. After two *Life* magazine covers, his name was no longer just a cue for never-ending jokes about baldness; now Yul Brynner was an established sex symbol, the masculine counterpart to Marilyn Monroe.

In the early 1950s, Yul had considered adapting *The Brothers Karamazov* for the screen. At the time, Billy Wilder approached him on Broadway and asked him to co-star with Audrey Hepburn in a project tentatively entitled *A New Kind of Love*. They also discussed *Karamazov*, and talked about a young actress Wilder was about to direct in *The Seven Year Itch* to play the role of the temptress, Grushenka: the actress was Marilyn Monroe. She herself discussed the possibility publicly on several occasions, suggesting that for this role she wanted to study with Lee Strasberg at the Actors' Studio. But neither Fox, with which she was under contract, nor MGM, which was distributing the Russian classic, would accept her for the role. According to Yul, the parasitical bastards were determined that she neither could nor *should* be treated as more than a sex symbol; having exploited her every way they could, they took care not to contaminate their "serious work" with her presence. And just when their seams were about to burst with hypocritical prurience, they muttered about how difficult she was, how late she was, and how the budget could not afford *two* demonically difficult stars.

Richard Brooks was directing *The Brothers Karamazov,* a man with whom Yul felt proud to work and completely at ease. Brooks was also responsible for the screenplay—he and Yul agreed to a couple of months' fishing together in Mexico so that Richard could complete the adaptation in consultation with Yul, while we got in a little water-skiing. By the autumn of 1956, Yul was the hottest star in the world. "Every studio wanted him," Ted Ashley was quoted as saying. "They were willing to pay tremendous prices. Never have I known another star so sought after."

No actor had ever had quite such a prestigious rise to stardom as Yul had had that year. It was apparent that he would be nominated for an Academy Award: the only question was for which role. No big surprise that the Academy nominated him for his shattering performance in *The King and I.* And Ingrid Bergman, in her Hollywood "comeback" after the Rossellini "scandal," was nominated as Best Actress for *Anastasia*.

Considering the competition he faced, Yul's victory was no foregone conclusion: in fact, he was the underdog. The favorite that year was Kirk Douglas, who had already won the New York Film Critics' Circle Award, as Vincent Van Gogh in *Lust for Life,* directed by Vincente Minnelli. He was already an established star who had paid his dues, having been nominated earlier for another Minnelli film, *The Bad and the Beautiful,* and widely praised for *The Champion* and for *Twenty Thousand Leagues Under the Sea*.

Also nominated for Best Actor was a kid in his twenties who had also made three films back to back: James Dean, nominated for *Giant*. Hedda Hopper, along with many younger Hollywood actors, was rooting for him; in her column she wrote that a shaved head "is a strange reason for giving someone an Oscar." But Dean had already died in his Porsche, and Sal Mineo, who was still like a son to Yul and a brother to me, came to stay with us briefly when it was feared he might become suicidal at the death of his idol and beloved friend.

But the most likely actor to win was the man usually referred to as "the greatest actor in the world," Sir Laurence Olivier, nominated for his portrayal of King Richard III. He had previously won an Oscar for *Hamlet*. The Hollywood handicappers were taking bets across the board. Yul was eager to start out as a movie star with the industry's ultimate validation, the Oscar. Since 1951 Yul's luck had not let up, and combined with his will power and perseverance, it seemed as if my father could achieve anything he wanted to—effortlessly. No one relished victory more than Yul, and this one would put him right where he had always wanted to be: at the top of the food chain. Only if there were a catastrophic error in the vote counting could he imagine that someone else might win what was his award. But, in the spring of '57, when Anna Magnani handed him his Oscar on the stage of the Pantages Theater, Yul wrapped his hand around the statuette and said, with a modest smile, "I hope this isn't a mistake, because I'm not giving it back!"

My father handed me the Oscar as if it were a trophy he had won in battle just for this moment, when he could place it in the hands of his son. His name wasn't even engraved on it yet.

"Dad," I asked, holding the cold metal in both hands, "how did you know that you were going to win? You told me you were going to win it. How do you manage to do that? It's as if you had some magic power."

Slowly, Yul nodded and smiled.

"It is, isn't it?" He thought for a moment, and when he spoke again, his eyes burned into mine. "I just want to make sure that you have the same power, laddie."

My eyes travelled from his piercing stare to the strange statuette in my hands, hard evidence of my father's absolute infallibility.

The Brothers Karamazov is generally considered the pinnacle of Fyodor Dostoyevski's art, published the year before he died, 1881, about the same time Jules Bryner first settled in Vladivostok. The novel recounts the relationship between the degenerate old man, Fyodor Karamazov, his four sons, and the large fortune which his deceased wife has left to them. In the characters of the four brothers, Dostoyevski shoots the human soul through a prism and refracts its colors into the personalities of the Karamazov brothers, a human spectrum born from the union between the corrupt Fyodor and his late, saintly wife. Foremost there is Dmitri, whose innocent soul is a blank slate, for God to write upon. Like Job, Dmitri is a litmus test for the power of God. And there are his three brothers: Alexey the monk, whose heart is devoted to God; Ivan the journalist, whose intellect is devoted to man; and finally Smerdyakov, Fyodor's servant and bastard son, whose body is devoted to itself. *Karamazov* is also a novel about *money,* about ethical transactions made with handfuls of hard cash, and the favors that warm-blooded women can bestow. Dostoyevski was writing at the end of an anguished life, after years in debtors' prison and decades in poverty. Most of the story revolves around the brothers' inheritance from their mother, which Fyodor has misappropriated. The plot involves envelopes full of roubles, the resale of IOUs, and visits to a pawnshop.

This was the most daring artistic undertaking of Yul's career. He and Richard Brooks were fully aware of the dangers of bringing Dostoyevski to Hollywood, but they felt that the romanticism of the story could be key to its universal appeal. If it could be told with clarity and emotional immediacy, the audience might not be troubled by its polysyllabic names and intricate class structures. What the story needed for the modern audience was a degree of urgency, which was utterly lacking in the novel. To Yul's mind, that could only come from the audience's knowing in their gut who they were *rooting* for. That audience identification was always the key to Yul's acting and directing technique.

"When we were working out his character in *Karamazov,*" Brooks said in an interview, "Yul must have asked three hundred questions a day. He was constantly aware of the importance of the picture and of himself in it." A far cry from the distant disinterest that was fashionable among stars during the days of contract-players.

The casting was curious, and yet it worked: Lee J. Cobb had the greatest problem, filling the Lear-sized boots of Fyodor.

Richard Basehart as Ivan and Albert Salmi as Smerdyakov were both effective, and a young William Shatner was a convincing Alexey. Claire Bloom brought a positive luminescence to the role of the aristocratic Katya, who must either possess Dmitri or destroy him: this early performance may have surpassed in depth and complexity her Lady Anne in Olivier's *Richard III* a year earlier. It was obvious to all that she found working with Yul an exhilarating, liberating experience, extending her career beyond classical roles. Her rapport with Yul was intense: "He is a tremendously subtle actor," she told *Newsweek*. "Without any tricks or outward gestures he can convey a thought precisely as he wants to. He's the most exciting man I've ever worked with, and I'd give my eye teeth to do something with him again."

Casting the central role of Grushenka was the biggest challenge: she is a nightclub owner with the smile of a virgin and the avarice of a madam. While she is Fyodor's mistress, she seduces his son Dmitri. The role went to the little known Swiss actress Maria Schell; she had the smile, all right, but she never caught fire. It is an amazing exercise to imagine what Marilyn Monroe might have done with the role, and what that would have done for the film.

Yul's performance as Dmitri fused Dostoyevski with Chekhov. He created an idealist, a character struggling to transcend what is lowest in himself, to reach what is highest. The performance is bathed in innocence—even when Dmitri is wishing for his father's death. What made this Russian saga even more personal to Yul was the fact that much of the story is set in Mokroe, the gypsy village outside Moscow where the aristocrats were known to throw their more decadent parties. Before the revolution, this was the very town where the Dimitrievich family had lived and performed. The musical theme of the film is one of the old gypsy songs, "*Inokhodetz*," and the Dimitrievich family sing it on the sound track just as they had when Yul first met them in Paris in the Thirties, just as Yul had performed it when he auditioned for Rodgers and Hammerstein.

The movie has a sumptuous look and feel, rich with dark velvets and drunk with exhilaration; it was Hollywood Dostoyevski à la 1950s, to be sure; but the result was about the best they could have hoped for. The whole film was shot in

California, using artificial snow: economics forbade any alternative. That is never apparent to the eye, neither is the discomfort of the actors as they trudge through the summer of 1957, wearing heavy wool coats. The other thing that is not apparent is that Yul made the film while suffering the worst pain he'd ever known, sleeping barely an hour or two a night, and hardly able to climb out of his Mercedes' gull wing, because on his first day of shooting he broke his back.

He was filming a competition with a Russian officer who is wooing Grushenka, a race on horseback, in which the contestants slice melons with swords, swinging their weapons from side to side. They started early that morning, and Yul noticed a crick in his back when they were done. An hour later, his body pitched forward on to the carpet of the dressing-room: his back and stomach muscles had contracted, and the cramps were so strong he was unable to breathe. At first they thought he'd had a heart attack. In fact, he had two cracked vertebrae. On the next day, Friday, he missed work, but he was in front of the camera first thing Monday morning—broken back and all.

Over the years, Yul battered his body many times, but it was his spine that suffered the most injury, beginning with his circus accident in the 1930s. Scar tissue along his vertebrae already made it difficult for doctors to decipher his X-rays. The threat of constant, acute pain along his spine was just another challenge of daily life to Yul, and yet there was not an ounce of self-pity in his nature. With boyish defiance, he tackled each new onslaught of physical pain as if he relished it: but where the masochist enjoys surrendering to pain, for Yul pain was something he could compete with, something he could defeat. His past accidents had already determined that his spine would always be vulnerable. But his performance on the screen speaks for the power of concentration he had developed under Chekhov's training. Although it is a very physical performance, nowhere does he betray the pain he was suffering.

For years, Yul's contract with MGM and producer Pandro Berman for *Karamazov* was legendary in Hollywood. It wasn't as long as his contract for *The Buccaneer* —250 pages—but the details were excruciating. Item: Yul was to have *the* star dressing-room, on the very spot where he had visited Judy Garland while testing as Valentino ten years earlier. But the contract also specified that, without failure, he was to have a hammock available in that dressing-room and, *contractually*, the hammock had to be able to support twice Yul's weight. When workmen went to install it, they discovered the walls could not possibly support the weight. The studio offered him another dressing-room. He refused, and pointed to his contract. Eventually, they had to reinforce the walls with exterior beams and cut through the dressing-room walls to gain access to them. Yul got his hammock.

Another item spelled out in the *Karamazov* contract was that the studio had to provide Yul with *his own private Russian historian*. The historian was none other than Count Andrei Tolstoy, nephew of the novelist, whom we visited at his orange grove near Anaheim. Yul felt that authenticity was crucial, and that only such an expert could assure them cultural accuracy. He was also happy to use his clout to force the powerful studio to support the frail old Russian émigré. Yul's feeling was that a company that behaved like a bully deserved to be bullied back.

My dorm mother allowed me to call home on her phone, for I was choking to death on my own tears, unashamed, after only three days at Chadwick, my first boarding school. I was nine years old.

My mother answered the phone à la Dorothy Parker:

"Hel-lo, and what fresh Hell is this?"

She was looped, that much was ominous. Instead of crying more, I toughened up my act the way Dad would have done, and asked if he was home. Of course, he was not. I was aloof and distant when she asked how I was, as if preoccupied with greater things, matters pertaining to the fifth grade. But I finally allowed her to pry the news out of me—just the way Mrs. Anna pried news out of the King—that I had fallen in love with a girl in my class, a little girl with a long ponytail and huge black eyes. Her name was Liza. Liza Minnelli.

Yul visited me at school a week later. "Gin tells me you're pretty crazy about Liza,'' he said, as we passed the gym on the long drive up to the dorms.

"Guess so, Dad. From the first time I saw her."

"Oh, you met Liza years ago. As a matter of fact, you were practically in the crib together. You see, Rock, for a little while, when you and Liza were about a year old, Judy Garland was my girlfriend."

After I was born? When we were babies? But that meant . . . What about Mom? I simply didn't know what to do with this information. But I couldn't wait to tell Liza.

Liza and I first met on a hot autumn afternoon, and an orchestra seemed to be playing our own musical score, I swear to God. This was two years after Judy Garland's triumphant screen comeback in *A Star Is Born*, and it was the year Yul had arrived as a movie star. Liza and I were like princess and the prince of adjacent Hollywood kingdoms: even adults felt compelled to watch how we responded to each other. And, it seemed, even they could hear the orchestra.

Chadwick School, near Marineland just south of Los Angeles, was a strange and wonderful phenomenon in the mid-Fifties. Three hundred acres were kept immaculate for three hundred overprivileged kids, many emotionally deprived, with a large proportion from the entertainment industry. It was the only high school I ever saw where as many students subscribed to *Variety* as to *Mad* magazine. In the 1950s, by the way, Yul Brynner jokes about bald heads and billiard balls were regular features of both publications. Nonetheless, Liza agreed to go steady with me.

Alas, our first blush of romance ended in fisticuffs on a dormitory lawn one afternoon, as Liza rehearsed a bunch of us mercilessly in a dance routine for "There's No Business Like Show Business," taunting me cruelly for being too clumsy to copy her complicated dance steps. But by then we had already shared our first kiss, and danced in the moonlight to "Tammy." I figured I was well on my way toward second base when an event occurred that changed things between us for a little while, an event that echoed an earlier romance.

For my tenth birthday, my parents had arranged a surprise

party at our home. With all my friends assembled, Yul presented me with a special gift, something I had always wanted because Sal always wore one: a St. Christopher medal. "Wear it next to your heart for ever, laddie," said my father. So, in the best romantic tradition, I strode across the room and draped the medal around Liza's neck.

A day or two later I was dispatched in ignominy to the big house on Mapleton Drive—next to Mr. and Mrs. Bogart's house—and ordered "to get the damn St. Christopher back." My father hadn't given me the order: he was happy to see his son with Judy's daughter. It was my mother who was so angry. I could not understand why.

I rang the door and stood in ghastly shame, waiting. Judy Garland opened the door. Oh Lord. This was not just Liza's Mama, it was also Dorothy from *The Wizard of Oz,* all grown up. The fact that my father was a star did not make me blasé about other stars. But Judy had always been very sweet and patient with me. So I suffered the full impact of my absolute humiliation.

"Oh hi, Mrs. Luft," I said, about as nonchalant as any ten-year-old who's about to wet his pants. "Say, is Liza in?"

In fact the whole sorry little scene, as ordained by my mother, had been carefully scripted. Liza came to the door, bruised on my behalf but also enjoying my anguish. She handed me the medal with a pout that was both sympathetic and scornful: we knew that our friends would never let me forget my disgrace, and that our budding romance was over. The social pressures for Liza to break up with me would be overpowering. Although I'd been receiving some romantic encouragement from a blonde in the sixth grade, I was devastated. As Liza handed me the St. Christopher, my whole life flashed before my eyes. F-f-f-t.

Yul rented a large summer house in Malibu while he was shooting *The Brothers Karamazov.* Although his cracked vertebrae had put an end to our skiing once and for all, it began as mostly a happy summer for everyone. Gin and Yul remained loyal to old friends, during good times and bad: they invited the artist Julio deDiego to come to stay; and Chris Forster, the New York cop, spent a few weeks with us. Friends dropped by for drinks at almost all hours, and I often stationed myself at the bar overlooking the ocean, pouring drinks for the adults and, like any good bartender, listening to their boozy woes. They didn't seem to notice that I was prepubescent. Late night grunion hunts were organized, followed by jokes and stories and gypsy songs that lasted till dawn. Marty Ritt, with whom Yul had worked at CBS, came frequently with Irving and Harriet Ravetch to work with Yul on the screenplay they were preparing of Faulkner's *The Sound and the Fury*. Yul's agent Ted Ashley, with his partner Ira Steiner and Ruth, were perhaps our closest friends in those years. I fell deliriously in love with a young ingénue named Angie Dickinson, who often came with Richard Brooks. Alex North, the film composer, dropped by with his wife, Sherle. And sometimes our neighbor Rock Hudson came to our parties, though we were never once invited to his. Despite the fact that Dad was filming with an aluminum cast strapped to his broken back, it was the most sociable time he and Mom had ever spent, and they seemed to be reveling in it.

Every morning, Dad woke me at five, and by five-thirty we were sitting in a diner near the spot where Topanga meets the Pacific Coast Highway. The place was a run-down greasy spoon called the Step Inn Café, managed by a grouchy woman named Margaret, who'd just as soon throw your plate in your face as serve you. By the end of the summer she owned the place: Yul was a very big tipper. We started each day with a huge breakfast there in comfortable silence and then sped to MGM, where I spent the rest of the morning before returning to the beach.

That summer, Yul failed in one endeavor: he had sworn to give up cigarettes and, with Richard Brooks, had taken up pipe-smoking in a serious way. Until this time he had smoked three packs a day of Old Golds, since Gauloises were unavailable in America, and while on Broadway he had begun smoking fine cigars, and keeping an extensive collection of Havanas in the humidor room at Dunhill's. Smoking was a big part of Yul's life, and of his image of himself. Before every posed photograph, without exception, he lit a cigarette, even in character, whenever possible: as Dmitri Karamazov, or Bounine in *Anastasia,* or the major in *The Journey.* The sight of a camera was often enough to make Yul light a cigarette.

* * *

"Dad, how old do I have to be before I get to smoke and drink?" I was still only eleven.

No reply.

"Dad, how old do I have to be before I can taste all these drinks I've learned to mix?"

"The law says you have to be twenty-one."

"Well that never stopped you, did it, Dad? You were already working in a nightclub when you were fifteen."

"That was different."

"Why?"

"That was Paris, 1935. This is LA, 1957."

"So?"

"Well, laddie, you're the son of a movie star. If you wreck a car, or get a girl knocked up, it's gonna make headlines." How well I knew, even then. My hyperactive imagination had long since supplied me with a chilling array of garish headlines for both of those very options.

"There are many advantages we have because I am famous. There are also many disadvantages. I share them all with you, in the hope they will balance each other. If that means you can't live quite the way I did at your age, so be it."

"So be it," I echoed. "I hope that doesn't mean I'll be very different from you. Sometimes, Dad, it seems as if all that growing up means is that you can have fun doing sinful things, like smoking, drinking and being unfaithful to your wife."

"Of course you'll be different from me, Rock. For chris-sakes, don't you realize how hard I've worked just to give you all the advantages I never had? And you know what? I'm as big and hot a star as I'm ever going to be, and I'm in debt! Seventy thousand dollars worth of debt, just because of taxes. And all that just to provide you with the one thing I lacked most as a boy—a secure home."

I thought about that. "Then, Dad—why am I in boarding school?" Again he did not reply. "I'm sorry, Dad. I'm really not ungrateful." As we reached the San Diego Freeway, he gunned the gull wing.

* * *

In the autumn of 1957, Yul began filming *The Sound and the Fury*, directed by Marty Ritt, and co-starring Joanne Woodward, Margaret Leighton, Ethel Waters and Jack Warden. Adapting Faulkner was as daring an artistic endeavor as Dostoyevski: so much of this novel took place within the characters' minds. It was nothing less than noble in the attempt—though nobility was probably not exactly what had motivated Jerry Wald to produce the movie—and it was an abysmal failure on most counts, though no one was shamed by the effort. Joanne Woodward, in her seventh month of pregnancy by the end of shooting, was somewhat unconvincing as a sixteen-year-old virgin. Yul, in his wig, was just credible as white trash. Perhaps the most memorable feature of the movie was Alex North's jazzy, sensuous, offbeat score. The film was released quietly and made very little stir, before it vanished. It was Yul's first flop since he had reached stardom.

I returned to Chadwick, where Liza and I prepared to co-star in a school play together. Sputnik had orbited, and Elvis was everywhere. The Brynner family had achieved a certain stability that only broke down when Mom got too drunk to hide the fact: the rest of the time, everything was fine. Yul treated his dressing-room as a home away from home, and met with friends and girlfriends there, just as he had been doing for years. I was at school making friends and learning how to get along with eleven-year-olds; and Mom stayed home to drink. A stability of sorts, however temporary.

Occasionally, we had a visit from Yul's Aunt Vera and her daughter Irena who by then was supporting herself as a jeweler. They had recently moved from San Francisco to New York City, where Yul's sister, Vera, my beloved aunt, still lived, performing and teaching opera. It was always strange to me, as for all children of immigrants, to hear their animated Russian, for it bespoke distant worlds I would never know. Older Vera, who had been present when Yul was born, had become to Yul the embodiment of all that was good in our heritage, and he made sure that I shared that emotional bond. Still, whenever I asked Vera about my dad's childhood, there were always variations from what I'd read in interviews with him, and sometimes her accounts were different from what he had told me. If I asked him about the discrepancies, he would gaze

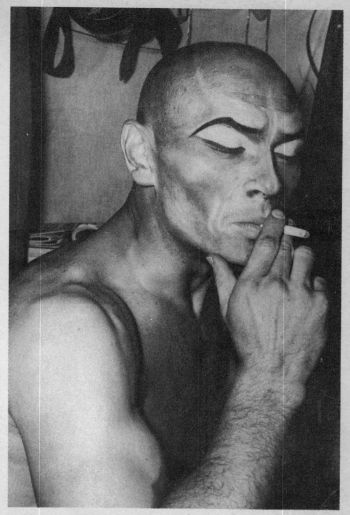

1 The King, as Yul conceived him, represents the soul of an angel struggling to escape from the body of a beast.

2 Jules married Natalia Kurkutova, the daughter of a Mongolian Prince.

3 Boris and Marousia were an attractive couple.

4 In anguish and shame, Marousia left the Bryner compound in Vladivostok with her children, Vera and Yul.

5 Yul was only four when his father Boris Yulievich fell in love with an actress.

6 Boris hardly ever visited his two children.

7 Women of all ages succumbed to his teenage charms.

8 By the time he was sixteen, the most reliable institution Yul had ever known was a nightclub full of gypsies.

9 With Mary Martin starring in *Lute Song*, the producer was looking for an actor with an "Oriental quality."

10 Goldwyn described Virginia as "an honest-to-God American beauty with brains, who even writes poetry."

11 Virginia's costar in *Truckline Café* was an exciting young actor fresh from Nebraska named Marlon Brando.

12 Michael Chekhov was Stanislavsky's codirector and the nephew of Anton Chekhov.

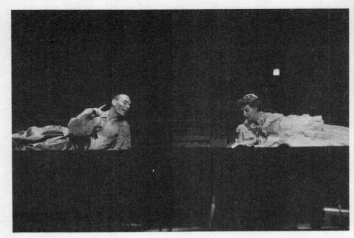

3 Rodgers and Hammerstein wrote, "The strength of their story lies in the violent changes they wrought in each other."

14 With the play's success, Yul began meeting all the stars.

15 Since anger expresses power most effectively, it was largely for Yul's Old Testament temper that the studio executives hired him.

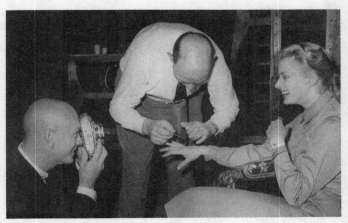

16 He and Ingrid lapsed into soft-spoken French whenever my mother left the room.

17 "His eyes glower with imperial rage, they widen with boyish curiosity, they dance with amusement at his own simple jokes."

18 When Anna Magnani handed him his Oscar, Yul wrapped his hand around the statuette and said with a modest smile, "I hope this isn't a mistake, because I'm not giving it back."

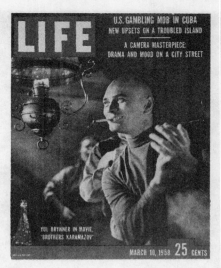

19 *The Brothers Karamazov* has a sumptuous look and feel, rich with dark velvet and drunk with exhilaration.

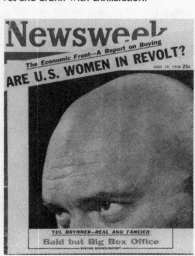

20 *Newsweek* magazine ran a cover story on Yul that had many consequences.

21 When Doris and Yul were married, a fiesta was held on the set of *The Magnificent Seven.*

22 It was Yul who presented the Oscar to Elizabeth.

23 Cocteau immortalized Yul as a wingèd angel, hovering above the altar.

a Yul son ami Jean Cocteau
X 1961

24 "Yul Brynner must be mad to imagine that he could be Yul Brynner."

25 Yul worked hard to create a rich, robust character for *Taras Bulba*, the ultimate authoritarian who murders his own son for disloyalty.

26 When Yul saw the final cut of *Taras Bulba*, something inside him broke.

27 Yul, who often supplied Cocteau's opium in the 1930s, now watched his son reenacting Jean's struggle with addiction.

28 He conveyed greetings to me from Liza, who had visited him backstage.

29 "Who'd a ever have thunk," said Ali, "that the son of the Phar-oah of Egypt would be protectin' a little black boy from Louisville!"

30 With Mia and Melody, the new home in Normandy which Jacqueline chose was filled with laughter and merriment.

31 Virginia never remarried: she lived alone for almost three decades.

32 Michael Jackson attended a party at which Yul Brynner announced that he had conquered cancer.

33 Some nights Mary Beth Peil had virtually to carry him through the energetic polka as he moaned with pain.

34 He posed for a cameraman doing a yoga handstand, which only aggravated his suffering.

35 Yul sometimes refused to make his final curtain call if the audience failed to give him a *standing* ovation.

36 "The reason I'm not alive today is because I smoked cigarettes."

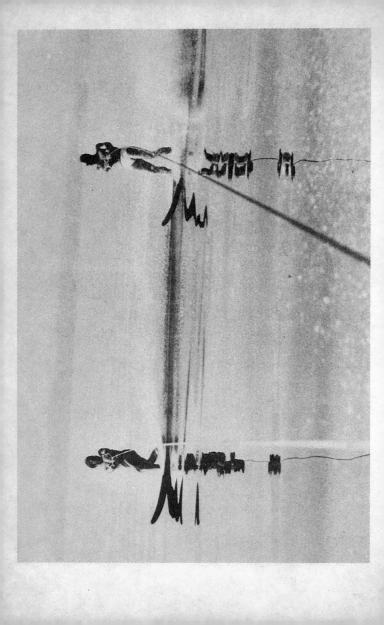

IL FIGLIO DELL'EROE

off to the horizon and reply impatiently: "The facts of my life have nothing to do with the realities of my existence."

That always shut me up.

Life went on with stunning normality for weeks at a time: the effect of our travelling years began to wear off. We were recovering a sense of neighborhood and community, of a network of friends, of continuity and of seasonal change—even in Southern California. Occasionally, we took holidays back east to catch up with the theater—it was the year of *West Side Story, Auntie Mame* (with Bea Lillie), and Gielgud's one-man show, *Ages of Man*. My parents made sure that, "now that I was almost a young man," I could have access to all the books, plays and films I might absorb. I was on a cultural tear through all human civilization, hungry to learn more, and anxious above all to shed what seemed to *this* hypersophisticated ten-year-old to be the burden of childhood. It was generally apparent to American kids in the 1950s that the right to smoke, drink and have sex was the primary benefit of adulthood. I, and many like me, just couldn't wait to be formally entitled to sin. And we didn't wait.

In early 1958, Yul and Gin went to Vienna together, where he was about to shoot *The Journey,* and my mother was going to continue her studies in cytology, which she had begun with enthusiasm at UCLA the previous autumn. She wanted to convince herself that she could learn anything she wanted to, and that nothing, not even alcohol, could stop her.

The Journey was an attempt to bring a contemporary event to the screen quickly—the subject was the Hungarian uprising of 1956. Filming began just a year after the uprising, and the story told of a Russian officer who prevented the escape of Hungarian freedom fighters from Budapest. Deborah Kerr played an Englishwoman intent on helping a rebel, her lover, to escape, but unable to resist falling in love with the Russian officer. In many respects, it was a latter day *Casablanca,* directed by Anatole Litvak, his first film after *Anastasia.* It featured Jason Robards, Robert Morley, Anne Jackson, E. G. Marshall and Anouk Aimee, in small roles. The character that

Yul created was a variation on the type he most liked to play: the bastard with a heart of gold.

While they were in Vienna, *Newsweek* magazine ran a cover story on Yul that had many consequences. The photograph of Yul on the magazine's cover did not even show his face, just his bald head and his eyes, and the words "Bald but Big Box Office: Yul Brynner—Real and Fancied." The title of the article was "Yul Brynner—Golden Egghead." It's difficult in retrospect to understand how extraordinary it seemed, in the 1950s, for a man to shave his head. This was, historically, the biggest decade in the toupée maker's trade. Two years after he had won an Oscar, a national magazine was still treating him like a freak for shaving his head. Yul gradually began to realize that the subject of his bald head might *never* go away, and that fact began gnawing at his innards.

The article itself was really the most serious attempt yet to identify Yul, and it started off with a bang, as it were:

"I was born out of wedlock in Sakhalin, an island east of Siberia, on July 12th, 1920," Yul Brynner said last week, offering yet another highly romanticized version of his fantastic life. "My father was a rich Russian, my mother a gypsy, and I lived with her until I was 10, when she died. My father, who was then living in Peking, refused to see me. But his real wife, who was separated from him and later divorced him, accepted me as her own son. During the Manchurian war she decided to leave Asia and took my half sister Vera and me to Paris. The years there were difficult. We had little money. My exotic appearance, my physique, and my restlessness came in handy. Learning always came easily, and I spent my days studying philosophy at the Sorbonne and my nights alternating between jobs in the circus and in night clubs . . ."

But *Newsweek*'s reporter had been in touch with his sister, Vera, and when she learned that Yul was calling her his *half*-sister, she erupted—and *Newsweek* printed the result. "Vera Brynner, now a concert singer, laughingly dismissed most of the foregoing. 'That must be variation number nineteen,' she said with a sigh. 'I love Yul, and I don't mind anything he concocts until he brings the family into it. Our father was a Swiss businessman working in Manchuria. Our mother was a Russian-Greek actress-singer. They were married before we were both born.'" Because of that quotation, and the "public betrayal" it constituted, Yul swore he would never speak to his sister again. But there was more to the article to enrage him, very possibly because he had been so hostile to the journalist who wrote it, Michael Mackay. Mackay continued with relentless fascination about Yul's scalp:

Brynner created his visual trademark, the bald-as-a-lie head he has since electric-shaved every day. Although his hairline was only receding a bit by the time the king role was offered, he decided to appear with the gleaming pate because he felt it was more suitable to the appearance of a barbaric Siamese. It was an immediate hit, particularly to women. "He's ugly magnetic," one ardent feminine fan said recently, and added with savage glee, "Look at his face. The bone structure suggests cruelty and women love it. There are very few male animals like him . . ." "You can look into his eyes and go back centuries . . ." "He would be the most attractive man alive even if he grew grass on his head . . ."

The article went on to examine his personal character, in terms he had never seen printed before.

"He is so full of hate for incompetence," says a friend, "that he often becomes downright violent . . ." "He has to be top man," says a close friend. "His entire bravado, his enormous inflated ego compensates for his own well-hidden inadequacies. He won't admit that he is not a perfect person. He is relatively humorless and never spontaneous. If you level with him you come out second best and only get contempt for your inadequacies. When I think of Yul I think of reputations tumbling, balloons being pricked, façades being torn down—the Brynner Wrecking Co. always at work. But he is so honest and unafraid in this dishonest and frightened town that I find what he says and does is refreshing. At times

he can be gentle and even chivalrous . . . impossible about
setting to rights the true record of his childhood. His bizarre
and often conflicting accounts of his early life have trapped
writers for years.''

In my boarding school, copies of the magazine circulated, but
the gist of the article was quickly paraphrased as a schoolyard
simplicity: ''Rocky's the son of a bastard.'' That was a big
deal in the 1950s.

Of course, I proudly defended my father's bastardy, even
as I doubted it. Why did Aunt Vera, who was present at his
birth, tell me a story that was different from what my father
told the world? But then, why would my father invent the story
that he was a bastard? Surely he wouldn't say something like
that just to make himself more . . . conspicuous? In any case,
thinking and saying crazy things like that seemed to be the
right thing to do, and I'd fight any kid to *prove* my Dad was
right. And as soon as I grew up I'd say some crazy things,
too, with just as much swagger. Hell, I might not even wait . . .

Fade in.
  ''*C'mon, Rocky,*'' *shouted Liza. ''I'll show you how to do
cartwheels.'' As Liza tells it, the philosophical young Rock,
his posture already slightly stooped from the burden of his
learning, walked on. Still, the frolicsome girl continued pestering, and had to be acknowledged. So came his reply, as he
knelt to pick up a handful of dust:*
  ''*Dirt. Do you see that, Liza? Dirt! We begin as dirt and
we end as dirt. AND YOU WANT TO TURN CARTWHEELS?*''
  Fade out.

Since both my parents were abroad, I spent alternate weekends
at the home of film composer Alex North, and his wife Sherle.
Since their son was at school in Switzerland they welcomed
me warmly several nights a month into their avant-garde household; Ruth and Ira Steiner also cared for me, as did other
friends. I was as complicated, confused, misguided, over-
protected and arrogant a little tyke as you ever saw. After all,

by the age of eleven, I already had my own car. And chauffeur.

My parents weren't there, so they made sure I would never want for a thing. Yul sent me a couple of hundred bucks pocket money each weekend, remembering how little cash he'd had as a boy in Paris. So on Friday afternoons I would give Liza a lift into Los Angeles in my limo and drop her off at her house, then go by the Norths' home to bathe and change. Then, after cocktail hour at Alex and Sherle's I'd pick up Liza again and we'd drop in on a few other Hollywood cocktail parties, usually the only children there. Then, after dinner at Don the Beachcomber's, perhaps a *nouvelle vague* film from Europe, or dancing (hardly my forte). Then I would kiss Liza good night on the doorstep of her father's big pink house on Sunset Boulevard opposite the Beverly Hills Hotel, and ride home in wondrous bliss, tipping the chauffeur generously. Often I'd spent my whole allowance by Saturday afternoon. Naturally, I was a big tipper, for an eleven-year-old.

Those brief, magic times that Liza and I shared were consolation enough for all the fears, anguishes, and insults that our lives at home and at boarding school had inflicted during those lonely, unsure days, when parents, hers and mine, had turned cold with each other, and all the sensitive, old subjects had new edges to them: money, work, drink, and even fun. Together, once in a while, Liza and I could be Prince and Princess of Hollywood, and delight in each other's company. But we were more than that, too. For it occurred to me, using that brand of logic peculiar to children, that if Yul and Judy had fallen in love together *before* marrying others, then Liza and I might have been . . . *the same person.*

Yul remained in Vienna a little longer, after Gin returned to the States to rent a house at East Hampton for the summer. Meanwhile, he fell in love with an Austrian singer named Frankie. When she became pregnant, Frankie told Yul she was eager to have a baby, their baby. He offered some financial help, but they both understood that the child would be Frankie's responsibility. Early the following year their daughter was born; together, they named her Lark.

When Yul returned to America in the summer, he was miserable, angry, and broke. He complained that the more he earned, the more he was taxed. After starring in six films back to back, he was in debt for almost a hundred thousand dollars, for chrissakes, how was he ever going to break even? Europe beckoned to him now, all the time, a remedy for all his woes.

We spent the summer of 1958 in East Hampton, where we water-skied, went shark fishing off Montauk Point, and, most days, socialized. Yul suggested a new hobby we could share: stamp collecting. We started out with a standard album, but within weeks this hobby had become an investment. Yul's secretary was instructed to write letters to the chiefs of state of every government in the world, requesting a corner block of each nation's most treasured stamp. He also asked that each chief of state sign the corner block, as a personal favor. Within six months the collection was worth hundreds of thousands of dollars. Then we began concentrating on United Nations stamps.

In the fall, *The Buccaneer* began shooting at Paramount. It was the story of the French pirate Jean Lafitte, and the help he gave to America at the battle of New Orleans during the war of 1812. Yul was not the director, as planned. De Mille had been unable to arrange that, with whatever forces he had to contend with at the studio. At the same time Yul realized it was not at all the movie he would want to make as his first directorial effort. It had already grown to be a huge, unwieldy production.

Like *The Ten Commandments, The Buccaneer* was a remake of the 1938 film, which had starred Fredric March, and co-starred a kid named Anthony Quinn. Twenty years later, the director whom De Mille assigned to the remake was Anthony Quinn. Andrew Jackson was to be played by Charlton Heston, because he was a bankable star. Also in the cast were Charles Boyer, the chivalrous, threadbare pirate; Inger Stevens, the Southern belle; and, again, Claire Bloom, freed from her usual aristocratic casting to play the scruffy pirate girl who wins the love of Jean Lafitte.

In the autumn, I went back to boarding school and Mom went back to heavy drinking, and life continued smoothly until Tyrone Power died. He had been in the middle of shooting a huge epic in Spain, *Solomon and Sheba*, with Gina Lollobrigida, and now the insurance company was obliged to offer a huge salary to any actor who would replace him in a role that Yul, among many others, had long since turned down. The difference was that now they were ready to pay him one million dollars. The way personal income tax was structured in the 1950s, his tax bill on that million would be nine hundred thousand dollars. But there was a solution. The government allowed a total exemption to citizens who resided abroad for a minimum of five years. Yul saw this as his chance to pay his debts: one million dollars tax free was all the money he'd ever need, then he would be free to give up stardom and return to directing at last.

Virginia would not hear of it. It was unpatriotic, or worse. It was dishonest and immoral and unredeemable. "All you want is to be a gypsy millionaire," she screamed, since the kid was away at school, "without a care or responsibility in the world. Well, I'm sorry, *Mr. B*, but you have responsibilities, whether or not you care to notice. And if you can earn money ten times faster, you better believe me, I can spend it faster still!" Or words to that effect.

I came home from Chadwick for Thanksgiving, to be met by my dad, who wanted to go for a walk. We had lived there four years without ever going for a walk before. Dad didn't even like walking. I knew that. But we went for a walk.

"I guess you understand what's going on, don't you, laddie?"

"Of course, Dad," I lied.

"I'm going to be in Europe, and as soon as you want, you come and join me there."

"To live?"

"Yes, of course, if that's what you want."

"What about Mom?"

"Gin is going to go back to New York, to work on the stage. You know, that's what she's always loved best."

"Are you going to get divorced?"

"Yes, laddie, after a while, I think we probably will."

"How soon can I come live in Europe?"

"Well, your mother is going to need you. Things have not

been easy for her, and they'll be even harder for her now.''

"Oh c'mom, Dad. I can't take care of her; Mom has a drinking problem. I'm eleven years old. So how soon can I come live in Europe?''

"Probably in a year. But you can come visit sooner—maybe even for Christmas.''

"And until then, where do I go at weekends, and for holidays? Alex North's?''

"If that's what you want, laddie.''

"Yes, please. And Dad?''

"Yes?''

"Can I keep the limo?''

"Of course.''

"Then I'll be OK, Dad. I won't need Mom, so long as I can have the limo . . .''

7

Gypsy Millionaire

"The gypsies remain by their own definition 'hunters,' with hunters' privileges."
—Jan Yoors, *The Gypsies*

Yul flew first to Switzerland to establish his residence in Lausanne where, more than twenty years earlier, he had received medical treatment for his opium addiction. Soon his secretary, Diana, relocated there with him, and he called upon his dresser, Don Lawson, to join him. Now money was plentiful, and convenience was his guiding principle. Resettling in Europe solved a variety of his problems with a single stroke: it made money abundant, returned him to his beloved Europe, and triggered the end of a marriage he no longer enjoyed. But divorce was a difficult step in the 1950s, legally and emotionally, especially after fifteen years of marriage. At thirty-eight, Yul had been married to Virginia most of his adult life. So, as convenient as it might be, the move left his soul tugged and torn. Though he told himself he was born to be a wanderer, and that any attachment could be broken, still, he felt at home in America, and he shaped his values according to the cultural precepts of American democracy in general, and liberals and social reformers in particular. He had been an avid Democrat— as well as a fan of Li'l Abner, hot dogs and baseball. Yul had no problem putting the best face on things, and the fact that his own grandfather, Jules, had set out for the Orient almost a century earlier from Switzerland lent a dizzying sense of destiny to this move. But while he had never fully *belonged* to any place, Yul could not escape a sense of expatriation this time.

Tax exiles and other transplants from both America and Britain were numerous in those years, especially in that corner of Switzerland: Charlie Chaplin, Noël Coward, Charles Lindbergh and William Holden, to name only a few of our best-known neighbors and friends. Soon after we arrived, a larger flood of these reverse Pilgrims settled on the edge of Lac Léman, from Geneva to Montreux. Their shared values put a premium on internationalism, and a low priority on nationalism.

Before settling down as a millionaire, Yul first had to make *Solomon and Sheba*. Here, for the first time since the beginning of his stardom, was a piece of unmistakable crap, on an aesthetic par with Steve Reeves as Hercules. Just two years after *The Ten Commandments*, the zenith of the genre, came this nadir. Gina Lollobrigida, with a ruby in her navel, had all the sex appeal of a fist. George Sanders, in his sixties, appeared so feeble in battle that he turned to camera as if soliciting comfort from the audience. And Yul, as the young Solomon with Tyrone Power's hairstyle (to match previously filmed sequences), spent most of his screen time trying to keep a straight face. Both Michael Chekhov and Cecil B. De Mille had died, mercifully, before *Solomon and Sheba* was released.

The experience of renouncing the values and loyalties that had guided him for two decades was not an easy one. At least he was out of debt and putting aside a nest egg that would allow him to become the director he always wanted to be, while feeling secure that he could guarantee his son, and even his grandchildren, a college education. But the extravagance of his daily life grew as fast as his earnings: whenever he had the wherewithal, Yul Brynner was one of the all-time great spenders. "I have no respect for money, Rock," he always reminded me. "I piss on the stuff." I took careful note of this, as part of my moral education.

The move to Europe had accomplished something else: it put him within range of a young lady named Doris who had struck his fancy when he visited Paris from Vienna. In her twenties, with long, straight hair the color of a strawberry roan, Doris Kleiner had spent most of her life in Santiago, Chile, though her parents were from Yugoslavia. In the 1950s she had come to Paris as the guest and protégée of Arturo and

Patricia Lopez, Chile's greatest contributions to high society. Thus the circle of intimate friends and esteemed acquaintances with whom Doris mingled was, socially, *la crème de la crème*. This was the stock from which the first Jet Set was born two years later, when passenger jets first came into service.

Of course, Doris's appeal to Yul was romantic, not social. Still, she lived within the only social milieu that had ever attracted Yul and still held some fascination for him. He had seen this crowd, in some cases the same individuals, seated in Paris clubs since his adolescence; he had sung beside their tables in the Thirties, and then again in 1948, when he lost his plane ticket in a poker game. Their ranks included several Rothschilds, and the group was spearheaded, so to speak, by Marie-Hélène, Ali Khan, Prince Rainier and Princess Grace, Prince Michael of Romania, Her Royal Princess Maria Pia of Italy, Gianni Agnelli of Fiat, Porfirio Rubirosa, and a limited number of other knights of industry, arts and entertainment. At the pinnacle of this Parisian pyramid reigned Wallis Simpson, Duchess of Windsor, and her husband Edward, formerly the King of England.

Yul's attitude toward this crowd was ambivalent, even paradoxical, for while he studied and admired the understated elegance of these bona fide aristocrats, he had momentarily to forget his own past, and ignore the fact that these included some of the very *gaje* the Dimitrieviches had taught him to despise. But of course, forgetting his own past was one of the things Yul did best. *Newsweek* had made him famous for it.

But Yul was having trouble ignoring the pain from the collapse of his marriage, and from missing his son. Sleeping had become a big problem; when he reached a point of real exhaustion, his doctor prescribed a sleep cure in Switzerland, said to produce a sense of rejuvenation. Both doctor and nurses warned Yul and those who worked for him that he would be emotionally vulnerable if he became involved with a woman just after the cure. When he awoke after the ten days, Doris Kleiner was there to visit him.

Meanwhile Virginia had gone to New York with one simple plan: to bankrupt Yul, by spending faster than even he could earn. She rented a duplex on East 65th, and had an architect draw up plans for a *ballroom*, with a fountain in the middle.

Her friends rallied to her support, most especially Gloria Vanderbilt, Pucky Violett and Carol Saroyan. They spoke or gathered together almost daily, often at Orsini's, and Gloria made sure that Virginia always had an interesting array of suitors or dinner dates. One evening, quite without warning, it was Sir Laurence Olivier who appeared at the appointed hour to take Virginia out on the town.

And then there was Rocky, still in boarding school in Southern California, feeling very abandoned, though far too sophisticated ever to show it. I flew to New York quite often, on the ten-hour prop plane flight—and of course, I had my limo. But at the age of twelve, I had no idea where I was going to live next. The trips to New York *seemed* like a great luxury, but they were long and unsettling. Still, I had to take care of my mother. And besides, I began doing what all the *hip* adults in first class seemed to do on those flights: I got drunk. No stewardess ever even thought to stop me: I was dressed to the teeth, and I appeared to know just what I was doing ordering a daiquiri, while I flipped through catalogues of rare stamp auctions.

Our stamp collection had several consequences. Yul had become aware that the United Nations had designated 1959–60 World Refugee Year, to create greater global awareness of the massive and expanding problem of refugees warehoused in camps around the world, from Hong Kong to Jordan. So Dad and I began a special collection of stamps commemorating World Refugee Year from every UN country. Naturally, Yul wrote to the UN's High Commissioner for Refugees, Dr. Auguste Lindt, and then one thing led to another. The more he learned about the refugee problem, the more he recognized a political problem to which he could respond emotionally, since, for much of his own childhood, he had been a political refugee, or DP (displaced person). Of course it was good for Yul's image, but he did not let that dictate his actions, and it was not what motivated him. Yul devoted most of a year to traveling in discomfort to camps around the world for a book, *Bring Forth the Children: A Journey to the Forgotten People of Europe and the Middle East,* and a television special, *Rescue— With Yul Brynner,* produced and co-hosted by Edward R. Murrow. This was an action motivated by simple, human concern for the helpless people he met. Yul was appointed special consultant to the High Commissioner for Refugees, and granted both a United Nations and a United States Diplomatic passport. He took this very seriously.

I never saw him prouder than when he handed me the first copy of his book. It was filled with photographs of refugee camps by Yul and by Inge Morath, his friend and colleague. The desolation that scars the faces of these abandoned people proves there is purgatory on earth, for those who have fallen in the gap between governments and become political lepers.

The words on the first page read:

This book is dedicated to Rocky, my son,
in the hope that he will observe, learn, and give something
of himself
in order to earn his place in society.

I rushed off to my room to read my dad's book, starting with his preface:

When I was fifteen, and a circus performer in Paris, we gave a matinee for orphans. I worked as a clown and an acrobat at the same time, flying as an acrobat but dressed as a clown. I still remember the day because of the contact, the rapport I had with those youngsters . . . Though I was at first asked only to assist in the making of a documentary film to give some advice about the postage stamps that were to be issued during the World Refugee Year . . . I entered a two-year contract with the Office of the High Commissioner.

He also donated all profits to the refugee cause.

Since most of the text was written in collaboration with experts, it painted a very accurate report of what the future would hold for those living out their whole lives contained in refugee camps:

The refugees did not choose their lot. They are the result of our world's madness . . . every day when my work in the camp was finished I wanted to wipe my eyes on a piece of

clean landscape—anything, after the drabness of those bar-
racks, the hopelessness that strikes you almost physically
whenever you look down a camp street . . .

I was so proud of my dad. This was not the voice of some
lame-brained hunk popping in for a charity gig.

Yul chronicled the plight of the ten thousand Tibetan refugees, devotees of the Dalai Lama, and of more than one million
refugees from Communist China along the edges of Hong
Kong, estimating that:

> nearly 15 million refugees around the world still need as-
> sistance . . . As long as we live in a world that indulges in
> war and the kind of rivalry and strife that substitute for war,
> I feel that we really have to make ourselves responsible for
> the results . . . It is important that we do not simply develop
> a bad conscience about them and let it go at that. These are
> our fellow human beings, displaced and deprived of their
> means of making a living, through no fault of their own . . .
> There is no disgrace in being a refugee, but there is certainly
> disgrace in trying to forget that refugees exist.

On the edge of the Dead Sea Yul played guitar and sang "Two
Little Fishes and Five Loaves of Bread" for a crowd of children. Later Yul wrote:

> Take a youth of seventeen who lives in a camp and is unable
> to go on to a vocational school. He has time on his hands.
> All he does is think about his hatred and his desire: his hatred
> for the people who have deprived him of his homeland, his
> desire to push them into the sea.

The point that Yul made about these young men during the
television documentary, in which Edward R. Murrow posed
questions to him, was that they would be compelled by the
hopelessness of their situation to turn to terrorism, if they could
find no other way to change their circumstances, warehoused
in camps. "More than 500,000 of these people are in Jordan.
When I visited King Hussein in his palace in Amman, he
pointed out that more than one-third of the people in his king-

dom are refugees . . . The Middle East refugee clings to the belief that one day he will go home.''

Dad had already told me about his visit to the King of Jordan, the 24-year-old descendant of Muhammad. Don Lawson had been with him. What remained vividly in my mind was an anecdote Don told me about a mild pleasantry King Hussein had made regarding a summit between Jordan and Siam. ''The real king came about as close as he could to calling your father a king.''

Some time after the documentary aired, I walked into Dad's office to find his eyes brimming with tears. Before him was a sheet of paper:

Appointed special consultant to the United Nations High Commissioner for Refugees, 1959–1960

Rescue with Yul Brynner

by Marianne Moore

''Recital? 'Concert' is the word,''
and stunning, by the Budapest Symphony—
    displaced but not deterred—
listened to by me,
    though with detachment then,
        like a grasshopper that did not
    know it missed the mower, a pygmy citizen;
        a case, I'd say, of too slow a grower.
There were thirty million; there are thirteen still—
healthy to begin with, kept waiting till they're ill.
History judges. It will
salute Winnipeg's incredible
conditions: ''Ill; no sponsor; and no kind of skill.''
    Odd—a reporter with guitar—a puzzle.
    Mysterious Yul did not come to dazzle.

Magic bird with multiple tongue—
five tongues—equipped for a crazy twelve-month tramp
    (a plod), he flew among
the damned, found each camp
    where hope had slowly died
        (some had never seen a plane).
    Instead of feathering himself, he exemplified
        the rule that, self-applied, omits the gold.
He said, "You may feel strange; nothing matters less.
Nobody notices; you'll find some happiness.
No new 'big fear'; no distress."
Yul can sing—twin of an enchantress—
elephant-borne dancer in silver-spangled dress,
    swirled aloft by trunk, with star-tipped wand, Tamara,
    as true to the beat as *Symphonia Hungarica*.
    Head bent down over the guitar,
he barely seemed to hum; ended "all come home";
    did not smile; came by air;
did not have to come.
    The guitar's an event.
        Guests of honor can't dance; don't smile.
    "Have a home?" a boy asks. "Shall we live in a tent?"
        "In a house," Yul answers. His neat cloth hat
has nothing like the glitter reflected on the face
of milkweed-witch seed-brown dominating a palace
that was nothing like the place
where he is now. His deliberate pace
is a king's, however. "You'll have plenty of space."
    Yule—Yul log for the Christmas-fire tale-spinner—
        of fairy tales that can come true: Yul Brynner.

*Mom and I spent Christmas alone together on a flight to New
York. We took turns crying through most of the ten-hour trip,
and by way of consolation she let me have a couple of glasses
or more of champagne, since I had turned thirteen at last two
days earlier. So Mom and I spent our first Christmas without
Dad on board some airplane, crying and getting loaded together.*

* * *

Yul had formed his own company, called Alciona, to produce the films that he hoped to direct as well as star in. (Alciona was Greek for "halcyon"; Yul commissioned Jean Cocteau to design the logo for his company's stationery.) The Mirisch Brothers at United Artists had guaranteed Yul some twenty-seven million dollars in production funds for Alciona over the following nine years. There were two projects he planned to start with: the first was a huge production of Arthur Koestler's epic novel *The Gladiators,* which recounted the slave uprising in ancient Rome and the story of its leader, the gladiator Spartacus. But just when Yul optioned the rights there was an announcement that another version of the same story, owned by Kirk Douglas, was to be made.

Now these two stars were on a courtroom collision course: but Kirk was holding all the cards, and he quickly beat Yul to the jump with the rights, the package and the deal. Yul swiftly shifted to a sour grapes stance on the whole project, claiming he was relieved not to be saddled with another huge, quasi-biblical epic. Since he was not in Hollywood, it was easy enough to put the whole fiasco out of mind. Yul was very good at putting unpleasant things, and people, out of his thoughts. But he also suffered sleepless nights of bitter anger and tormented vengefulness that left him exhausted the next morning.

The Gladiators was one of many deals Yul tried to put together for Alciona that fell through. That's not unnatural in a business which calls for collaboration from many people, but it happened partly because Yul was not available for meetings and conferences in Hollywood, where the deal was being negotiated. And also because Yul had established his reputation for being too difficult to deal with.

The second project involved an idea that had occurred to Yul before he left California, and it became Alciona's greatest success. One afternoon when I was home from school, he asked me to come to see a movie with him, warning me that it was in Japanese, with subtitles, and that it was long. It was *The Seven Samurai.* He explained that he wanted to buy the rights to adapt the story as a Western. My first reaction was exactly the same as everyone else's: a bare-scalped cowboy was sure

going to look funny. But he was determined to demonstrate
that if it was a great project, his shaved head would make no
difference. With the Mirischs' money, Yul optioned the rights
to Kurosawa's masterpiece, and hired a writer for the adaptation.

The first film he made after *Solomon and Sheba* was neither
epic nor Western but, even more unlikely perhaps, a stage
comedy still playing on Broadway. It was called *Once More
with Feeling,* written by Harry Kurnitz, and it was very funny.
The story cast Yul as a self-centered megalomaniac: a world-
renowned orchestra conductor ''with an ego as big as your
average-sized aircraft carrier.'' Yul's co-star, who played his
long-suffering wife with a talent for placating members of the
orchestra board, was Kay Kendall, an incomparable comedienne, who made the film her own. The film was shot in Paris,
and directed by Stanley Donen.

Once More with Feeling was shot at Studio de Boulogne,
mostly, where the daily shooting schedule was very unlike
Hollywood. Instead of 7 A.M. make-up calls, the French started
at noon, and then worked without a break until about eight in
the evening—a routine better suited for nightlife. Harry Kurnitz
created an ambience of sly wit, especially in the company of
Kay Kendall and, to a lesser extent, her husband Rex Harrison.
Harrison was consistently moody and ill-tempered, but the reason for that became apparent a few months later, when he could
no longer hide the fact that Kay was suffering from leukemia.
By then she had just managed to finish the film, and died a
few months later. After Gertrude Lawrence, she was the second
leading lady Yul had lost to leukemia in just a few years. He
did not talk to me about it much: the death of this vivacious
English comedienne was just too painful to discuss.

In those days the established American culture in France
frequented a restaurant called Moustache's: Hemingway, James
Jones, Irwin Shaw, James Baldwin, Sidney Chaplin, Norman
Krasna, Richard Condon, Art Buchwald, Oscar Levant, Stanley Donen and Harry Kurnitz, among them. This was a sophisticated crowd, more ironic in style than cynical—but pretty
cynical, too. They had plenty of other places to meet around
the city as well—including Harry's Bar, the Rosebud and New
Jimmy's—but Moustache's was their usual hangout by the end

of the Fifties. The atmosphere at Moustache's was noisy, smoky, crowded, rude, and sexy—everything a kid like me would enjoy. At thirteen, I was usually the only child present. While my father allowed me only a sip or two of wine with each meal, there was usually at least one lush present who enjoyed the novelty of pouring a drink for a kid.

Visiting my father in Paris that spring meant a twenty-hour prop flight from Los Angeles that stopped in Chicago, Gander and Shannon. It took days to recover, but I had a terrific time, mostly because Dad was relaxed, comfortable, and just plain happy for the first time in years. With Doris by his side, as she had been most of the time, and a string of friends and associates, he was beginning to feel better about the choices he had made. Most of all, he was glad to be back in Paris.

That visit to Paris had a profound effect on me. Returning to California, I solemnly vowed that someday I would return to live in Europe, and that I would become a great writer, the way Dad said I would be. I'd marry, have a number of mistresses, and be one of those glamorous people who drank too much most nights, and had serious, adult-type hangovers. So, my future was decided. I finished the school year in California, already disdainful of all things American, especially anything my mother valued.

At forty, Virginia was struggling to rebound as an actress, even as she was struggling to control her drinking. She'd landed a temporary role in a soap opera, *The Edge of Night*, which really took guts in front of her friends in the theater. Needless to say, I was unimpressed. By now, I had set my heart on living in Europe with my father, even if that meant leaving my mother alone in America. But legally she had custody of me, and she would not let me move to Switzerland; she just could not bear it. She insisted to Yul that I try a prep school in New Hope, Pennsylvania.

"There's no choice, laddie. The best I could do is make her agree that if you weren't happy, you could come to school in Geneva next year."

"But I hate America, Dad. It's so . . . passé."

"Whoever said you got to enjoy everything in life? Haven't I told you before? Life is like a long, wild party, occasionally interrupted by an examination. You're a teenager now, Rock. You have responsibilities, including responsibilities to your mother. I am not lying: she needs you."

"Well, if it's just a year. What kind of school is it?"

"It's, uh, excellent, academically. You even get to study Latin. It's called Solebury. It's a Quaker school."

In her way, my poor mother was doing her tipsy best to provide me with a stable background. In his way, my father was teaching me how to adapt to other backgrounds. No matter how hard they competed to please me, Dad always won. Being with him was simply more fun than being with my mother.

Yul had rented another beautiful house near Geneva on Lac Léman—so that we could water-ski. As with other rich folk, our hobbies had become our priorities. He rented a speedboat, and sent a plane ticket to Chris Forster in New York, so that we'd have someone to talk to about things like baseball and politics. Chris not only drove the boat: he provided our life with some token of continuity and normality. Just a few years earlier we had all skied together in Connecticut. Since then our lives had been turned completely upside-down, but at least there was still Chris Forster. In the rarefied social climate Yul had now settled in, Chris was a breath of fresh air, like a Bronx raspberry.

Switzerland remains a preserve for a particular style of élitism that seems like an endangered species—century after century. The aristocracy of the world gather in anti-egalitarian splendor from Geneva to Montreux to visit their doctors, school their children, and bank their money. From Klosters to Gstaad, the thin mountain air is heavy with what Samuel Johnson called "the insolence of wealth," companion to the arrogance of power. But that summer we did not mingle much socially. Mostly we water-skied—a few hours in the early morning, then again at the end of the day, still singing "Up a Lazy River."

It was the first time I'd seen Dad living with a woman other than my mother, and it took some getting used to. Doris was, of course, as friendly as she could be toward me, and I had to admit that, even from my youthful point of view, everything about her style was classy. But I was a complicated, pseudo-intellectual spoiled brat and she was a nascent society figure, halfway between Yul's age and mine. While cultured, Doris never pretended to be a great reader of books. She accomplished many things with her daily life, mostly of a social nature. There was always a luncheon at Longchamps with Ali Khan and Bettina, or a wedding party in Klosters for Deborah Kerr and Peter Viertel, or a charity ball in London. Her delight and tireless occupation was games of chance, especially backgammon and gin rummy. She could and did play for hours of an afternoon and an evening; and so did Yul. Soon enough, so did I. Doris was certainly not obsessive about gambling. She simply enjoyed playing games, hour after hour, day after day, year after year.

In the autumn of 1959, Yul made *Surprise Package*, with Stanley Donen directing a screenplay adapted from a novel by Art Buchwald. Shot largely on a Greek island, it was meant to be an amicable time filler until *The Magnificent Seven* was ready to roll. Yul played a convicted mobster who is repatriated by the Justice Department to his native island in Greece. There he awaits a bundle of cash from his old mob. Instead, they keep his money and send him his dizzy, blonde girlfriend, played by Mitzi Gaynor. The story had a subplot which featured Noël Coward as the king of some lost little principality; Noël even sang an incongruous title song. The film was so inconsequential, it was filmed in black and white; that alone did not bode well.

But Yul did not seem to mind. He was preparing funds for his divorce from Virginia, and paying for that ballroom of hers on East 65th Street. Through her lawyers, she refused his offer of a percentage of his next film, *The Magnificent Seven*, replying that she had no confidence in that film or in his career. She would accept only a lump sum. The bargaining continued.

* * *

I was now attending a school in Pennsylvania which I disliked so intensely that I skipped the eighth grade, just to express my contempt. At twelve, I was studying James Joyce in earnest, especially all the naughty bits. My girlfriend Robin was a sixteen-year-old blonde bombshell who introduced me to the Beatnik culture and a couple of other things, too. Weekends were spent with Robin at coffeehouses in Greenwich Village, or Down in the Depths at the Dwayne Hotel listening to Mort Sahl talk politics, or Dave van Ronk sing "Cocaine," or to the Beat poets read their own works: Corso, Ferlinghetti, and even Ginsberg himself reading "howl." Pretty heady stuff for the Eisenhower years. But my strategy worked: by running away from my mother's apartment, disappearing in the Village, and returning drunk and disheveled after twenty-four hours, I demonstrated that I needed Yul's paternal guidance, and won my passage to Europe. Virginia agreed that the next year I could go to live with my father, and attend the International School in Geneva.

On a visit of Yul's to New York we stayed up late talking in his usual suite at the Waldorf Towers. I'd been smoking cigarettes for several months. Since it was obvious that I wanted to become a heavy smoker like my parents, it seemed ridiculous to wait till I was grown up. Yul wasn't upset about my smoking, so long as I was never seen smoking in public, which would reflect upon him. When we were alone together he didn't mind at all.

"Rock, how do you feel about Doris?"

"I love Doris, Dad. I think she's swell. And the two of you are happy together."

"How would you feel if I married her?"

"I think that would be terrific, Dad."

"Well, with your blessing, we'll get married in Cuernavaca, while we're filming Mag Seven." *It didn't seem to me that he needed my blessing. Why was he asking? The responsibility made me uncomfortable.*

"Dad, who's going to play the other cowboys in Mag Seven?"

"Why do you ask?"

"Well, I heard you say you were still looking, and there's this guy on TV who's really cool. He carries a sawed-off shot-

gun, and—I don't know, he's kind of like a teenager. His name is Steve McQueen. He'd be really good. He's already starred in one movie: The Blob.''

''*Any other recommendations?*''

''*Well, how about Sal?*''

''*He's shooting* Exodus *in Israel with Paul Newman. And he looks too young.*''

''*How about Alex North to do the music?*''

''*We already signed up Elmer Bernstein. Remember how much you liked his score for* Ten Commandments?''

''*My taste was a lot less mature when I was eight, Yul.*''

''*And now that you're thirteen . . . you're old enough to call me Yul?*''

I nodded, just a wee bit unsure.

''*In that case, I suppose, you are no longer a boy. You have become a young man.*''

Sudden and unexpected as it was, I beamed with pride.

In preparation for all the gun work in *The Magnificent Seven*, Yul began studying quickdraw with the world champion, Rodd Redwing. Redwing, a Native American, had trained Steve McQueen how to use handguns, along with many other Hollywood actors. But no one took it more seriously than Steve, who practiced hours each day and, at his peak, could fire two rounds into a one square foot target in just eleven hundredths of a second; Redwing's championship time in 1960 was, I think, seven hundredths. At the age of thirty-nine, Yul's speed was twenty-five hundredths.

Yul and Steve were friendly with one another, as were all the others on the set. James Coburn was a relative newcomer to the big screen. Charles Bronson advanced from heavy to leading man with his role. Since Yul had personally selected these men for the film, much as his character recruits them in the story, Yul's position of leadership was secure, and so the whole shoot was blissful, compared to most. Yul had rented a luxurious house in nearby Cuernavaca, notable for its mosaics by Diego Rivera, which was quite a distance from the hotel where the rest of the cast stayed; there was always that distance. In March 1960 Doris and Yul were married, and a fiesta was held on the movie set; the festivities merely added to the family atmosphere there on location. There was a feeling all-around that this was going to be a big hit, and so the congeniality was palpable, and a casual, good-natured mood prevailed—an atmosphere not always present on Yul's movie sets.

When *The Magnificent Seven* opened, it was not an instant, universal hit with the critics, mainly because of its pacing. The *New York Times* review in November 1960 called it:

A pallid, pretentious and overlong reflection of the Japanese original . . . Mr. Brynner plays a mysterious man among men, ambling about Texas in black Western togs suavely accepting a money deal from some Mexican farmers . . . Just why [he] decides to "chase some flies from a little Mexican village" we never really know. Not for money, he implies repeatedly. For that matter, why is such a blandly intelligent man simply bumming around?

Notwithstanding the added remark that "Mr. Brynner just is simply not a cowboy," the box office grew, gradually and steadily, and principally by word of mouth. Within a year or two the film was widely considered to be among the all-time great Westerns. It was also among the most successful, with one of the best-known musical themes ever: United Artists later sold Elmer Bernstein's theme to Marlboro cigarettes for television commercials, complained Yul, for a mere $5,000. It was one of the first "buddy" Westerns. Yul, who named his character after his buddy Detective Chris Forster, worked hard to cut his own dialogue to the bare bone: The Man of Few Words was already an established Western tradition. Yul took that tradition to the limit wherever he could, starting with the first scene of the movie, between Yul as Chris and Steve McQueen as Vin.

> VIN
> Where did you ride in from?
> CHRIS
> [With his thumb he points backward over his shoulder.]
> VIN
> Where are you headed?
> CHRIS

[He aims his forefinger straight ahead.]
End of conversation.

Much later, the seven mercenaries, working for peanuts, are about to confront the band of two hundred Mexican bandidos.

CHRIS
How are you feeling?

VIN
Kinda like the fellow who jumped off a twenty story
building: on the way down, people on every floor heard
him say, "So far, so good. So far, so good."

"Your father's got exactly the right idea, Rock," McQueen said to me one afternoon on location outside Cuernavaca. Then he paused. "Perfectionism . . . Your dad's perfectionism is legendary. Just learn to do one thing better than anyone else, doesn't matter if it's ping-pong or drawing a six-shooter real fast. Work to be best. Oh you'll lose plenty of friends that way. Like Yul says, 'So, I won't win the Nice Guy of the Year award.' Anyway, I heard you'd seen me on TV, and put in a plug with your dad. I just wanted to thank you. You've got quite some father, Rock." As he paused again it occurred to me, my dad was a hero to my own cowboy hero. "He's gonna be a tough ol' man for you to live up to, all right." I didn't need Steve McQueen to tell me that. "'Specially if he ever gets mean with you. He's real competitive."

"Nah! Not with his son! Anyway, I could never compete with him. And he'd never feel competitive toward me, why would he? I'm his closest friend."

"I'm glad to hear you're good friends; he sure talks about you a lot. It's just that, sometimes that has a way of changing, down the road a piece. You're still a kid." He paused a good long while. I was dying for a cigarette. "It has a way of changing, between a father and a son. Especially with perfectionists. Anyway, you're either a spoiled brat or you're not. It's not gonna be easy, either way."

Plenty of other folk had tried to warn me that I was, well, hellbound: it was not news, and it was not helpful. I left before the next pause.

* * *

For the summer of 1960, Yul's fortieth year, he rented another large house on Lac Léman, which the Genevois naturally call the Lake of Geneva. Now that he and Doris were Monsieur and Madame, a new protocol began to arise, and it came quite subtly. Meals became more formal. Even breakfast, our private ritual, now began to conform to a code of manners and etiquette that remained as mysterious to me as the first time I ever saw algebra. I had never before seen my father acknowledge that there was any authority higher than common sense and virtuous conduct. Now, suddenly, fine etiquette seemed proof of a houseguest's integrity, and certain kinds of wealth were accepted as evidence of character—especially *old* money. This change in my father's values was more than I could grasp or assimilate, much less copy all at once. It was the unspoken assumptions about our values and priorities that were suddenly different, and changing weekly. Four years earlier, Dad had been a Stevenson Democrat—a defender of social justice, civil rights, and good ol' American equality. Now there was a staff of eight just to care for the newlyweds, including a driver for the Rolls and a maid for the three apartments in Lausanne.

Of course, I did not consider Doris responsible for the change in Yul, who was ten years her senior. Even to suggest that would have been to imply that Dad was not choosing his own lifestyle, when it was obvious he was under no coercion whatsoever. Yul's happiness was a top priority for Doris, and she brought to his life a taste for the best of everything she was acquainted with. Eventually, however, that meant having one room of the house just for arranging flowers. Quite apart from differences of language and culture in his new married life, there was undeniably a distinction in *class* between Yul's old lifestyle in suburban Brentwood and his new lifestyle in the midst of old money. Just ten years earlier we had been living over the dry-cleaner's.

Yet what else, exactly, could Yul have done? Joined the Swiss middle class? Become the first socialist movie star? His global politics were gypsy truisms and gut reactions, not studied positions. Most of his political beliefs were just extensions of the concept of free enterprise, hardly different from those of his uncle Felix, who had pulled Lenin off that podium in Petrograd in 1917. Most of Yul's views resembled those of others who had fled Bolshevism and Stalinism.

The clearest expression I ever read of Yul's anti-socialism was written by another political reactionary: "I am the first man who would not do penance for my virtues or let them be used as the tools of my destruction. I am the first man who would not suffer martyrdom at the hands of those who would wish me to perish for the privilege of keeping them alive. I am the first man who told them that I did not need them . . . they would have to exist without me, as I would exist without them . . ." That's a passage from Ayn Rand. Soon I too began refining views that were politically *correct*, especially with regard to those pesky social issues.

With some of his earnings from *Solomon and Sheba*, Yul helped finance the final film of his friend Jean Cocteau, now seventy-one years old. It was called *The Testament of Orpheus*, a very personal and uncommercial autobiographical fantasy, in which a number of the important figures from his life appeared. These included Picasso, as a mourner at Jean's byre, and Yul, as a diplomatic footman, who ushers Cocteau in to see the goddess who awaits him. This is a covert reference to the way their friendship began, when Yul had often made trips to the docks to procure his opium for Cocteau. A few years earlier, while painting frescoes in the Chapelle de St. Pierre at Villefranche-sur-Mer, Jean had immortalized Yul as a wingèd angel, hovering above the altar, just to the left.

That fall I began tenth grade at the International School of Geneva, and Yul was delighted to have his son that much closer. I quickly became quite popular at this school, where the sophisticated adolescents were as standoffish as I was: all except my best friend, Harry. Harry Dalton was a self-effacing English boy who enjoyed being my sidekick: he was not much taller than I was, and almost as clumsy. He had a big smile, huge feet and a heart that could hold the Hindenburg. *When I introduced my best friend to Yul, I thought that huge heart of Harry's was going to burst with excitement.*

I was pleased to live with Yul, and glad to be away from my difficult mother, though I missed her at the same time. I did not miss the drunk that she had become, only the angel she once had been. I missed my first boarding school, I missed American food, and most of all I missed Liza, as I often confessed to Yul on the telephone. It had been two years since we had seen each other, although once I had seen her dancing with Gene Kelly—on television.

At the autumn half-term, a week after Kennedy's election, Yul told me to catch a plane to Paris. There to greet me at the airport, as a complete surprise, was Liza. She was now living with her mother in London, and this very weekend Judy Garland was performing in Paris. Yul had been in touch with her and cooked up this plan, with Doris's help, just to cheer me up. I don't think Judy realized that Yul had arranged adjoining rooms at the Hôtel Meurice for Liza and me. Notwithstanding our maturity, our innocence survived the weekend intact. On Saturday night, we went to Judy's concert at the Palais de Chaillot. Liza joined her mother on stage to sing "For Me and My Gal," and then returned to the seat beside me in the front row. It was the happiest I'd ever been—even better than being drunk. If there were stretches of lonely confusion that were part of being Yul Brynner's son, there were also moments of exquisite joy, thanks to his love and care.

8

European Aristocrat

"In café society, the major inhabitants of the world
of celebrity—the institutional élite, the metropol-
itan socialite, and the professional entertainer—
mingle, publicly cashing in one another's claims
for prestige."

—C. Wright Mills, *The Power Elite*

Rejoice, rejoice! A new age has begun! Ring out the old, ring
in the new, ring-a-ding-ding. Now *Some Like It Hot,* but cool
is hot and square is out. "Suàve" is the thing to be, like
Brubeck's "Take Five"; and the name of the place is "I Like
It Like That."

John Kennedy was only a few years older than Yul and,
while the two were hardly fast friends, they had met on several
occasions when Kennedy was a Congressman, and to some
extent, they moved in much the same social circles. Yul and
the President shared the same physician: Dr. Max Jacobson,
whom Marlene Dietrich had introduced to Yul. Max's famous
vitamin injections, to which he secretly added amphetamines,
became something of a political issue when it was learned that
Max was spiking the President with his "cocktail syringes" at
about the time of the Cuban missile crisis. Jacobson had treated
Yul with his cocktail syringes during the years my father was
onstage, and he continued to write Yul any prescription he
wanted.

Kennedy's inauguration transformed the nature of authority
in America, as well as its perception, and validated all that
was modern and scientific. Not much had changed since Eisenhower had been elected in 1952, but now the paradigm was

shifting, and the rules were different. John Foster Dulles was supplanted by James Bond. Rock 'n' roll had become respectable since Elvis had served in the Army. Thanks to the Pill, good girls didn't have to be so good. Playboy clubs were inaugurated as fast as bunnies. Color television reached a national majority. Passenger jet service had begun: our friend Harry Kurnitz was on the first commercial flight of the Boeing 707. Inevitably these changes seemed to come *from*, not just with, the young new President. But if there was a single piece of evidence that things had changed overnight in America, it was the fact that now the President of the United States was a friend of Frank Sinatra's. Sinatra, more than any other cultural figure, set the style for the Kennedy years.

Yul and Frank had met in the early 1950s, while *The King and I* was on Broadway, but it wasn't until the early Sixties that they became fast friends, about the time that Frank made the movie *Ocean's Eleven* with a bunch of his pals: Sammy Davis, Jr., Peter Lawford, Dean Martin, Joey Bishop. Together they were called the Rat Pack, and for about fifteen minutes or so they didn't mind that name. By the time they made *Robin and the Seven Hoods,* the Rat Pack were the longest established floating crap game in the world, bonded together by their commitment to "get the booze, get the broads, and get the hell out of here."

The single-minded devotion to the pursuit of *fun* amounted to a game of hedonistic chicken: who could survive the bad hangovers, the oversexed women, and the near-wins on the point spread? Not to mention all the bad jokes. ("Hey Dean, I hear you're not drinking anymore." "Well, I'm not drinking any less.") There were some defined limits on what was acceptable behavior. No drugs whatsoever were tolerated in this crowd: no uppers or downers or powders or even "tea" were tolerated around Frank no how, no way. Those things were all in the same bag with heroin: musicians had seen what "horse" did to people. But you had to be able to hold your liquor. For a young drinker just learning the ropes, this was pretty confusing. As far as I could tell, there were different standards of inebriation for different times of the day—falling down drunk, for example, might be all right at 4.00 A.M. but not at 4.00 P.M. The comedian Joe E. Lewis, one of Frank's main barroom mentors, put it this way. "You can always tell you've had too much to drink," he said, "when you are unable to lie on the floor without holding on to something."

This was a world of earnest drinking, from the first Bloody Mary of the morning to "One More for the Road." With nonskid elbow patches so you could lean on the bar without slipping, to a collection of jokes, stories and yarns that could fill a millennium, these guys were having a party: the most contagious, widespread, nonstop binge in history. It was The Party That Would Not Die, fuelled by Jack Daniel's, fed by Mike Romanoff, and committed to all those old slogans that celebrated inebriation: "If you don't swing, don't ring," "Get down in the gutter with us sinners," and, of course, "I'd rather have a bottle in front of me than a frontal lobotomy . . ."

What Yul admired most about Frank was his talent, and the hard work and high standards that had gone into it. He had worked on his sound since the days when his fans were bobby-soxers—when Yul had arrived in America. Without his underlying respect for Frank, he probably would not have joined this free-wheeling fraternity—Yul was never much of a joiner. But, in Yul's eyes, Frank's power entitled him to swagger and even misbehave, just the way another saloon singer, in another time and place, had swaggered: Ivan Dimitrievich.

Yul also admired Frank's acting on those special occasions when Frank really took the job seriously, as in *From Here to Eternity,* or *The Man with a Golden Arm,* or *The Manchurian Candidate,* which was directed by Yul's assistant from television, Johnny Frankenheimer. On some of his other films, it almost seemed as if Frank's intention was to detach himself completely from the film-making process, as if he were trying to make a movie without ever noticing. On one film location Frank had a putting green *grown* on the soundstage before shooting began.

There is a moral chasm between the best and the worst in each of us: you have your chasm, I have mine. Frank has his. I always figured that somewhere along the line his heart was *so* big and got broken *so* bad that he had to have a second one installed, just to keep all his warm blood separate from the cold. I always thought of his caring, thoughtful personality as Frank, and his cold, tough posture as Sinatra. Inevitably, as with Yul, how you felt about Frank depended mainly on how he felt about you: if he did not like you personally, the chances were slim that you would like him much either.

Frank did like me, and I idolized him. Much about him reminded me of my father, but much was different. Frank was a great professional, but he did not profess or even aspire to be an expert in all fields. I was especially struck by the contrast in the way each of them looked at art. After being captivated by a particular painting, Yul usually sought advice from experts, took months considering the painting in relation to the artist's other works, and monitored the value obtained by other paintings at auction. He would choose to leave a wall bare rather than hang a painting he didn't love.

Not Frank. I was a guest of his just before a large Christmas party—so large he didn't have enough bedrooms in the "compound" of houses at his Palm Springs home for all the houseguests he'd invited. He called his lawyer and said, "Hey, Mickey, I need a couple of extra bedrooms. Would you have someone deliver a guest house with a couple of bedrooms? Something in beige? I need it by the weekend."

Sure enough, on Friday morning the new guest house was there, and while plumbers and electricians hooked it all up, Frank turned to me and said, "The walls look pretty bare. Let's drive into Palm Springs and get some art."

Now, of course, if Frank wanted serious art, he would have acquired serious art: all he needed right then was something to cover the bare walls, as a matter of consideration for his guests. So we drove to town and strolled into a cramped, tiny gallery, where the owner was chatting intently with a lady.

"Hey, buddy," Frank interrupted.

The owner didn't recognize him at first. "I'll be with you as soon as I'm available," he answered.

"How much do you want for all the art on the premises?" said Frank.

Now the gallery owner recognized him. "Sorry, lady, I'm closed," he said.

The owner walked us through the gallery and storeroom, and Frank pointed out which canvases he wanted: landscapes, a few portraits of teary urchins, à la Keane, and the like.

"What's that gold frame facing the wall?"

"Oh no, Mr. Sinatra, that's a mirror."

"I'll take it. How much for the lot?"

"That comes to twenty-two thousand."

"I'll give ya twenty. Come hang the stuff tomorrow and I'll have a check ready for you."

"Yes sir, Mr. Sinatra. Are you sure you don't need a little more art? I could make a fast run to LA and get some more. There's lots of art there, ya know."

"Nope, that's all the art I need. See you tomorrow."

The next day the gallery owner turned up with a truckload of art, and Frank walked him through the new guest house, pointing out where he wanted each painting hung.

"Do you have hooks, Mr. Sinatra?"

Frank stared at the gallery owner, eyes wide with disbelief. "You didn't bring the hooks?"

"I'll get the hooks! I'll get the hooks!"

"Hey, Dad, can I ask you something?" We were furling the mainsail on the new five-point-five meter formula sailboat with the special maintenance ropes, which Yul had designed and spliced himself, using ski rope. Now forty-one, smoking three or more packs of Gauloises every day, he found sailing more pleasurable than skiing.

"What?"

"It's about women."

"Ah-ha. Older women?" He offered me a Gauloise, and a light.

"Well, four years older. She's eighteen."

"Ah-ha."

"I can take care of business pretty good on the sofa. But, well, exactly how do I get her into the bedroom?"

"And do you know what to do when you get there?"

"Yeah, I think so. About as much as anyone else, I guess. But until I figure out how to get her there . . ."

Yul set down the ropework and went into his oriental squat beside Lac Léman; I did likewise.

"It's very simple, lad, once you develop the power . . ."

"Power?"

"The power of concentration, and the power of imagination."

"Um, what does concentration have to do with it? I mean, I'm concentrating all right."

Dad laughed. *"No, that's not it. You've heard my advice many times on how to deal with women."*

" 'Give them everything they want.' "

"Right. So you begin your evening together with that premise well understood. In the noblest tradition, the gentleman conveys to the lady the growing sense that he will do all that he can for her."

"And that's what gets her to the bedroom?"

"Not at all, nothing to do with it. The keys to seduction are imagination and concentration. As the evening begins, give all your concentration to the lady: fill your mind's eye with her presence, till there is nothing left in your thoughts, nothing at all, except for this woman you desire. As you gaze at her loveliness, freeze that moment in your imagination, capture it for all eternity. Now, once you have done that, imagine this: the two of you are in bed together, and you have just finished making love, passionately, for hours. Imagine you are both resting, smoking a cigarette, and recalling how beautiful it all was."

"What do you mean, Dad? All I do is imagine what it would be like if we had just made love?"

"That's it, Rock—that's the whole trick. First, capture that moment of her loveliness; we'll call that Point A. Second, use your concentration to imagine the wonderful afterglow you would be sharing together right after making love. Call that Point B."

"And then what?"

"That's all there is to it. If your concentration and imagination are powerful enough, everything will take care of itself. The evening will steer itself, effortlessly, from Point A to Point B."

I stared at him until I realized that was all he had to say on the matter.

"Really?"

Yul smiled and nodded. It sounded pretty unscientific,

*frankly. But I had complete faith in my dad, because I knew
that he would never intentionally steer me wrong, and so I put
all my trust in his method. Well, when you put all your faith
into any enterprise, it has the greatest chance to succeed.*

Despite the worldwide success of *The Magnificent Seven,* Yul's
career was half-stalled. Most of a movie actor's professional
life is spent *waiting*. He waits months to get the part, weeks
for The Deal to be consummated, days for the schedule to be
set, and hours for the scene to be lit. With a *bankable star,*
the problems are even more time consuming, since the financing
may depend upon whether the star approves of the screenplay—
a decision that could take the star *time*. The star knows this.
And so the producer is potentially at the mercy of any star with
a whim of iron. Like Yul.

The few scripts being offered to Yul were mostly dreadful
Italian epics, like *Hercules This* or *Jason That*. Yul had suc-
ceeded in being *so* different from the ordinary that he was never
given serious consideration for ordinary roles. He was still
considered "just your average, clean-cut Mongolian kid."
There were some films offered to him that he might have
made—but they were being filmed in Hollywood, where he
could not work as a foreign resident. So his strategy of moving
to Europe was starting to look like a serious misjudgment in
his career. Angry at his situation, Yul demanded that his at-
torneys find a loophole whereby he *could* make a few films in
Hollywood. As a result, Yul and Doris spent the summer of
1961 living in Bungalow Number Twelve of the Beverly Hills
Hotel, while Yul filmed *Escape From Zahrain* which, at Yul's
insistence, costarred Sal Mineo. He was a star by now because
of *Exodus;* his romance with Jill Haworth was still top-grade
gossip.

For the first time, Yul was prepared to acknowledge Hollywood society. Thanks to Doris's considerable social graces
and her unfeigned admiration for the talents of show business,
it became a summer of newborn camaraderie with many of
Yul's professional peers, including Sinatra. Closest of all, just
two bungalows away, were Elizabeth Taylor and her husband,
Eddie Fisher. Yul and Elizabeth had met briefly several times

during the 1950s, first while he was on Broadway, when she came to see *The King and I*. That was about the time of Elizabeth's first Oscar nomination, for *Raintree County*. Then she was nominated for *Cat on a Hot Tin Roof* in 1958, followed by *Suddenly Last Summer*. She won nothing. Finally, in early 1961, after the loss of Mike Todd and her marriage to Eddie, she almost died from pneumonia. *Then* the Academy finally honored her work. "Hell, *I* even voted for her," said Debbie Reynolds. It was Yul who presented the Oscar to Elizabeth.

The friendship that Elizabeth developed with Yul and Doris lasted across decades and continents. It was especially important the following year, when Elizabeth and Richard Burton were socially excommunicated for their passion. After that, the Burtons settled semi-permanently in Gstaad, a few hours from our home near Lausanne, and became part of our daily lives.

Of all the great raconteurs whom I had met in my short life, none was as hypnotic as Richard Burton: when silence fell over a room, Richard could not help but fill that void with anecdotes. But even if he was silent, a glance at the adoration in Elizabeth's eyes would be enough to make you love Richard yourself. Some force great as Nature bound these two lovers together.

Among the talented and wealthy people who bumped into each other at homes and resorts around the world, there was a growing sense that a new global community was emerging, known first as the Jet Set, then as the Beautiful People. Doris was an important founding member of this community, and she excelled in providing a bridge for aristocrats and would-be aristocrats to meet entertainment figures, and vice versa. Doris radiated her delight in her role, as if aware how blessed she was to be princess of every fairy tale she'd ever dreamed of. That summer ended with an extravagant birthday party for Doris at Romanoff's. It was also Yul's way of repaying the hospitality they had received, and an attempt to cement their standing in Hollywood—the very world from which he had exiled himself.

The notion of filming Gogol's classic *Taras Bulba* had occurred to Yul years before. Now he approached historian and novelist Howard Fast to write the screenplay. Fast, however, could not bring himself to overlook the historical reality that the victims of Taras Bulba's Cossack army were Polish Jews. Yul could overlook that fact, in order to tell this story of a father who destroys his greatest treasure: his own son.

Eventually Waldo Salt wrote the screenplay for producer Harold Hecht, with J. Lee Thompson directing. The relationship of father and son was usually central to Yul's films, and there was a reason for this paternal aspect to his image: he often played authoritarian characters. This sweeping epic that spans thirty years depicts the ultimate parable of authoritarianism, as a devoted father murders the beloved son who betrays him. Yul worked hard to create a rich, robust character for Taras, whom he described as a mythical figure. "In my mind he is fifteen feet tall, in order to make the things he does convincing. He has the facility to mesmerize his Cossacks into doing what he wants them to do. He has a great love for his son. Taras has a peasant streak in him, but even though he kills Andrei, his son, for betraying the Cossack cause, he learns something from Andrei. His world is changed, broadened, he places more value on people." At some considerable cost.

Yul wanted to track this character over the decades, to show how his idealistic nationalism exceeded his paternal instinct. He even proposed that the movie be filmed strictly in sequence: that way, when he was playing Taras as an old man, he could have the caps taken off his front teeth. There was never a film Yul cared about more, not even *The Brothers Karamazov*. It might have been the best performance he ever gave on the screen, but in the end that didn't matter. *Taras Bulba* turned out to be a terrible movie.

A lot of factors contributed to this bitter failure, including some stupid dialogue and the *worst* painted backdrops of medieval Poland you've ever seen. Yul's carefully crafted performance was edited without reference to the timing and emphasis that Yul and the director had planned in detail. Finally the film was butchered in the editing room, to make it short enough to show on a double bill.

The single irrecoverable blow to the film was the casting of Tony Curtis as Yul's son Andrei. Curtis had given a number of excellent performances in films such as *The Defiant Ones* and *The Sweet Smell of Success*. He had acquitted himself well in *Spartacus*. But in *Taras Bulba* his performance just didn't work. Part of the problem was that, at the beginning of the story, Curtis had to play a teenager; in trying to summon up a childlike quality, he created a character who was only childish. During the filming, Curtis fell in love with his costar, Christine Kaufmann, and ended years of marriage to Janet Leigh. Not only was Tony Curtis *in* the film—on the movie marquee, *he* was its star. For the first time in his career, Yul had accepted an extra hundred thousand or so, to take second billing. Even though Yul was playing the title role, *Taras Bulba* had become a Tony Curtis movie.

When Yul saw the final cut of *Taras Bulba*, something inside him broke. The end result was so far from his original dream as to be unrecognizable, and for several nights thereafter he hardly slept. His aesthetic trust had been violated, and no professional undertaking would ever be quite the same again.

"There's too much money, and there are too many idiots in-volved, Rock," he said late one night, sharing a beer. "I can't put my heart that far out on the line for an industry that no longer cares enough to be proud of the result. They're hacks, just earning a living. The cocksuckers ought to be parking cars—instead, they're calling the shots for the whole film busi-ness.

"Well, to hell with it. From here on in, I'm just there for the money, like everyone else. I can't go on being the only one who cares. I'll just pick up my check and go my way. A great performance in a lousy picture is not going to get seen by anybody. So? The real value of a film, or any work of art, is how many people it inspires, how large an audience it reaches, how big its box office is. Ninety-three percent of audiences surveyed have proven it." (He loved to invent percentages like that, to bolster his assertions. They sounded so scientific.) "That is what the power of stardom is all about. More people come to see a movie because of its star—so the movie has a greater impact. That is what makes it a greater movie."

"Does that mean The Sound of Music *is a much greater movie than 8½, Dad? Are you sure?"*

I guess he didn't hear me. "But as the star, I can't ensure the quality of a film. And, because of the editing process, I can't even ensure the quality of my own performance. From now on, that's all they're going to get from me. No script revisions, no directorial help. Fuck 'em—''

''—and the horse they rode in on. Right, Dad?''

''That's the spirit, son.''

My mother was costarring with Henry Fonda on Broadway in a mild comedy called *Critic's Choice,* directed by Otto Preminger. Her drinking was under control, more or less, during the run of the play. Mine was not, especially when I visited her, once or twice a year. She had an occasional boyfriend, but I know very little about her romantic life. She lived alone, in a two-bedroom flat—in case her son decided to come back to live in America. She struggled to survive with the grief of a mother who has lost her husband and her only child. What remained for her seemed nothing more than a leftover life to kill.

In the spring of 1962, Doris learned she was pregnant at last, but was told she would be wise to remain in bed for several months. Now Yul began househunting in earnest; until then he had only rented houses beside the lake. The property he found was not for sale, and he could not have afforded it if it had been; but he signed a very long lease. Named Chanivaz, it was a nineteenth-century landmark on the lake, a formal, imposing structure in stone, with three stories, including the servants' quarters, and several outbuildings. The decor chosen by Doris would be admired by many guests in time to come. The walls were hung with ''padded'' fabric, the coffee tables littered with *objets d'art* by Fabergé, and the front hall was dominated by the obligatory Vidal-Quadras portrait of Doris. Nothing was missing. Large as the house was, though, I myself did not have a room of my own there. I stayed in the guest room, when it was free. Or sometimes at a nearby motel.

Of course it was a huge place to run, with gardeners and groundskeepers, maids and upstairs maids, a chef who doubled as pastry chef, the chauffeur and his wife, Don the valet, and the secretary, Diana. Between supervising her huge staff, and all the *arranging* that she personally had to do—the lunches and dinners, travels and agendas; why, even the flowers needed arranging—it's a wonder Doris had any time left for backgammon.

Yul spent the summer of 1962 in Japan, filming a forgettable movie called *A Flight From Ashiya*. Throughout the Orient, Yul was considered the only oriental-born ever to become a movie star, and he was greeted throughout the Far East like a home-town boy who had made good. In fact, we were nearly killed on arrival at Tokyo airport by an uncontrolled crowd that almost pushed us through a plate-glass wall. Every time we ended up in a crowd scene like that, Yul's "higher sense of love" for humanity lost more of its ardor.

We spent much of our time in Kyoto, but on our way we stopped in Yokohama for a night, to visit an elderly man named Etoh Naoasuke. He had arranged a special dinner party for us at an aristocratic geisha house. Like Yul, this serious Japanese businessman was a grandson of Jules Bryner. Here was a child of the family that Jules had abandoned in Japan almost a century earlier, before he settled in Vladivostok with Natalia. Naoasuke-san was Yul's first cousin.

In Kyoto I lost my innocence to an Australian blonde who had misplaced her own some time earlier. She was thoughtful, and I was grateful—and clumsy, even for a half-drunk fifteen-year-old. Fortunately, it did not take much concentration or imagination to lead this sweet, young semi-professional from the sofa to the bedroom. Much later, I learned that Yul had arranged the whole thing.

We travelled together a little in the Far East, hoping to retrace the trip Yul had made with his father Boris through China in 1940, twenty-two years earlier. But that was politically out of the question: China was closed for the Cultural Revolution. We visited Hong Kong. Near Aberdeen we passed opium dens, and Yul told me about his own addiction to the drug, and how his friendship with Cocteau began. That trip represented a rare period of reflection about his past, and it helped to arouse further my growing curiosity about the discrepancies in the stories of his childhood.

In November, Doris gave birth to their daughter, Victoria,

in Lausanne. Greetings came from around the world. Yul was in Rome, still shooting interiors for *Flight from Ashiya,* but he arrived within a few hours of the birth. Among the first visitors to greet Victoria were Elizabeth Taylor and Richard Burton, who had just finished shooting *Cleopatra.*

With Victoria's birth, Yul began developing a stronger sense of his new family, and a desire to achieve greater financial security. But just as he began to enjoy new responsibilities, he began to feel confined by them. His own stardom, he had learned, might not necessarily last forever. Once that became clear, he began to experience waves of insecurity that sometimes kept him awake at night, wondering how he would meet his huge obligations if his star-power suddenly evaporated.

Since he was to begin shooting his next film in Mexico in January, and since Doris was taking the baby to visit her family in Chile, Yul decided we should spend Christmas in Acapulco. There we could ski some, relax, and join a circle of friends and acquaintances who were taking bungalows at the Las Brisas Hilton. Other friends, including Loel Guinness, the British industrialist, and his wife Gloria, owned homes on the hill below. This incongruous, impromptu Christmas gathering included acquaintances and complete strangers. Among those present were Chairman of the Board Frank Sinatra; Porfirio Rubirosa, the world's oldest playboy; the Maharini of Jaipur; the French industrialist Paul-Louis Weiller, and a softspoken man named Dr. Moody.

For Yul, Acapulco was a reinvigoration. Together we went back to the fronton where we had watched jai alai in the early 1950s, before he was recognized in the street. Now it was very different, for he was identified everywhere: identified, stared at, pestered, poked with pads and pencils, shouted at. That had not happened the last time we'd been there, six years before.

"It's as if they were throwing peanuts in your cage, Dad," I said.

"Throwing peanuts in my cage." Yul was powerfully moved by the image, and repeated the words aloud several times.

Two days before Christmas, I turned sixteen, and it became legal for me to drive one of the little pink and white striped jeeps that Las Brisas hired out. And so it was on Christmas Eve that I began my driving career. Lo, on the sixth night of

Christmas it came to pass that most of the party flew to Merle Oberon's home in Cuernavaca where, it was deemed, I would not have fun, and where the quiet Dr. Moody was not invited. I was enlisted to drive Dr. Moody around the clubs of Acapulco on New Year's Eve. Unfortunately, I was still very clumsy behind the wheel of the jeep, especially when I got drunk. I almost gave Dr. Moody whiplash, just from lurching through the gear shifts. To sober me up, Dr. Moody pushed me off an underwater bar stool at Villa Vera. I almost killed him a half-dozen times on the way home.

Good thing I didn't. Much later on I learned who Dr. Moody really was. He was a Cosa Nostra *capo* from Chicago. So, there I was, at sixteen—driving for the mob. I didn't even have a learner's permit.

Dr. Moody's real name, by the way, was Sam Giancana.

9

Swiss Collector

"Under the influence of materialistic concepts, the contemporary actor is constantly . . . suborned into the dangerous practice of . . . overestimating the significance of the physical."
—Michael Chekhov, *To the Actor*

While the quality and quantity of scripts offered to Yul diminished, his expenses continued to grow rapidly. Cash was still coming in from his percentage in numerous films, especially *The Magnificent Seven,* and so, like his friend Edward G. Robinson, Yul decided to invest in art, beginning with the profits from our stamp collection. "I'm selling all those little pictures to buy a few bigger pictures," he explained to me.

Like his wealthier friends, Yul had a special fondness for Impressionists, and indulged himself with leisurely afternoons in Paris visiting the galleries of *premier qualité.* Yul was always happy in Paris, with money or without: strangers in restaurants gawked less blatantly, autograph hounds were less pushy, and children didn't point and shout at his bald head. His anger with such displays had grown more and more acute with the years. Any joking reference to his shaved head threatened to transform his image from artistic superstar to a sort of sideshow freak. It was inevitably demeaning. In Paris, as in Switzerland, the populace usually behaved better, but whether that was because of their manners or their self-absorption remained unclear.

Yul's love affair with France and most things French knew no bounds. Considering his voracious appetites, and all the sensory delights of France, including cuisine, this was no surprise. But now Paris had become the hub of his social world.

One aspect of Gallic tradition that appealed directly to Yul was its enduring respect for class distinctions. The subtle and not so subtle stratifications of French society are always appealing to those who are welcome at its upper reaches. And, whether the political left or the right is in power, the *métro* in Paris still has a First Class and a Second Class, a fact that gave Yul great pleasure, even though he did not actually *ride* on it.

At its apogee, Yul's art collection included two Picassos, one from the turn of the century, a Modigliani portrait, a Utrillo windmill, a powerful nude by van Dongen, a Terechkovtich landscape, a sailboat by Boudin, and a Dufy fauve, *Le quatorze juillet*. But Yul's favorite was a tiny masterpiece by Paul Cézanne with a mildly erotic scene beside a lake entitled *Baigneur et baigneuse*. Painted in 1870–71, it was one of the few paintings of his career Cézanne had signed in red, his highest accolade.

Yul could not afford an Impressionist collection to fill all the walls of Chanivaz, so he began a second tier of *living* artists in the collection, starting with two oils by Bernard Buffet and, eventually, perhaps a dozen by Jean Jansem. He had a huge number of drawings, sketches and objects by Cocteau, of course, as well as most of Jean's books, handsomely bound and personally inscribed. Later, he added a wall-size tapestry designed by Alexander Calder, a modest Chagall, a series of tiny Rouaults, and a fascinating series of Yugoslav *naïfs* painted on glass.

Objets d'art abounded on the corner tables and coffee tables of the various sitting nooks in the *grand salon*, the *petit salon*, and the veranda. Yul's Fabergé collection—items designed and executed by Fabergé's studio in imperial Russia about the time Jules Bryner arrived there—was not large. It began modestly with a translucent stone letter opener with a hint of gold trim, followed by a delicate onyx picture frame lightly encircled in braided gold wire. There was a hiatus before the next Fabergé: a carved stone toad about the size of a fist, with a baby toad mounted on her back. It was actually a bell for summoning the servants.

Of course all the tables were laden with the other fine bricà-brac that one finds strewn about the homes of the wealthy: the Tiffany carriage clock, the Cartier table lighter, the Asprey cigarette case, and the uneven mounds of overweight art books. And there was more, still more. As a child I marveled how often, in many of the homes we visited, the clutter on the fine tabletops was identical, as if mandatory.

Alas, I lack the necessary knowledge and appreciation of gems and their settings to do justice to the tasteful, understated elegance of Doris's collection of personal jewelry. Much of it was designed by Jean Schlumberger and executed by Cartier. Some was designed just for her. The gentle wing-shaped gold settings for symmetrical white and canary diamond earrings were always flattering, especially with the necklace in a matching pattern. Possibly her most stunning piece was to be carried instead of worn: a small cylindrical make-up case, or minaudière, that could fit in the palm of the hand, in a wicker-weave with a diamond ornament on each end. That pattern was compatible, almost identical, with her wedding-ring, a series of gold bands, diagonally bounded by slim bands of diamonds, ever so fragile . . .

Yul was never interested in owning a large collection of fine cars: he wanted one or two superb vehicles, from the finest carriage house. He acquired the 1956 limousine, the longest low rider that Rolls-Royce made in those days—I've forgotten the exact name of the model. When we rode in it, I always felt as if I were travelling in a gyroscopically balanced opera box, complete with crystal bar, note table, Agry stationery and Cartier pencil. Yul actually complained occasionally to our chauffeur, Philippe, that the noisiest sound in the ear was the clock. The other car was a convertible Bentley Continental that Yul had had built for Doris in 1960 when they were married. The color was gold, but *tasteful* gold, more a metallic beige. Discreet. With the top down, and her long, perfect, auburn hair playing in the wind over a simple cashmere combination in pastel, Doris was as lovely as a vision. Ah yes, the cashmeres. Not long after they met, Yul discovered that Doris did have one idiosyncrasy: an insatiable passion for pastel cashmeres in matching pairs of pullover and cardigan. He began augmenting her collection, filling in the missing shades, adding whole new *ranges* of color to her expanding spectrum.

I am hopelessly ill-equipped to describe the *haute couture* gowns that made up Doris's renowned wardrobe. It would not be too much, perhaps, to say that she was among the very best dressed women in all the world, in the opinion of those very few who *really* mattered. The handmade Diors were, of course, divine, but the prize of her collection at that time, I would say, were her several Balenciagas. They were in solid colors, of course, like most of her Chanel suits, with just a touch of trim. Then there were the pearls, hand-picked from the sea. And Doris's luxuriant hair, often coiffed by Alexandre in a clever French bun, was topped off, for formal outings, by the same pillbox hat that Jacqueline Kennedy had made her trademark.

Yul's personal wardrobe was growing, with a definite emphasis on basic black; but that wasn't the only color he wore in those days, though he stayed within a conservative range of charcoal, navy and dark brown. Except for his formal suits and tails, tailored by Knize, most of his wardrobe was cut by Doug Hayward in London, Charvet in Paris or Sulka in New York; Sulka was also his shirtmaker, naturally. The double cashmere blazers, navy or black, were from tailors at Dunhill. He tended to shop in bulk for everything he bought, holding the salesman—usually the owner of the store—responsible for anything wrong with the product. Yul was always perfectly happy to pay the top price for everything he bought—since he knew that's what they were going to charge him, anyway. But the day that one of his purchases failed—a juicer, for example— the shop owner would receive an irate, personal phone call from Yul Brynner himself, telling him to get his ass over to the hotel—and be ready to squeeze oranges.

As the untaxed income from *The Magnificent Seven* washed in with each tide, Dad started designing a speedboat just for water-skiing, with more than enough power to stand the combined weight of our crisscross slaloming. In the spring of 1963 it arrived: a thirty-five-foot Riva with two Chrysler engines, 175 horsepower each. We christened her the *Seven*. With Don at the helm (just as he had been in Connecticut a decade earlier, when "Mr. B" stitched up his own head wound), Dad and I skied all over that lake, from Rolle to Lausanne, Montreux to Évian, Geneva to Nyon and back.

But Dad was becoming more interested in sailing, since this

lake was so perfect for boat races. Through his friend Sadruddin Khan, he became interested in the five-point-five meter class Olympic formula sailboat, which was raced extensively on the lake. Soon enough, we were the owners of a beautiful racing boat named *Alciona*, like Yul's company.

The *cave* at Chanivaz was modest in size, but presumptuous in quality, and it grew perhaps faster than any other of Yul's collections. Christmas was often celebrated with a Château Margaux 1934, quite rare by the Sixties. But for really special events, Yul always had one or two bottles of a 1928 Lafite Rothschild on hand.

One of the most attractive and endearing of Yul's attributes was his boundless love for animals. His passion for pets was an intense and important part of his life that related to his power of communication: the same power, I expect, that had enabled him to become a television director in New York before he could even speak much English. So it was that Yul communicated with dogs and horses, birds and monkeys, goats and deer, *much* better than he communicated with studio executives. And nary an obscenity.

Along with a series of Yorkshire terriers, to whom Doris was every bit as devoted as the Duchess of Windsor was to her Yorkies, Yul took a special delight in raising big dogs at Chanivaz. He chose a noble local breed, the *berger des Pyrénées*, an all-white cousin of the Saint Bernard. The dogs weighed eighty to one hundred twenty pounds each, and ate two pounds of beef apiece each day: at one point we had more than half a dozen. To see them scrapping and gambolling across the acres of trim lawn, you might have mistaken them for a crazed flock of carnivorous sheep.

Yul was a masterful horseman, as he demonstrated in numerous films: but he did not have that special passion of the truly horsy. Nonetheless, he and Doris had two Falabella *miniature* horses imported from Argentina—their backs were two feet from the ground. They were meant to tow an irresistible little carriage, which was specially built for them to pull.

We were in the estate car, driving to meet Don in Bellegarde, on the French side of the Swiss border. There we would transfer

*Yul's paintings to this small van, which Yul personally would
drive across the border into Switzerland. "If the customs official starts to look in the back of the truck," said Yul, "I'll
just take off my hat. Gypsies don't pay customs duties."*

"Dad, can I ask you something?"

"Shoot."

*"Sometimes . . . the stories you tell me about the family are
different from what Irena and her mother tell me."*

"Ah-ha."

*"I used to love spending time with your sister Vera. She
used to tell me about Russia and China and Paris. Aren't we
ever going to talk about her again?"*

*Yul's eyes welled up with tears. "I already have spoken to
her, Rock. She just had surgery, for a malignancy." Even
when my mother had been studying cytology, Yul could barely
bring himself to utter the word "cancer." "We'll visit her
together, Rock, next time we're in New York. I don't think this
is the right time, son, to try to explain it all to you. But someday,
if you like—when you're ready—I will answer every single
question."*

*"Well, Dad, I am ready, and we've got a three-hour drive
ahead of us so, do you mind if I just fire away?"*

"Well, Rock, I don't know that this is—"

*"Let's start with your grandfather, Jules Bryner, from
Möriken-Wildegg, a hundred miles from here."*

There was a long, long silence.

Then slowly, he began.

*"Jules was one of several children of a Dr. Johann Bryner
and his wife, Verena Linck, and he set out from the village of
Möriken-Wildegg. I've recently met with members of the Linck
family . . ."*

*There were just the two of us in the car, with no gaje to
tease. The inconsistencies did not survive the bright light of
my questions: I was determined to know who my grandparents
were. Gradually, as we drove, it all came together, all the
pieces of the puzzlement.*

Yul was the perfect sort to own so much property, because he
had an indispensable talent for maintenance. This was true even

before he became a rich man. As a kid, I thought all men's shoes were *conceived* with shoe trees in them, like Dad's Gucci shoes. Sometimes Yul stayed up late at night building custom racks for storing water-skis and tow ropes, or drying the spinnaker.

But as his goods and chattels reached some kind of critical mass, the time and energy required for their maintenance grew even faster. There were only so many boats, cars, paintings, ponies, dogs and servants a family of three could maintain. Gradually, signs of entropy began to appear everywhere: accessories rusted, paint chipped, oil leaked, threads gave, gadgets broke, pathways eroded, whiteflies infested and fungus spread. It seemed as if there was no end to Yul's maintenance problems, which were often the direct result of his own methods of overkill. For example, he used imported soundstage fog makers to blast the mosquitoes from a small pond, and then ended up with a garden that stank of dead frogs. Mainsails ripped. Engines died. So did pets.

Slowly, it began to close in on Yul. He was the sole qualified maintenance man for his little empire beside the lake. I watched as it slowly evolved, for it took a couple of years. I had seen it happen before. As it set in, I studied the staleness, thinking: this is important to understand, I must watch carefully, and learn from my father's example exactly how marriages end. Watching my father, it was obvious to me that all human relationships were disposable. When they went bad, as they all seemed to do, there was nothing to do except scrap them. It seemed clear enough to Yul. Love was a form of nourishment. And when food has gone bad in the refrigerator, you don't leave it there, hoping it will get better again. For him, a relationship gone bad was like a flower, torn petal from petal: it was impossible to reconstruct.

The same rituals that gave Yul stability as a vagabond seemed to clutter and choke him whenever he tried to settle down. More often now, business matters drew him to Paris, where he kept his business manager's office, at Place de la Madeleine. Usually he stayed at the Hôtel Meurice, or the more exclusive Lancaster, but that was getting as expensive as maintaining an extra residence. Now he had to keep finding films to make all year long, just to offset his overheads and still have a little left over, for pissing on.

His latest film, *The Kings of the Sun,* was released at the end of 1963, and it was pissed on by everyone. Many of Yul's best performances were in movies so bad you can hardly bear to sit through them. This film featured Yul as an American Indian chief captured by the Mayans, to be sacrificed to their gods. The Mayan king who conquers him was played by George Chakiris, the talented young dancer from *West Side Story,* whose physique and self-assurance suggested about as much threat to Yul Brynner as a plastic coffee spoon. A nice man, but casting him as Yul's adversary was the greatest insult Yul's career had endured. So far.

At sixteen I graduated from the International School of Geneva. Desperate to have me within her reach, my mother took a sheaf of letters I'd written, bristling with literary allusions, to Yale University. I was accepted there without even an application. It was obvious that, apart from my relationship with my mother, life was going to be a breeze. Virginia lurched unpredictably from being the most caring of mothers to the most vicious of scorned women, and when she drank, she often confused me with my father. Then, from the depths of her tipsy grief, she would hurl at me all the insults and epithets that she had reserved for him. So I came to resent her more and visit her less, even though Yale was just a short train ride from New York.

Yale was not for me. The place was crawling with jocks. I was looking for a more medieval academic environment— some place that wouldn't interfere with my drinking. So I applied to Trinity College, in Dublin, the following year, where my pal Harry Dalton was studying. Harry was still my best friend, even though I could be as abusive toward Harry as Yul was toward his valet, Don Lawson. I had watched that relationship carefully all through my childhood because, apart from being Yul's valet, Don was also his best friend.

Yul's eyes twinkled with anticipation, and so did mine. We cut swiftly through the crowded nightclub, past the balalaika players and violinists, to a back room. There, at last, I met Valia

*and Aliosha Dimitrievich, who embraced me as Rom, not gaje.
In minutes, Aliosha, now almost fifty and wasted away by
tuberculosis, became my mentor in songs, sayings and strat-
egies. Yul poured the vodka. He picked the glass up in his teeth
and threw his head back, downing the spiced liquid. Then he
took a bite out of the glass, breaking it off between his teeth.
He chewed thoughtfully for a moment, then spat it out, with
only a trace of blood. The remains he smashed against the
wall, just as I had seen him do in* The Journey. *Aliosha laughed,
recalling how they'd done this as teenagers. He too drank, and
broke the glass between his teeth.*

Then it was my turn.

*"Don't try it, laddie," said Dad, and so I didn't. Not until
the fourth vodka. Then I got a half-inch gash inside my lower
lip, and bent the braces on my teeth. No one noticed, though,
because another old friend of Yul's had arrived, a Tzigane
named Kyrili, whom they called The Millionaire. Time had not
been kind to The Millionaire. Unlike the Dimitrieviches he was
disheveled, stained and a little smelly, albeit friendly as hell.*

*"Dad," I whispered, "he couldn't really be a millionaire,
could he?" Yul whispered my doubts to Aliosha, who became
indignant and nodded vehemently, with a burst of words and
gestures. "The reason they call him The Millionaire," Yul
explained, "is because he has spent more than a million." We
collapsed in laughter together.*

*Aliosha brought out the guitars. For hours, Yul and he played
and sang together—for each other, and for me. And that night,
through the smoky prism of time, I could just barely make out
my father as a young man. Suspended beyond time by the gypsy
rhythms, Yul was sharing with me the white heat of his own
adolescence and, for just that moment, my father and I were
teenagers together.*

In the autumn of 1964, the United States Internal Revenue
Service ruled that Yul Brynner, American citizen, had not
fulfilled the requirements for foreign residence, and could not
claim that he had been a permanent resident in Lausanne since
1958. Factors cited included his frequent visits to the United
States, for both business and pleasure, as well as Alciona's

corporate structure, whose primary function appeared to be the evasion of American taxes. Yul had the option of defending his case in court, but that could take several years to resolve, during which the IRS would freeze his assets and seize all the film royalties paid to him in the United States. If he lost the court case, the interest and penalties would bankrupt him for life. It was an immensely complicated case, but it all boiled down to a simple bottom line: this was a fight that Yul could not win. Although the numbers changed with Yul's anger, he told me that his earnings had been near five million dollars for the five year period, largely from *Solomon and Sheba* and *The Magnificent Seven*. The taxes owed were close to two million dollars, including penalties. Paying the amount owed would take every penny of his savings, he explained. It also completely vitiated his original purpose in giving up his home in America.

He felt betrayed. His lawyers and accountants had studied the rules of residence abroad, and he had stuck to every letter of the law; now the US government was acting like a bully, winning the fight before it even began merely because of its size and its power. Yul despised bullies, and he despised the IRS even more than he despised studio executives.

As the cost of their maintenance grew, it was almost as if his own possessions were turning against him. Even his cigars, sitting in dark, humid rooms at Dunhill's, had to be rotated every six months. Dunhill didn't do that for free. To add to Yul's aggravation, many of his possessions began requiring more maintenance at about the same time he began wearying of them. And once in a while he would chuckle, and remind me of the penniless gypsy millionaire, half-enviously.

Before the IRS ruling arrived, Yul had already made another film, entitled *Invitation to a Gunfighter*. Filmed in Hollywood and produced by Stanley Kramer, it was only Yul's second Western. The story is set in a Western town after the Civil War, dominated by a rich bully who owns the dry goods store, the bank, the pawnshop and the jail. This bully hires a passing gunfighter, played by Yul, to run the town's only Rebel (George Segal) out of town; then it becomes a story of how one bully replaces another.

Yul's character is named Jules Gaspard d'Estaing, and he

hails from Louisiana: just the look in his eyes scares off other hired guns. Attracted to the wife of a local shop owner, the dark-skinned gunman sits at her clavichord one afternoon, singing a gentle French lullaby, and explaining that his mother always wanted him to learn music, and literature, and culture. He explains: "My education was the most important thing to my mother, and she pestered my father to pay for me to go to the best schools. She kept pestering him, and pestering him . . . so he sold her."

As the story progresses, this bitter Creole gunman takes over the town, picking up every poker pot, stealing and smashing whatever he pleases. When Jules realizes he can't bully the shop owner's wife into loving him, he finally runs amok, walking down the main street tearing the whole place down: he levels one wooden building with his bare hands. Finally the tables are reversed, and the town bully is forced to ask the Rebel to kill the gunman. In a final three-way shoot-out, the Rebel wounds Jules, who dies in the village square, half hero and half brute.

The film was a total bomb. Apart from Yul's performance, which was hypnotic, it was a bore: the editor failed to make scenes deliver their punch, and the result was tendentious and heavy-handed. The town and its inhabitants seemed like abstract metaphors in an intellectual exercise. Pat Hingle as the judge and bully and Janice Rule as the shop owner's wife were both excellent, and yet they lacked a crucial element of identity. George Segal was more successful, but an implausible Southern accent made a lie of the performance. As usual, Yul planned the development of his own character carefully; even though he declared he was only there for the paycheck, he was still compulsive about creating and preparing a character. And, in this case, he had great respect for Stanley Kramer, or at least for Stanley Kramer's track record. So, as usual, he had weeks of coaching with George Shdanoff.

Why did my father make so many lousy movies? He had had remarkable training with Chekhov, years of working experience onstage and as a CBS director, and the star-power at his command to finance any reasonable project—with all that going for him, *why did Yul make so many lousy movies?* If there was any single reason outweighing all others, it had to be his growing preoccupation with the business negotiations that precede the film-making, known as The Deal.

I was five years old when I first heard adults around a dinner table discussing The Deal. I thought they were talking about some elusive, mythical beast: a fierce carnivore that required exotic sustenance before any movie could be made. Soon though, I came to know that The Deal was not only an important part of film-making, it was the very *raison d'être* of the movie industry. Yul liked to joke with Billy Wilder that the Academy should create an Oscar for the Best Deal of the Year. There would never be a problem with disgruntled losers, he said, because no one would ever win: if The Deal was that good, making the movie would probably be impossible.

Yul tried his best, even after *Taras Bulba,* to make good films, but he had realized that the final product was beyond his control as soon as he had accepted The Deal. Unless, of course, he was also the director. Why, then, did he not direct? Often when I asked him that, Dad replied that "the system" was rigged to make sure no star ever got behind the camera, but year after year we watched other stars do just that. I couldn't imagine that he had lost confidence in his ability to direct. Sometimes he answered that he just hadn't found a project that inspired him enough to endure months of pre-production and post-production, as well as the shooting itself. Once in a while he said that financially he could not afford to direct, even though that was what he really loved. To myself I wondered how directors like Marty Ritt or Sidney Lumet could afford it, since they were not as rich as Yul.

A major part of The Deal, of course, is The Billing. This is no mere trifling matter of professional ego. The issue of which star gets top billing determines the destiny of stars, agencies, business managers—even local Porsche dealerships. In 1964, Yul committed himself to shoot a film in Hollywood, and he was glad for the work. Entitled *Morituri,* the film was not the sort of thing he'd usually get excited about: it was a Second World War story in black and white, with a screenplay that was suspiciously intellectual. And, Yul's financial needs prevailed over his need to be top dog: he accepted second billing to Marlon Brando, with a small stipend. Neither he nor Brando had had a major hit for quite a while—Brando's film career was reeling, as it were, from the effects of *Mutiny on the Bounty* and *One-Eyed Jacks*. Wisely, the question of top billing was fully resolved before the two gentlemen were brought together for a press conference to announce The Deal.

The studio was good ol' Twentieth Century-Fox, an institution that had never forgotten Yul, and vice versa. Dad never started a grudge he couldn't hold. But at the press conference he was generally on his best behavior: he didn't once call the studio "16th Century Fucks," and hardly ever called the studio executives "parasitical cocksuckers." Brando, too, was said to be at his affable best, but as the two men arrived at the hall through different doors, the whole room suddenly seemed much smaller. For anyone present that afternoon, the anticipation made it feel as if one were watching a huge catastrophe in slow motion—a collision of blimps. The two men made their entrances after the journalists and photographers had been made to wait a few minutes, which raised the anticipation even further. At last, the stars approached each other from opposite sides of the hall, scowling at fifty feet, not like wary boxers, but with the compelling thunder of sumo wrestlers.

Then they cracked up laughing. They hugged, they danced a little, and then admitted to the press that they had staged the whole thing—poking fun at themselves the best they could. There had been so much speculation about whether these two dragons would survive each other that they could not resist hamming it up. Of course, they had known each other for eighteen years: Virginia had costarred with Brando in his Broadway debut just before she became pregnant with me, in 1946. They had long since decided never to lock horns, even if they were not close friends. They had little in common with one another, except the pleasure they took in teasing the *gaje*.

The whole of *Morituri* was set on a German merchant ship carrying vital supplies of rubber to Germany; Yul played the ship's captain, Brando the American saboteur disguised as a German undercover intelligence agent. Also in the cast were Trevor Howard, Janet Margolin and Wally Cox, of all people, as the ship's doctor, who is also a morphine addict—that's right, Mr. Peepers the Junkie. The German director, Bernhard

Wicki, spoke little English, and anyway *he* thought he was making an art picture. Unfortunately, the film was not being made near the coast of, say, Bremen, where everyone spoke German. Instead, the ship was anchored off the coast of Catalina, California, twenty-six miles across the sea, so simple communication was tricky enough, let alone a serious exchange of ideas.

Brando chose to live mostly on the ship, or in a motel in Catalina, like everyone else working on the film. But Yul and Doris did not wish to spend the summer in a Catalina motel, or on a cargo ship off the coast: so Yul persuaded the studio, contractually, to build a landing pad on the back of the ship. Every day Yul awoke in town, drove to an empty lot at Robertson and Santa Monica, and took a helicopter out to the cargo ship. The trip took about twenty minutes; most days I went along. Needless to say, this routine was not economical.

Marlon Brando was not a happy man, not that summer anyway. I could not guess what was happening in his life to create such a melancholy mist around his shoulders. It was a gentle sadness, but powerful. Often he would sit in his cabin for hours between takes with a pillow in his hands, face buried in the pillow. Gradually, Brando's melancholia appeared to get the better of him during the filming, and his concentration seemed to drift further afield. One night toward the very end of the shoot he busted up his cabin. A little unhappy, that's all; blowin' off steam.

The ship and all its crew members were meant to be German; several talented German actors flew to California to play sailors. They all had thick German accents. So, Brando played his role, that of an American saboteur, with *similar* thick, throaty sounds. Yul, however, added hardly a trace of accent or altered intonation to his customary speech: scene after scene they appeared to be acting in different movies, and no one had the guts to raise an objection. The result was a mismatched mishmash, a phonetic hodgepodge.

By now, my mother's melancholia was worse than Brando's. She was rarely sober by late afternoon, and had developed such an uncontrollable cough that she could rarely watch a play, much less appear in one. Off and on she worked—she played *Sweet Bird of Youth* in summer stock, and kept attending acting classes. She had affairs, all of which she kept quite secret, especially from her long-gone son, who visited reluctantly and unhappily once or twice a year, until our arguments grew too fierce. Then, all over again, she endured the trauma of driving her only child to the airport and sending him off to his father the movie star, returning in solitary desolation to her two-bedroom apartment to get drunk and begin waiting for her boy's next visit. Her son, taking after his dad, did not seem to notice the enormity of her anguish. I could not afford to. I could have helped her some, I certainly could have helped her more: but as long as she was drinking, I could not have done enough to make her happy. I was seventeen, and just a little confused myself.

With a smile and a big hug, my father examined my face carefully: he was concerned. It was obvious that I was not well, as I prepared to leave for college in Ireland, and yet neither Yul nor anyone else had a clue that I was drinking myself sick. When I visited Yul's dressing-room on the Fox back lot on the way to the airport he handed me a big wad of cash as well as a check to cover my tuition and expenses for the next twelve months.

I flew to New York, where I made an unscheduled stop for a few days to visit my girlfriend, a literature major at Columbia University. Just like my dad, I took a suite at the Waldorf Towers and ordered a selection of wines and liquors for the wet bar in the suite. For convenience, I kept a hansom cab on call for transportation. I bought a splendid new wardrobe, and some exquisite boots from John Lobb. I even bought a meer-schaum pipe. I was going to be Yul Brynner, Jr., if it killed me.

By the time I got to Dublin I was almost broke, and three months later, just after my eighteenth birthday, I had a complete nervous collapse. Since I was the only one who knew how much I was drinking, my problem was not properly diagnosed: after all, I only drank about the same amount that my father did,

*and everyone could see that Yul Brynner didn't have a problem
with alcoholism.*

*Dad came to Dublin and took me back to a clinic in Lau-
sanne—to the same place where he had gone in 1937 when he
had collapsed, at about the same age, from a similar problem.
Was I subconsciously recreating my father's early collapse?
No one could say. When I needed him most that year, Yul was
there for me in a big way.*

*After a few days' observation in the clinic, I was sent home,
and Yul was told that I should take some time off. "You're
eighteen years old," said the old Swiss gentleman. "Go visit
Paris in the spring, and watch the men opening oysters beside
the Seine." I was given a yearlong prescription for a brand
new Swiss medication that would "take the edge off"—the
drug was called Valium. Of course, no one knew that I'd been
drinking myself into a stupor three or four nights a week for
a couple of years, even though my hands sometimes shook so
bad that I had to keep them in my pocket.*

As I left for a holiday in Paris, Yul gave me the telephone
numbers of several friends whose company I might enjoy,
including an older lady who had some books of Cocteau's to
give me, and a younger lady who was a surrealist painter and
novelist, a protégée of André Breton.

The older lady was named Andrée Peyraud, and even the
hall outside her flat was heavy with the smell of opium. It took
her maid several minutes to remove the steel bars across the
otherwise fashionable double doors. Madame is under the
weather today, won't you visit Madame in her chamber? It
appears Madame had been under the weather for some thirty
or forty years. I felt like a square American adolescent entering
a private opium den for the first time. That's exactly what I
was.

The first thing I noticed in the room was the pistol beside
her bed. Fine, just fine. There I was with an armed, drug-
crazed collector of rare books. *Why*, I wondered, did this lady
keep a gun so handy? I kept my eyes on the gun uncomfortably
as we talked about the art books that I was to convey to Yul.
Cocteau had died eighteen months earlier, and Yul had offered

to buy all Jean's first editions from this old lady, with whom he had smoked opium and sipped absinthe thirty years earlier. I flipped through the sketches she showed me nervously. When she asked whether I would like a whiskey I accepted eagerly. That's when she picked up the handgun and fired a shot into the air.

The maid appeared. "Oui, Madame?"

"Un whiskey pour Monsieur Brynner," Madame Peyraud shouted her command, and then explained to me that the maid was growing deaf. I could see why: a dinner party in that small apartment must have involved a lot of gunfire. I left the place with my ears still ringing, to visit the surrealist painter. It all felt very European and decadent.

She lived in an eighth floor flat near place Saint-Sulpice, where she painted erotically charged canvases. At thirty-six, twice my age and much shorter than I, she was a wild, impetuous spirit, with black hair to her waist, and a hands-on feel for conversation. We had a few drinks together and she showed me some of her visionary paintings. Among these startling, Daliesque tableaux, there was a crystal-clear portrait of Yul, in the sleek body and fur of a tiger, mounting her own naked figure. We went out to dinner, and later returned to her flat to listen to some new *musique concrète* by Stockhausen. During the chime solo, I heard the long, slow sound of the zipper descending the contours of her dress: that was music to *my* ears. Within minutes we were entangled together beneath her painting of a naked girl held captive in a wine carafe.

It was not until the next morning, as I was saying goodbye, that she mentioned she was my father's mistress.

10

Former American

"Ventilating anger is not sufficient redress for grievance; only ending the grievance is."
—Carol Tavris, *Anger*

In the summer of 1965, Yul travelled to Tel Aviv to work on
a huge production about the founding of Israel, in which he
was to play none other than Moshe Dayan, complete with eye
patch. The film was entitled *Cast a Giant Shadow*, the story
of Mickey Marcus, and while it recounted history, there was
so much concern about libel suits that they renamed all the
historical personages. So Yul's character was named Asher
Goren, and Luther Adler, who looked a lot like Ben-Gurion,
played a fictional Jacob Zion. A number of other actors had
cameo roles: John Wayne, Gary Merrill and Frank Sinatra, for
whom I tended bar that summer. But the star of the film was
Kirk Douglas, who played the role of Mickey Marcus, an
American hero of Israel's War of Independence.

Over the years, Yul and Kirk had crossed paths many times.
Each time they met, they started off their relationship anew,
somewhat tense and insecure with each other; within days they
were sharing a warm friendship. Over the years, their encoun-
ters grew warmer, but each time they had to become reac-
quainted, almost as strangers.

The same was true of Michael Douglas and me. We were
about seven when we were first introduced, sitting beside a
giant squid. That was on the set of *20,000 Leagues Under the
Sea*. And we had spent time water-skiing together at Puerto
Marqués, near Acapulco, in 1956. Now Kirk and Yul were
working together for the first time, if only in one or two fast,

busy scenes; during this stint together they seemed to seal their friendship at last. And once again, Kirk's sons were there, and the few times I saw them all together I envied the love and fraternity and even the rivalry they shared: I envied it more than I could ever express. Michael was an especially diligent, hard-working, second assistant director: next to him, I was definitely the fuck-up, playing piano in a bar called the Omar Khayyám in Jaffa and poker all day on the set. And drinking too much almost every night.

It wasn't until about the third week of shooting that Frank arrived, with Harry Kurnitz, for his two-day cameo. Frank was to play a daring pilot with no weapons, dropping seltzer bottles on Arab positions as his plane went down. But Frank was in no happy-go-lucky mood that summer: generally he was in mean and lonely spirits, though he always treated Yul like a pal, which is also how he treated me. Once or twice before, he had raised hell in Europe with his friend Jilly Rizzo: according to the press, someone in Frank's limo had pitched cherry bombs into carfuls of paparazzi pursuing him. But on this trip he was not in the mood for pyrotechnics or headlines. Besides, Frank had signed on for this gig partly to fulfill a long standing promise he had made to his mother, an ardent Catholic. And so it was that one day Frank, Harry Kurnitz, Yul and I set out from Tel Aviv to commemorate the opening of the Francis Albert Sinatra Orphanage, in the holy city of Nazareth.

On June 22, 1965, the *New York Times* ran a piece with the headline: BRYNNER GIVES UP HIS U.S. PASSPORT FOR FAMILY'S SAKE.

  Yul Brynner said today that he had returned his United States passport "to normalize his family life." The actor, who, like his wife and daughter, holds Swiss citizenship, said his "affection and loyalty to the United States can never change," and added that his move is "just a formality . . ." Travel, to film locations or privately, required different passports from different countries and visa applications at different places. "This situation complicated their lives enough

in normal times, but in times of international tension, the
family might be split up altogether.''

Because his grandfather Jules was Swiss, Yul was born with
the right to Swiss citizenship, by patrimonial privilege: now
having decided to remain in Europe, Yul was giving up his
naturalized American citizenship. Of course, the decision had
definite tax advantages, but if Yul had expected to live in
America again, he probably would have remained American.
The fact was that he regarded citizenship the way the Dimitrievich family did, as nothing more than a bureaucratic ne-
cessity. And so, for the first time since the early 1940s, Yul
was neither a resident nor a citizen of the United States. And,
in accordance with Swiss law, Yul's passport did not mention
his birthplace, Vladivostok: instead, it named his ''place of
origin,'' Möriken-Wildegg, because that was the village where
Jules had been born more than a century earlier. So at the heart
of the mystery of Yul Brynner's origin lay this incongruity:
this fierce, exotic wanderer in fact belonged to Switzerland,
the gentle land of milk chocolate and cuckoo clocks.

The reaction to Yul's renunciation of his American citizenship was generally muted, with a few exceptions: according to
one biographer, ''[talk-show host] Ed Sullivan had called Yul
a hypocritical ingrate. He said that Brynner 'takes our money
and then runs off to Switzerland. I say they can keep him.'
Yul had to be constrained from hiring demonstrators to picket
Sullivan's apartment house.'' This story of demonstrators is
something Yul himself added on at a later date. Typically, Yul
assumed that demonstrators were for hire, and took home paychecks, like everybody else.

*I poured us each a Johnnie Walker. We both stared out over
the Mediterranean across the coast of Tel Aviv.*

''Does this mean you'll never live in America again, Dad?''

*''I don't expect to, no. I feel very settled in Switzerland,
don't you?''*

*''Sure. I mean, no. Well, really, Dad, you and I are just
'birds of passage,' right?''*

''Right.''

"And Ed Sullivan can go stick a rusty fork with mustard on it up his ass."

"Right, Rock. My concern was to be sure that my whole family would be of the same nationality: Doris, Victoria . . ."

"Uh, Dad? What about me? I am American."

"Don't you want to be the same nationality as me? Switzerland is your fatherland, now. You weren't thinking of returning to America to live?"

"Well, no."

"Well, I've already asked my attorney in Paris to draw up documents so that you can receive your Swiss passport whenever you choose, and repeat the procedure I performed at the embassy in Bern. You visit there one afternoon and—chung!" He made a neat chopping motion with his hand.

"You mean, renounce my American citizenship?"

"Right. Exactly the same thing that Elizabeth did after she married Richard."

"But, Dad, maybe it's different for you. You're both stars. Neither of you was even born in America. I was."

"We're both superstars. And you are my son—whatever power I have, you share."

"But that's not true, Dad. Not with star-power."

"Of course not. That can only be earned."

I struggled to reconcile this fractured logic with my image of a flawless father. But I knew that if I kept pressing Yul on the issue, he would become, well, cranky. It was worth heaven and earth to keep Yul from getting cranky.

"By the way, Rock, how did you like . . . that lady I sent you to visit? The surrealist painter?"

Clunk. *"Oh yeah, hmmm. Hmmm. Nice lady."*

Yul chuckled. *"She told me all about it. She was never really my mistress, by the way. I just dropped over to see her once or twice, in a friendly sort of way. You know what I mean. And that's over now."*

Clearly he was not as upset as I'd dreaded. Later though, when I looked in the mirror, it was not Dmitri Karamazov I saw, but Smerdyakov . . .

*   *   *

That autumn, I repeated the "procedure" my father had performed with the State Department; since I was legally a minor, my renunciation should never have been accepted at all. Couched in bureaucratic language, I found it relatively painless to cease being American. I had lived in Europe since I was thirteen, and I was beginning to feel it was the place where I belonged—my fatherland. The war in Vietnam was a factor, too. After a year in Dublin I knew damn well, as did my friends, that I had a serious fondness for alcohol. Obviously, military service would interfere with my drinking: for that reason alone it was not even a serious option. From the drinker's perspective, which I had acquired from some real pros, even boot camp was unthinkable. So, I did exactly what Yul had done before me. I wrote to tell my mother about this "mere formality." It was a while before I heard back from her. She did not address the issue directly. Instead, she wrote that she had developed an allergy to alcohol; now, with a group of caring friends, she had decided to remove alcohol from her life. That evening, at my local pub, I drank a toast to her courage and resolution. I think.

Preparations continued for a sequel to *The Magnificent Seven,* called *Return of the Seven.* When Yul had first hired Steve McQueen for the original film, McQueen had promised, informally, to appear in any sequel. But when Yul sent him the script to *Return,* McQueen's agent went back on Steve's word. My cowboy hero had backed down on his word, and the little faith I had left in heroes was shattered. Yul had half-expected him to fink out, and went about finding a whole new cast for the sequel. In the meantime he accepted another cameo role in a film called *The Poppy Is Also a Flower,* which was made in cooperation with the United Nations' Drug Interdiction unit. Everyone from Mastroianni to Rita Hayworth did two or three days' work on this uneven, ungainly narco-epic, directed by Terence Young.

At forty-five, Yul had a string of mediocre films behind him to contemplate, while he lived in the museumlike atmosphere, the suffocating serenity of Switzerland—living like the *gaje.* He had already abandoned his first wife, his adopted homeland,

and Hollywood. Now Yul was deep into his variation on a mid-life crisis. The part of him that had sought security, living like landed gentry in Switzerland, had long been in control of his vagabond soul, but that started getting old quickly. Yul had actually taken up golf, sailing and backgammon—and it was all just a little too tame.

He began to feel gypsy again: the call of the tziganes beckoned loud. Both personally and professionally he began to feel claustrophobic, and that is how he began to behave. He became more demanding and more quarrelsome with everyone, severing his ties with many old friends and associates. Even Don Lawson, his loyal friend and valet for most of two decades, was fired abruptly, as was his longtime secretary Diana Baron. He grumbled often about the overhead that he had saddled himself with; and by now, of course, almost everything he owned needed to be fixed.

In the spring of 1966, Yul went to Alicante, Spain, to shoot *Return of the Seven*: the cast was a bunch of young, interesting men who, everyone assumed, would soon be as famous as Steve McQueen, Charles Bronson and James Coburn ever were: they were Bob Fuller, Claude Akins and Warren Oates. There was no obvious reason why this could not be as good a film as the original—indeed, so much had been learned on the first film that the second should have surpassed it. The fact that it was shot in Spain instead of Mexico need not have made much difference. There was the great Emilio Fernandez as the bandido this time. The director Burt Kennedy was no slouch. Why then did it have a *cut-rate* feel about it? It was as if an idea that had proven itself was now exploiting itself.

"Hey, Rock!" Dad shouted impatiently for the third time. Reluctantly, I picked up the pesetas I hadn't lost from the poker table, downed my cognac, and ran to join him for the ride back to the hotel. We didn't talk. Staring out the window, Yul whistled a tune: "Lazy River." We noticed at the same moment and smiled together.

"So, kid, what are you going to do when you graduate from college?"

"I don't know, Dad. I'd like to be a writer. But it's going

to be a long time before I can support myself.''

"That's OK, Rock. I've told you right along, I'm happy to help while you start out developing your craft. Where do you want to live?''

"Between London and Paris I suppose. I'd like to do some acting, as well.''

"For that, you'll need to study acting with someone. You'll also have to stop drinking. Some mornings your hands shake bad enough to spill coffee.''

"Yeah, well, you know what Dean Martin says, Dad. 'I'd rather have a bottle in front of me than a frontal lobotomy.' ''

Instead of laughing, Dad looked out at the bleached Spanish hills. Guess it didn't sound as funny, coming from his teenage son.

That summer Yul played an aristocratic German officer to Christopher Plummer's British counteragent in *Triple Cross*, directed by Terence Young, whom Yul liked personally so much that he even admired him. The script was only so-so, but The Deal was excellent. By and large, Yul was earning about a quarter of a million dollars per film through the 1960s.

Yul and Chris Plummer became and remained friends. At first they were drinking pals, too; but they were different kinds of drinkers. After a while, Christopher and I were more likely to be found drinking together. We seemed to have some sort of unspoken understanding about drinking that Yul did not share. There was something else Yul did not share: a secret of some kind or other. He disappeared for several hours each day or evening, without explanation or remark, and the few times that I inquired what he was up to, he brushed aside the question. Clearly, there was a new lady in his life. This much had changed between us: he no longer wanted to confide in me about his romantic life, but I could never say for certain why that was. However curious I might have been, Yul made it clear that I would not learn who the Mystery Lady was. Not until he was ready to let everyone know.

At the same time, Yul looked in upon my world, and spent more time with people he met through me. Since my best friend, Harry Dalton, needed a job, Yul hired him to be his personal aide, chauffeur and valet. Ironically, by behaving like my father with Harry, I had already unwittingly trained him to behave like Don Lawson: the kind of subordination that Yul demanded came naturally to Harry. And my best friend had another piece of luck: with his big feet, he wore the same size shoes as my father—which I did not. Pretty soon, Harry had a closet full of half-worn Gucci shoes, a couple of sizes too big for me. Now he fitted in perfectly with Yul's entourage.

By the mid-Sixties, Yul enjoyed being with my crowd of friends, who mostly revolved around the groovy new phenomenon of Swinging London. So, in a short time, Yul had fallen in with the Beatles and the Rolling Stones. That all began with Tara—the Honorable Tara Browne. Tara was heir to the Guinness family of Ireland and Britain, producers of the stout. By the age of twenty, he was generally credited with fostering the aristocratic foppery that was key to the King's Road fashions of the Sixties, from the Chelsea Antique Market to Granny Takes a Trip. Tara was always believed to have been the first to turn John Lennon and the other Beatles on to hashish and LSD. When Tara died in a car accident at twenty-one, they paid tribute to his short, swift life with the finale to *Sergeant Pepper's Lonely Hearts Club Band,* ''A Day in the Life.''

I had known Tara and his wife in Dublin, and stayed with them regularly in London. Tara helped create Sybilla's, London's trendy club of 1965, possibly the first place outside France to call itself a ''disco.'' By 1966 it was already a cheap parody of itself, with knock-off fashions supplied by a tasteless conspiracy called Carnaby Street. But in 1965, Sybilla's was really *groovy*. It was there that Yul and I got stoned on marijuana for the first time. Together we had a number of evenings of silliness and hilarity with Brian Jones and Ringo Starr, who was a sometime houseguest of the Burtons.

Like Paris in the 1930s, Swinging London was the center of everything that was happening in the Sixties, setting trends for the rest of the world with its music and fashion—specifically the mini-skirt and the ''Carnaby Street look'' (bell bottoms, dress shirt with long, pointy collar and flowered necktie). London was the creative heart of most of Europe and the world. Yul's new circle of friends was a rich, young, avant-garde crowd that commuted between Paris and London once or twice a month, migrating to the Mediterranean in summer and the mountains in winter on a highly predictable basis. Each April they gathered at Cannes, for their molting and laying, as it were. Yul had no admiration for the Cannes crowd, and his attitude toward the avant-garde was uncharitable, at best. He could make the name Antonioni sound like an obscenity. More and more he had come to believe that the only proof of a film's merit was its success at the box office. An avant-garde film might achieve greatness, like Cocteau's *Beauty and the Beast*, if *eventually* it sells enough tickets.

Since Yul believed that earnings were the simple proof of a movie's universal appeal, and that that appeal proved the artistic value of a film, he ended up his more quarrelsome evenings defending *The Sound of Music* as the greatest movie ever made. And he also became decidedly more open-minded toward shaggy-haired musicians, so long as they were extremely successful. At Sybilla's, fortunately, the music was much too loud for much conversation anyway; about the only exchanges he had with these rockers at this stage were a few baldhead-longhair jokes. There were a number of younger talents toward whom he reached out in a friendly way, especially among those who had defected to Europe from communist countries, including Rudolf Nureyev and Roman Polanski. For a time there was even talk of Yul *adopting* Rudolf Nureyev, then in his twenties, just to provide him with a passport.

Yul's wardrobe began changing with the times: he added a wider range of styles and colors to his usual muted blends of charcoal, navy and black. These superficial changes in Yul's style reflected tectonic shifts, deep in his soul. He was tired of the society that Doris had introduced to his life: he had lost interest in backgammon, gin rummy, and golf, but he had not yet discovered a style of life that he preferred. Now, that would depend largely upon the Mystery Lady; because Yul phoned me in Dublin in November 1967 to tell me that he and Doris had separated. I caught a plane that evening to join him in Madrid, and for a couple of weeks, as he burned away his pain, we caroused across Madrid with his friend and costar, Bob Mitchum.

Mitchum had, of course, been Hollywood's bad boy since serving time for grass in the early 1950s. In the atmosphere of the late Sixties that made him seem like a bold pioneer—but you had to get pretty stoned to agree with that loony point of view. Of course, if you hung out with Mitch in Spain in the late 1960s, you probably did get pretty stoned. During that film Mitchum was dating a pair of identical twins from London, whom he referred to as his "bookends." And so, night after night, we sat up listening to Mitchum retell a million different yarns you could never forget—and never remember.

Over the coming months, Yul slowly cauterized the grief of his second ended marriage. And much grief there was, too. No one could deny that he and Doris had given all they had to give to this marriage. They had lived together the better part of eight years and, with the birth of Victoria, they had both shared their fondest dream come true. But from now on Yul's time with Victoria would have to be measured, negotiated and scheduled. With the financial obligations he'd taken on, his net worth was about the same as when he had first arrived in America nearly thirty years before. Now, of course, he could sometimes earn big money fast, making lousy movies. In fact, he was still a bankable star, for a low-budget film: which meant that all he had to do was accept a second-rate script, and it could probably be financed.

So Yul was a vagabond again, of his own making. He was devastated and relieved, in equal measure. Christmas was going to be a little lonely, so he rented a house in Palm Springs adjoining Sinatra's, as far from Switzerland as we could get. But first we stopped in New York to see Yul's sister Vera, to whom he had not spoken since she told the truth to *Newsweek*. Vera was dying.

We visited her in the same apartment where she had cared for me as a child, just blocks from our old apartment on Central Park West; but that seemed like a million lifetimes ago, and just walking with Yul in the neighborhood where we had lived when he first became a star seemed like travelling through time. When we arrived at Vera's we sat beside her bedside. Her skin was dark now, for the cancer had already reached her liver. For stretches of time she was comfortable and lucid, thanks to large doses of morphine. Yul's primary concern for her was that she be assured all the freedom from pain that medicine could provide, and that Yul could afford to pay for. He held her hand for hours, stroking it gently, and they reminisced about their childhood, and their years of revelry in Paris. Everything that was gentlest and noblest in the man rose up, seeking without words his sister's forgiveness for his years of silence, and she did not withhold it, as she lay dying. There were no recriminations between them now, none whatsoever, only tenderness and care. When we left her apartment and the neighbors gawked, the transformation in Yul was sudden and palpable, as the part of him that hated being eyeballed like a freak overcame what was gentlest and noblest. As the neighbors stared in admiration at him, Yul scowled, and slammed his sister's door behind him as we left. It was Vera's overwhelming last desire to sit among trees; so she was moved to the country, where she could rest in the company of an oak, and an elm, and a birch. In December of 1967, Vera passed away.

A letter, forwarded several times, arrived from my mother: at the time I was in New York where she lived, but I hadn't visited her, even for my twenty-first birthday. I had shut her out of my heart exactly the way I had watched my father shut his sister out. And by now I was too committed to my own drinking to appreciate the news that she had completely turned her life around since she had become sober. Virginia was now teaching drama at Yale, my old stomping ground, along with Robert Brustein, Stella Adler, and all the new lights in the School of Drama. Still, her years of drunken bickering had hardened my heart.

How much did I owe, at that stage of my life, to being the son of Yul Brynner? For better or worse, nearly everything. Had I performed a moral inventory, I would have found that most of my stock came straight from Yul Brynner's shelves. From childhood on I had loyally lived out my father's wills and whims: from water-skiing to philosophy I toed the line. Even my youthful rebelliousness was modelled on his, from Parisian cabarets to Swiss clinics. Yul gave up my mother, I gave up my mother. He gave up my country, I gave up my country. After all, gypsies don't belong to women or to governments. Besides, how could I fail to be grateful for such an amazing father?

There was an irony at play in my life, however. Much as I might *think* like my father, and however much my features resembled his, I remained several inches shorter than he, and scrawny. And, since I smoked three packs of Gauloises a day just like Dad, and rarely emerged by daylight sober, my face had a greenish pallor, and my shoulders were disguised in the humplike curve often affected by intellectuals. This, along with my shaky hands and social twitches, cut quite a decadent figure. Add to that image a near-terminal case of self-consciousness and you have most of the picture. There was also the question of the shaved head. The phrase *Yul Brynner's son* naturally begged the question, "Is he bald like his father?" No matter how much my face looked like my father's, the resemblance ended there. Put another way, apart from being short, weak and pale, with long hair, I looked just like Yul Brynner. But while I had nothing like my father's physique, one asset I *had* undeniably inherited was The Voice. Whenever I used my lower register, I *sounded* so much like Yul it was uncanny. Especially if I growled obscenities.

That Christmas, alone together in Palm Springs, it felt a little like the two of us against the world. But Frank Sinatra sang "Happy Birthday" to me, and I was proud as hell; then we all got on Frank's Learjet and cruised to Vegas to see Sammy Davis at Caesar's, and when I got to my hotel room, a young English blonde appeared at the door, and said Sammy had told her she'd enjoy my company, since it was my birthday. The next morning, I felt a little older and a good deal more experienced.

"Dad, I've decided to become an actor." We were having a drink at the Nineteenth Hole of the Tamarisk Golf Club.

"I thought you were going to be a writer."

"Well, I will be. But I'm going to need to earn some money some other way first, aren't I?"

"You bet your ass," replied Yul. *"Double or nothing."*

"Well, acting seems like a pretty nice way to earn a buck," I said, glancing around the club.

"Do you know how to act, laddie?" Yul asked softly, very serious. No, I did not know how to act, although I had spent

*many hours listening to Yul talk about Michael Chekhov's spe-
cific techniques, and taken detailed notes from a series of lectures Chekhov had recorded, covering all his work.*

*"I tell you what, Rock. For your birthday, I will treat you
to a few weeks of intensive lessons with George Shdanoff. That
way you will learn the craft just as I did—except you won't
have to drive a truck playing one-night stands."*

*"But that's just what I'd love to do, Dad. Isn't that just—
paying dues? Liza's out there doing summer stock."*

*"Well, she's American, Rock, and you aren't, remember?
You'd need a work permit to do that. Besides, no one in this
profession will let you forget who I am. This is no longer a
world of travelling Shakespeare companies, it's the age of the
drive-in."*

*"Well, I'd love to study with Shdanoff, Dad. And I'd also
like to pay my dues."*

"Happy birthday, then, Rock."

A few months later, after graduating from Trinity College Dublin, I settled in London, and began auditioning. I couldn't get
anywhere. After months without a job, I decided to write a
play that I could perform, about some contemporary issue. And
I remembered a book of Yul's that had been around the house
since we had lived in Brentwood. It was a notebook by my
"godfather" Jean Cocteau, entitled *Opium—Journal of a
Cure*. Written during his detoxification in the 1930s, the notebook described in wondrous language the effects of opium on
the artistic mind, the addiction, and the anguish of withdrawal
from the addiction. Along the way it chronicled the Parisian
culture of the 1930s. I translated and adapted his text, creating
a character based on Cocteau himself. Yul helped me secure
the dramatic rights just as, in the 1930s, he had helped Cocteau
secure the opium.

So in the fall of 1969, Yul loaded a jet in Paris with a dozen
close friends to come to his son's professional debut at the
Dublin Theatre Festival production of *Opium*: very chic *claque*,
indeed. Telegrams arrived from Frank Sinatra, Kirk Douglas,
Richard Burton, Peter Sellers, and many other old pros in the
business: it was as auspicious a debut as any 22-year-old could

hope for. Here was The Clumsiest Child on Earth, now a young lush, giving a two-hour solo debut, in his first professional acting job, with an untested play. It was fair to wonder if I could even memorize the text, much less perform it. Yul, who always suffered from nerves in the theater, was terrified that I had bitten off more than I could chew. As the curtain rose Yul, who was often Cocteau's source of opium in the 1930s, now watched his son alone onstage, re-enacting Jean's struggle with opium addiction. Yul sat in the audience, as the cameras of the curious clicked in his face, his stage fright and intense love for his son near to bursting point. That night he was there to lend his power to his son; to make it easier for me to find his eyes in the audience, he wore a bright pink scarf around his neck.

Backstage, an hour before curtain, Yul gave me the rabbit's foot that De Mille had given to him on the first day's shooting of The Ten Commandments.

"Dad, what happens if I just seize up onstage, and can't even move?"

"All I can do is to tell you what Chekhov taught me; it always pulled me through stage fright. He said that the actor must offer his work the way a child offers a drawing to a friend. 'It's a little wrinkled, maybe and a little smudged,' says the child, 'but I did the best I could—and with love in my heart, I made it just for you.'"

For Yul there had never been a doubt that I had inherited his charisma, his star-power: he always believed it. As far as he was concerned, I'd proven it at age six when I told Leopold Stokowski to go tune his cuckoo. But was it true? Had I really received that legacy?

That night, for Yul, the answer seemed to be yes. He collected the *Opium* reviews with consummate pride: "With a voice and presence of hypnotic quality, he had his audience spellbound as he recorded the tortures of heart and soul-searing withdrawal over a nerve-tingling two hours . . ." "An unusual personal grace beside the quick humor, a keen intelligence,

and an enviable stage authority . . .'' "Had the audience twist-
ing on its seats . . .''

One reporter seated near him wrote: "Yul Brynner was obviously very pleased. As the performance came to an end he
turned to one of his party of companions and murmured 'fantastic,' then he applauded delightedly. Throughout, he and the
delegation from the international film world that he brought
with him had watched his son intently . . . His familiar figure,
with the bare head topping off a black doublebreasted suit, and
a broad cerise tie, had dominated the intervals in the production.
But his son had definitely dominated the stage."

*Dad sat quietly in my dressing-room, as I had so often sat in
his, watching me remove the face of his friend, Jean Cocteau.
Every so often he'd actually slap his knee and smile with pleasure: and my father's delight was also my own.*

*"When the curtain went up, I almost puked from stage
fright," Dad told me.*

*"Me too, Dad." We chuckled, and just then I felt, or perhaps
imagined, that he was relieved of a burden: that, at the age
of forty-nine, Yul felt that he had lived to pass along the knowledge Chekhov had passed to him. But I may have been wrong.
Perhaps he was just relieved to think that I'd be able to support
myself from now on.*

*Fewer and fewer film roles were being offered to him now,
and he was deeply concerned about his future as a movie actor.
It had been fifteen years since Yul's last performance onstage.
But that night, as he watched his son across the footlights, Yul
began to reconsider his options.*

11

Betrayed Father

"The father, compelled as he is to subdue the son, would despise him if he stayed. The son, anguished as he is over fighting the father, remains undivided in his need to go. He wants the world, and if he must tear flesh and maim spirit to get it, so be it. Life is born out of force and denial at the hands of one's intimates. This is knowledge to be taken in manfully. In fact, the taking in of this knowledge is precisely what has always been called manful."
—Vivian Gornick, *New York Times*

The end of the 1960s was what remained after everyone had done everything else. In Europe, as in America, 1968 was the signal that everything had changed. After Martin Luther King, Jr. and Bobby Kennedy, assassination seemed the norm. Some fleeting apogee of peaceful imagination was reached as mankind touched the moon, and then celebrated a few weeks later at Woodstock. Within months, however, Charles Manson became the image of our age; then Altamont. Finally, in May 1970, came Kent State: the hippest T-shirt that year featured a bull's eye and the word STUDENT. Oh, by the way, Richard Nixon had become President, the Beatles had broken up, and Elvis was playing Vegas. The bash that began with Kennedy's inauguration had turned into a bawdy wake, before becoming a bloodbath. As for me, my salad days were about to turn to coleslaw.

Yul's personal life began achieving new stability as he slowly came to admit that he was really in love with his Mystery Lady, whom he had been seeing secretly for some years. Jacqueline de Croisset, like Doris, was in her mid-thirties, and they knew each other socially. Though Jacqueline was popular and respected in that same *haute société*, she did not conform to the social dictates of the time, but went her own way, courting no one's favor. She admitted to a somewhat melancholy cast of spirit, preferring the rainy weather of Normandy, for example, to the holiday atmosphere along the Côte D'Azur. But to Yul's life she brought both light and order: at forty-eight, he was more interested in peaceful days at home than wild nights out on the town. Yul began making his home in Jacqueline's Paris apartment, rue Boissy d'Anglas, and they were already inseparable by the time she accompanied him to Dublin for my debut, though I didn't realize then that she was Yul's Mystery Lady. Jacqueline offered me her friendship, and whenever I was sober I did my best to return it.

Yul gave an interesting performance in 1969 as a corporate predator in a film of *The Madwoman of Chaillot*, opposite Katharine Hepburn. This was subtle, devious and amusing, compared with Yul's earlier comedy roles. He had no meaningful scenes to play with the leading lady, and in the few exchanges they had, he came across as mostly deferential and chivalrous, just as he was with her in real life. The few people who somehow earned Yul's respect never forgot his wonderful manners.

By now, he told me firmly, he regarded himself as a character-actor, as if this were a rite of passage that the family ought to note. He was quite realistic about aging, and recognized that he had passed the point where he could play romantic leading men on the screen: such scripts just weren't proposed to him any more. Instead, he was being offered roles as villains that, more and more often, were extremely violent. But by this time, for a variety of economic reasons, the film business was in such dire straits that even Henry Fonda was making spaghetti Westerns; and so was Yul. These were Westerns, shot in Italy and Spain, in which only the famous star spoke English; all the other characters were played by gnarly looking Italians who merely mouthed the English dialogue, which was later dubbed. This was not the aesthetic goal Yul had had in mind when he had studied with Michael Chekhov, but he regarded it as a personal insult when I pointed that out, noting that I myself was being supported by these same awful movies.

The truth was, though, that by the end of 1969 there were simply no roles being offered to Yul, and he had to admit that he was desperate. Not only did things look bleak in the short term, it was not even clear that one or two great roles could give his career the boost it needed. At just about that time, it looked as if I were on a roll: I had performed an extended run in London of *Opium,* and now there was talk of a production to follow on Broadway. I tried to think of a film that I might write for Yul—something that might do for his later career what *The King and I* had done earlier. But what kind of role could work magic for Yul's career in the age of *Easy Rider*?

The answer had to be: a gypsy. So I wrote the proposal for a screenplay called *Rom,* in which Yul would play an older gypsy, and I would play a young hippie who falls in with him along the way and stays to learn the gypsy rules of the road. Yul loved the project, and the fact that I was writing it for him. Ted Ashley, Yul's former agent, was now the chairman of Warner Bros. studios, and was happy to commission me to write it. I tried, and failed: I did not have the experience to shape the characters and plot into something viable.

At about this time, Yul and I received another offer to work together. Not long after the premiere of *Opium,* we were approached by the curious figure of Conrad Rooks, a dangerously brilliant and wealthy young man who owned the film rights to *Siddhartha,* Hermann Hesse's epic retelling of the life of Prince Buddha. The greatest problem was, how could any actor plausibly portray sixty years of Siddhartha's life? To this, Yul proposed an ingenious solution: at the start of the film, he would play Siddhartha's father and I would play Siddhartha. Then, halfway through the story, as Siddhartha considers drowning himself, we would exchange roles: Yul would play the mature Siddhartha, and I would play Siddhartha's son. Thus we would share in the creation of the character of Prince Buddha.

Well, it never came to pass. It was an exciting idea, something fresh and promising at just the right moment in Yul's career. But there was a problem: The Deal. There was no way that Yul would accept a big enough cut from his customary salary to play this character on a low budget, no matter whose damn soul it was. He had too many people to support, he explained, as if they were to blame. And anyway, though I was still performing *Opium* with great success, no one realized that most nights I passed out drunk. The world was spared the vision of Buddha with a hangover.

I did open on Broadway in October 1970, at the age of twenty-three, alone on stage in *Opium—Journal of a Cure*, just a few blocks from where Yul had opened in *Lute Song* at twenty-six, the year I was born. For Yul, it was the confirmation of his ardent belief that he had passed his magic along to his son, having endowed me with the same star-power that had launched his career. He let me know that he wanted more than anything to be there, but he was playing a bit part in a war film in Yugoslavia, locked into a shooting schedule, and could not be there to see his son follow his footsteps all the way to Times Square. The *New York Times* review of *Opium* read, in part, "This excursion into a man's central nervous system, viscera and soul, an excursion solemnly, and yet with pompously exhibitionistic theatricality, transforming its honest observations into a bleak ego trip, is fascinating . . . Brynner impressed one with this sensitively observed portrait of the artist as a young addict . . . An evening of distinctive interest." Some of the other critics were as flattering, and others were not: "another play like *Opium* and I'll start smoking eggplant or snorting halvah," one TV reviewer said. But even unanimous raves may not have made much difference, whereas being in an off-Broadway theater might have made all the difference: this really was not commercial entertainment. As the ancient impresario Sol Hurok whispered to me at Sardi's bar, "Young man, it is the first fact of the theater: when the audience does not want to see your show, you can't stop 'em."

Yul was shattered. He was convinced *Opium* should have been a financial as well as critical success; he blamed himself for not walking off his movie set and flying in to help—with publicity or money. And he blamed me, for not doing everything in the universe to keep the show going: friends in show business like Sinatra would have helped, insisted Yul. But the truth was, the way I was drinking, eight shows a week would have killed me. I drank with commitment, the way a number of our family friends used to drink back then: Richard Burton, Peter O'Toole, Dean Martin, Christopher Plummer, Jason Robards, Bob Mitchum. Yul did not understand that, because he was not that kind of drinker: he lacked that solemn bond, The Deal which we *real* drinkers had each made privately with the bottle, early in the game. I had the impression that drinking was making me part of a distinguished club of stumbling talents, when, really, it was just making me stumble.

Yul and Jacqueline were very much in love, that much was clear. Because of his passion for France in general and her fondness for Normandy in particular, they found a house there in which they could settle, marry, and hope for children. By 1971, Yul's divorce from Doris was complete, and once again the ordeal left him without much money. Yul found the means to borrow the considerable sum involved to buy a large old country *manoir,* Criquebeuf, built of carved stone and ancient beams, which resembled a castle. Maintenance of the property, including the caretakers who lived there all year round, unlike Yul, cost more than a hundred thousand dollars per year.

In the autumn of 1971, Jacqueline and Yul were married in Deauville, where, in 1935, Yul had stood under the cinema marquee and decided to become a movie star. They spent their wedding night in their new home. They had already been in love for several years, and the companionship between them was so strong that, if they sat quietly side by side, one hesitated even to speak to them, for fear of interrupting their silent dialogue. I never saw my father happier than he was just then. They shared a powerful hope of having children together. Doctors whom Yul consulted began prescribing a variety of hormonal treatments. Of course, once he had an initial prescription, Yul got duplicate prescriptions in other countries. He had always been a master of self-medication, ever since he'd consulted Kennedy's doctor in the early 1950s. These hormonal treatments made him feel strong. He liked to feel strong. So he continued treating himself with testosterone.

* * *

*Dad picked me up at the train station in Lisieux. We were not
getting along very well. He could not understand why I looked
more and more disheveled and distracted since closing on
Broadway. Rather than yakking about things, we often sat in
silence now, even in the car, where we'd often had our warmest
conversations. Now, the car had become the place where we
could exchange our sharpest words without looking into each
other's eyes.*

"What's that godawful smell?" he grunted.

"Patchouli. It's a fragrance—"

*"I know what patchouli is. Stop using it. Throw it away.
It's vile."*

"I'll keep it in my room, then."

*"Your room, as you call it, happens to be in my house.
You'll throw it away. I will not have an accident where it will
spill and ruin my home."*

"OK, Dad." I became very quiet.

"I see you dress like a hippie now."

"Yes, Dad, I guess I do."

*"Well, you look miserable, Rock. No wonder you can't get
any kind of work. Look at your fingernails, for Chrissakes!"*

"That's for the twelve-string, Dad. Look at Aliosha's nails."

*"Aliosha is a professional musician. You are a hippie with
an earring. You're even wearing it in the wrong earlobe."*

*Suddenly, Yul had become Archie Bunker, and I had become
the Meathead.*

Actually, I was Red Hat the Clown.

I had tuned in, turned on, and dropped out, and hit the global
trail of vagabonds and urchins. Like Wavy Gravy and General
Wastemoreland of the Hog Farm, I had transformed myself
into a creature of my own imagination, a street clown named
Red Hat, who lived by a set of half-cocked principles and half-
crocked notions. By changing my identity, I had broken free
from the enchanted kingdom of my father, just like Prince
Booder. And with that, the burdens of adult responsibility were
lifted off my curved shoulders. As Tom Robbins put it, it's

never too late to have a happy childhood. Red Hat was no mere appendage of Yul Brynner, which meant that nothing I did would reflect discredit upon him. That was a great relief. But it also meant that I could keep all the credit for my achievements, however meager—and that was a new experience. Until then, I had assumed that all my accomplishments could be explained away by the advantages I had been born with—advantages of both blood *and* money.

When I visited my mother that summer in the Montecito hills above Santa Barbara, I lugged with me all the exotic paraphernalia of a global vagabond: wooden earring, henna-red hair, loose white garb, a maroon borsalino, and a fondness for smoking London-style joints. For a while there, I only drank wine; sometimes I was just too stoned to get drunk.

Suffering from emphysema, Virginia moved to California in 1971. Sober for five years, she had taken control of her life for the first time since Yul had left her. She was already an important figure to hundreds of people a year as a counselor, sponsor and central voice in Alcoholics Anonymous. She was such an appealing maternal figure to those who entered the program, especially young folk, that she was always in demand as a sponsor. Besides her devotion to Jesus, she participated daily in the meditative rituals of Vedanta, under the spiritual direction of the scholar Swami Prabhavananda, whom Christopher Isherwood canonized in *My Guru and His Disciple*, and whom Aldous Huxley had visited in the 1940s.

Confronting her own anger at Yul, she had hired an independent accountant to explain to her in layman's terms why the IRS had seized half her alimony. In a three-page document, he detailed how the IRS had, in fact, collected from her more than one hundred thousand dollars which was actually owed by Yul, before he had renounced his American citizenship. She shared the accountant's report with me, and as I read how she had paid a hundred thousand dollars of Yul's taxes, without his even knowing it, I joined in her anger. This was not some accountant's fiction. My father had swindled my mother, doubtless inadvertently. But now, as soon as I showed him the report, he would have to do right by her—even if that meant selling one of his paintings.

* * *

*On New Year's Eve 1971, after Jacqueline had gone to bed,
Yul and I sat up in Normandy, drinking and talking. I had not
been sober a single day in many months; nobody knew that,
not even myself. I had just spent Christmas in Paris with Liza
at the Hôtel Meurice, where we had stayed a decade earlier,
as teenagers, when Judy and Yul had brought us together.*

*"Dad, there's something we have to talk about. It concerns
my mother." I had to concentrate to keep from slurring, as I
poured a fresh drink for Yul.*

*"Virginia? You visited her? How is she?" He often spoke
in clipped, precise phrases when he was on guard, barely
glancing at my eyes.*

*"She's never been better. She hasn't had a drink in six years,
and it's obvious now that's what she needed. She's really all
better."*

"No, she isn't."

"What, Dad?"

*"If Virginia had really recovered, she would have written
to apologize to me for all the pain she inflicted on me."*

*"Well, Dad, that was a long time ago—you haven't spoken
to each other for fifteen years now, and I know she's forgiven
you for—"*

"What is it you want to talk about?" He was already angry.

*"I sent you documents, an accountant's report. It proves
that through some error in the early Sixties, the IRS collected
a lot of money from Virginia, money that in fact you owed.
More than a quarter of her alimony."*

"Bullshit."

"Well, I've studied the whole thing pretty—"

*"BULLSHIT! DO YOU HEAR?" I had never seen him so
angry. But I was defending my mother, with all the sympathy
I had finally found for her bitter loneliness, and with all the
guilt that I had accumulated in almost fifteen years. And I was
drunk, all thud and blunder. Rising unsteadily, I lurched across
the room toward Yul, coughing and slurring.*

*"This time, Father, you will not shout me down, you will
not intimidate me, you will not bully me. You have wronged
my mother, and—"*

"Your mother is no candidate for sainthood. Virginia has not redeemed herself in my eyes. If she had really regained her senses, she would have already begged my forgiveness for all the ways she wronged me, and all the men she slept with. And you, Rock, have the gall to stand in my home, half crazy with alcohol, and confront me with bullshit accusations about things you know nothing about! Well, you can go to hell!"

He swept out of the room. I left early the next morning, so that he wouldn't have the option of throwing me out.

Yul and I barely spoke for the next few years. Every so often I'd wind up drunk in a jam somewhere, and call his office to shout for help, and my old friend Harry Dalton would reluctantly wire me a couple of hundred here or there: he was more my father's employee by now than he was my best friend. At holidays I spoke to Yul in chilly tones. And on his birthday in July 1972, I sent him a letter:

Dear Dad,

My heart is always with you on your birthday, and I think back happily to other years: water-skiing in Connecticut, in Malibu, in Paris, in Switzerland. This year, I have written a poem for you.

THIRD WIND

Third wind, spiral wind,
Raise high the whisper from the alley to the throne:
You aren't isolated just because you're born alone;
Each moment of your life is a phase to be outgrown;
Remember how to learn and forget how to own;
Today has no debts and tomorrow's on loan,
And yesterday longs to be free; can't you see—
    That we're all just the same, and no one has sinned
    And no one is chilled by the third wind.
    Third wind, vital breath,
    Fill your lungs and realize:
    That all doors must be entrances and windows must be
        eyes;

For they who know how men's minds work must surely
   be the wise;
Serenity receives with awe all qualities of skies;
The poses, roles and façades must at last reorganize
And the structure of your life reflect humility, so you'll
   see:
That the pedestrian has tired feet, but the poet's wings are
   pinned:
Transcend and become yourself as you catch the third
   wind.

Third wind, final wind,
Unrehearsed and played by ear, another song is sung:
Superior Man decides his own case when the jury's hung,
But sorts the berries carefully before they cross his
   tongue;
He imagines life's cycles in a handful of dung,
And cherishes each blemish of the people he's among
And instead of forcing matters lets things be, now you
   see:
   When the ghosts have all vanished and the thickness
     has thinned,
   The ashes are scattered on the third wind.

     Love,
       Your Prodigal Son

It was a long time before Yul spoke to me again.

PART THREE

"Happiness, which depends upon the tranquility and contentment of a wellborn spirit and upon the resolution and assurance of a well-ordered soul, ought never to be attributed to any man until he has been seen to play the last, and doubtless the hardest, act of his comedy . . . But in this last scene between death and ourselves there can be no more counterfeiting, we must speak plain, we must show whether the bottom of the pot is good and clean . . . That is why all the other actions of our life ought to be tried and tested by this last act."

—Montaigne

12

Homebound Odysseus

"... the son of Arnold Schonberg reprimand[ed] his
father for scolding him, arguing that he is, after
all, the son of a great composer and hence someone
rather better born than Schonberg himself."
—Aristides, in *The American Scholar*

In the autumn of 1974, Yul made the first of two flights to
Saigon. He and Jacqueline were so eager for children, that they
decided not to wait any longer, and to adopt. In order to ac-
celerate the process, Yul wanted to meet with the South Vietnamese agency working to secure the adoption for them. This
was the same agency through which Mia Farrow Previn, a
close friend of Yul and Jacqueline's, had first found a child.
Yul returned from Vietnam with a daughter, and they named
her Mia. A year later Yul went back to Vietnam in the last
months before America pulled out: a second little girl had been
on her way to them in an airlift of orphans that had crashed.
When she arrived back in France safely with Yul, they named
her Melody. With Mia and Melody, their home was suddenly
all laughter and merriment. In a houseful of children and pets,
Yul's authoritarianism seemed silly and pompous, and he was
often forced to laugh at himself. Like most of us, Yul was
always at his best when he was able to laugh at himself.

Happy as that time was for him personally, there were no
film roles anywhere on the horizon. The public usually forgets
that movie stars remain free-lancers for life, unless under a
contract negotiated with a studio: that's what studio executives,
Yul's least favorite species, were there for. Like a fisherman,
Yul waited for a role. But patience was never exactly a forte

of Yul's, and now that he was in his fifties, with small children, he started to become—afraid. With Jacqueline's help he had begun to rein in his own extravagance, for his wife had no tolerance at all for wastefulness. Still, with no income, and a minimum overhead of a hundred thousand dollars a year, he had good reason to worry.

Reluctantly, Yul began to ponder his greatest role: the King. After fifteen years of aristocratic luxury in Europe, he could barely imagine returning to the grind of eight shows a week, so far away from his new home in Normandy. But he could hardly play the King on film *again*. Struggling with his options, he came up with another idea: he decided to transform *The King and I* into a television series. That way, he would only have to be away from his home three or four months a year. A fellow named Larry Gelbart had approached Yul, and together they developed and produced the first six episodes of *Anna and the King*. It was a half-hour show on CBS costarring Samantha Eggar, the perfect actress for a young Mrs. Anna.

The show was a flop from the start, for a variety of reasons. The scripts were a far cry from Oscar Hammerstein's. Second, it aired on Sunday nights, and was specifically geared to compete with *The Wonderful World of Disney,* so from the start the whole show was for and about children. The network's idea was that American kids would relate to all the King's brats running barefoot through the royal palace. The end result was the Americanization of Bangkok, eliminating the very charm of the exotic setting. The final kiss of death to this Siamese sitcom was the laugh track. It was just awful: the King scowled, a bug-eyed kid gasped, and canned laughter erupted. Yet Yul remained determinedly oblivious to the travesty in progress. He was simply happy to play his role again. From the first broadcast there was no denying it was a flop, even among those who collected at Larry Gelbart's house to watch his two new series premiere together, back to back. Gelbart did not seem too concerned about the trivialization of *The King and I* and besides, the other series he had premiering that night was M*A*S*H.

* * *

Yul was now returning to work in America for the first time since 1964, and paying American taxes just like every *gaje*. The films he made were mostly inconsequential, and so were the roles. Only one of these later films was successful: *Westworld*. The premise of Michael Crichton's script, which he directed himself on a shoestring, was an adult Disneyworld of the future, in which lifelike robots fulfilled the guests' fantasies. Yul's role was that of a robot in the Wild West realm of the amusement park. In fact, Yul was playing a robot version of his own character from *The Magnificent Seven*—the gunslinger in black, a brutal killer, like most of the characters he played in the late Sixties and early Seventies. Of course, Yul's friend Richard Burton was not exactly playing Shakespeare by this time either: he was making big-bang war movies with Clint Eastwood. The reason Burton made these films was no profound aesthetic mystery: it was for much the same reason Willie Sutton robbed banks.

The last film Yul made was also the most violent. It was called *The Ultimate Warrior,* and in it he played a mercenary warrior for a tribe surviving in the postnuclear wreckage of Manhattan. The director, Robert Clouse, who had directed several Bruce Lee movies, had a taste for the grotesque. The film ended with a scene in which Yul's character has his hand snared by the villains: to save his life, he uses a machete to lop off his own arm. Then he pokes the bleeding stump of his arm into a fire. Yul was finally working in films that he did not want his own family to see. Why would any self-respecting artist appear in such trash? Yul's reply was simple: he was just earning his living. Yul's costar in the film, incidentally, was Max von Sydow.

His stardom on the screen, which had begun with the King— the beast inhabited by an angel—had reached a point where the beast had no soul at all. Now all of Yul's roles were either killers or machines.

But when he was at home in Normandy, Yul's life was far removed from robots and murderers. While he faced growing financial concerns, with no great prospects of work up ahead, he began to fulfill a lifelong desire. It was another new hobby: pigeon keeping. Yul began to plan and build the largest, fanciest, best-cared-for bird-house in the whole damn history of

the world. It was larger than a trailer home, sixteen feet by
forty. It had a concrete foundation with built-in heating, and
brilliant drawerlike arrangements, designed by Yul in his wood-
shop, for up to one hundred pairs of *very lucky* white pigeons.
He chose a remarkable breed, the Tumbler. This breed's specialty was to rocket straight up in the air to a thousand meters
then fall backward, rolling and plummeting just to the treetops,
before rocketing straight back up to the skies. Yul never failed
to give his pigeons the utmost care.

At about this time George Shdanoff invited Yul to play
Othello on stage in Los Angeles, and Yul accepted the invitation
almost like a hostile challenge. Shdanoff, who had been Michael Chekhov's colleague for almost three decades, and Yul's
acting coach for as many years, arranged to finance the production on the basis of Yul's participation. Then just weeks
before rehearsals were to begin, Yul received an offer to star
in a new musical, for much bigger money. Almost overnight
Yul dropped *Othello,* and refused to take any future phone calls
from George Shdanoff. Forever.

*Red Hat, the street clown, wandered the world for many
months. He cursed all things, though he was himself The Accursèd, anathema in his own sight, banished from the only
source of power he had ever known: that of his father. No
longer the joyous prophet of a new age, he was now just one
more shaggy, sullen, road-weary shadow. You might even have
seen him yourself, Reader, without even noticing, for he was
just one of those figures on a street corner somewhere, with a
guitar and a bottle—except that most of the time he didn't have
a guitar.*

*After he pawned or sold pretty much every possession that
his father had given to him over the years, he mooched off
friends, picking at their refrigerators and haunting their liquor
cabinets. When he used up one city, he moved on to the next,
or was moved along by his hosts, for he had become The Thing
That Would Not Leave. Then he would live out on the street
for a few days, fancying he was "independent," busking for
money with his guitar, and sleeping under a movie marquee.
When he could bear it no more, he screwed up his courage*

and phoned his father's office, and Harry would send him a little more money, which never lasted more than a day or two. After all, he was a generous tipper.

This protracted, global binge started getting old after a couple of years. At twenty-six, his hacking cough grew more persistent until it never stopped, and the cold sweats became permanent, his hands shook bad, and that faint feeling after the second bottle of tequila lasted all day, along with the hangover that never stopped, no matter how much he drank.

Why did he think he had been designated The Accursèd, and cast out of the kingdom of his birth? Was it for abandoning his mother to perpetual solitude when he was twelve? For uncovering the nakedness of his father's mistress? For attacking Yul in his own home? Or just for pissing away all the extraordinary advantages of his life? By now all his separate guilts had merged.

Suddenly, on a cold night in London, broke and stumbling, I could go no further. By a doorstep in Knightsbridge I fell down and wept. Settling my head upon the pavement I thought to myself: "Now I shall die and no one will care, they warned me I'd die in a doorway somewhere." And, because it rhymed, I took comfort in this little ditty, and began repeating it to myself louder and louder, until I was shouting and giggling and puking in the street. Wild-eyéd, I stomped along the pavement, laughing like a vicious half-wit, approaching strangers, poking my smelly face into theirs and shouting, "WHERE'S MY FUCKING LIMO? HOW CAN I VISIT LIZA WITHOUT MY LIMO?"

At last I became very frightened. As fear suffused me, the scales fell from my eyes: I was a drunk, and I needed help. I struggled half a block to the telephone on the corner, where I made The Call.

"Can I help you?" asked a voice, and I began sobbing incoherently, uncontrollably. "It sounds," the voice said gently, "like you're sick and tired of being sick and tired."

Yul had been approached to play Odysseus the wanderer, who sought his homeland for twenty years, while his son Telemachus searched for him—not on film, but on stage. That much was exciting: Yul was returning to the footlights after twenty years. But there was also bad news. First, this was not merely an adaptation of Homer's *Odyssey*: it was a *musical comedy* adaptation, complete with a dancing Cyclops. Second, the author was not Homer, but Erich Segal. Third, the Broadway title was not the *Odyssey*. It was *Home Sweet Homer*.

Mitch Leigh, who had composed *The Man of La Mancha*, wrote all the music, before becoming a producer as well. This large round man, once a student of Hindemith's, shared Yul's fascination with the Bottom Line, a natural interest for a producer. By carefully planning road companies of *La Mancha*, which crisscrossed America with sophisticated TV ad campaigns, Leigh had already squeezed a mint out of that sucker, Cervantes; now he was ready to wring every last nickel out of Homer.

The first performance of *Home Sweet Homer* (initially called *Odyssey*) was in Washington, DC in December of 1974. It was abysmal. Worse, it was humorless comedy that was often unintentionally funny. Among the production's greatest liabilities was the director's wife, Joan Deiner, who played Penelope. In a different vehicle her operatic tremolo might have been perfect: *Twilight of the Gods,* for example. But here it was woefully out of place; and of course, the director could not see that.

All the Indian chiefs who produced this show were tugging in different directions: the choreographer gave Odysseus' leather-skirted crew a cute little dance to do, then the solemn-minded Mr. Segal objected, so Mitch Leigh came up with another song to compensate, and the director's wife pouted until she was allowed to warble it her way. Even Cyclops could see what the problem was. By the end, the story was so incomprehensible it might as well have been a musical of *Twenty Thousand Leagues Under the Sea*: then at least it might have had a dancing squid.

And how was Yul onstage, after twenty years? While nothing could save the first act from its own stupidity, Yul single-handedly rescued the second act and almost the whole show, as he portrayed Odysseus disguised as an old beggar. He delved back to his Chekhov training and he created a character that stood apart from all the other tomfoolery on stage. This old beggar was funny, endearing and imaginative, with a voice and manner all his own. It owed nothing to any part Yul had ever played, but perfectly expressed his unqualified delight at returning to live theater.

Home Sweet Homer toured America throughout most of 1975, earning its way in almost every town, regardless of how bad the reviews were. This proved to Yul that his name was drawing the people there: it sure wasn't the title of the play. After more than a decade of great Deals and lousy movies, this was a big boost to his spirit. Compared to the home comforts he and Jacqueline were accustomed to, the accommodations were predictably inferior on tour, but despite the discomforts, or perhaps thanks to sacrificing those comforts, Yul felt creatively engaged for the first time since *Taras Bulba*. He was working shoulder to shoulder with enthusiastic theater folk for the first time in twenty-five years, and sharing in the creative spirit. When the musical finally opened on Broadway and closed the same night, it was not the crushing blow to Yul that it might have been. He was reinvigorated, mingling and mixing amicably among the cast members—especially, of course, among the dancing girls. Yul was always a pushover for dancing girls.

After six months without a drink, I made plans to return to my homeland America and put my life in order. It was going to be a long haul. The only real job I'd ever held was a manager of the Hard Rock Café in London in the early 1970s. At twenty-six, I had neither driver's license nor credit card, nor the legal right to work in America. Liza, who had just won an Oscar for Cabaret, *did all she could to help find me work, despite my obvious lack of skill, determination, intuition, common sense or gumption. My mother helped me with immigration matters, so that I could become American again, more American than the day I was born. But making my daily life manageable was still going to be a long haul.*

"Hey Dad, it's me."

"Hey." *His voice was soft, coiled to strike.*

"It's been a few months since we've spoken. I thought you'd like to know, I'm working hard to turn my life around."

"Yes?"

"Yes I am, Dad. First of all, I figured out something important that's changed my life—something I should have recognized all along, except that I couldn't admit to any kind of weakness."

Silence.

"Now that I've begun making sense of things, I wanted to call you, to apologize for any and all the pain that I have caused."

Silence.

"The first thing I needed, just to survive, was to recognize the fact that's been obvious to everyone else for quite some time: I am an alcoholic."

Silence.

Then he spoke. "Oh, bullshit. You're no alcoholic, Rock. Trust me. You're my son, for Chrissakes. And I can assure you, my son is no alcoholic."

"Don't do this to me, Dad," I whispered, "not now, not now."

"You don't have the willpower to control your drinking, so you throw your hands up and declare that you aren't responsible for the failure you've made of your life. If you just have a glass of wine now and then, you'll be OK."

"Of course I'm responsible."

"Well, why can't you support yourself decently, then?"

"Legally, I can't work in America yet. So I've taken out a student loan, and started classes as a computer programmer. Maybe I can get a steady job with a bank . . ."

"A steady job? HA!"

"Listen, Dad, I've got to get off the phone." His scorn could have killed me dead. "I've learned one thing in my first six months without a drink: I am a survivor."

"Of course you're a survivor, for Chrissakes. Look whose son you are!"

"Goodbye, Dad. I love you." I tried to whistle a few notes of "Lazy River," but I just couldn't pucker while I cried.

Even as I grew stronger, Yul despised my weakness, and separated himself from my shame. I had been his accomplice when he had eliminated my mother from our lives—I had watched and even helped. Twenty years later he had still never forgiven her; I had never known my father to forgive anyone. Why should I expect him to forgive his son? The one gypsy ethic Yul had never learned from the Dimitrievich family was devotion to the clan. Having already terminated two families, Yul had severed so many loyalties that by now he defined clan by personal fiat, as if he could wish people in or out of our family. When he ended his marriage to Doris, for example, Yul decreed she was no longer my stepmother: though she and I had been in the same family for almost a decade, our relationship was instantly null and void, in his eyes. Wherever marriages end, ragged boundaries of loyalty are left behind. In Yul's mind, defining who was a Brynner was entirely his prerogative. Now, Yul had cast his only son out of his heart, as he had done with his mother, his father, his sister and two wives; not to mention his dresser, his secretary, his acting coach, and almost everyone else who had ever meant anything to him. Man is born alone, lives alone, dies alone . . .

Yul began preparing for the revival of *The King and I* on Broadway fully a quarter of a century after its original opening. *Home Sweet Homer* had not yet closed when he started to negotiate The Deal; a pair of summer-stock producers had approached Yul, and now he was ready to listen. He had one basic attitude: since the only reason the public was going to buy tickets was to see Yul Brynner live on stage as the King, he intended to keep most of the profits, and leave as little as possible for the producers.

In his customary manner, Yul readied himself with extensive preparatory maintenance on his body before the tour of *The King and I* which preceded the Broadway opening. In New York for a couple of weeks he had daily appointments with specialists of every bodily region, as well as a dentist building new bridges, and an acupuncturist poking new holes. The acupuncture was supposed to reduce the severe back pain that sometimes damn near crippled him. It was diagnosed and treated in different ways at different times; whether it was sciatica or the result of his injuries as an acrobat, no one could be sure. Yul had an extremely mechanical conception of his own body, which came from his enormous faith in medicine as a perfect science. This was an extension of the exactitude he expected to find in all dimensions of daily life. Indeed, like the robot he had played in *Westworld,* he held to a sort of modular, mechanical view of his body. Now, at the age of fifty-six, that was more true than ever: he relied upon doctors simply to fix anything that was not aright.

As ever, Yul appeared almost to enjoy the challenge of pain: not as a masochist might, but rather as an adversary. Once I walked into Yul's hotel suite and heard the sound of his power drill: I thought he was doing some carpentry. Instead, I found him leaning forward in a chair, driving the electric drill through his big toenail, as wisps of blood flew off the spinning drill bit. He smiled when he saw the shock on my face, and calmly explained that he had dropped a camera case on his foot, so, to avoid losing his toenail, he was putting a hole in it, to relieve the pressure. What struck me most was Yul's detached expression as he pressed on the drill—as if it were someone else's big toe.

During his various medical examinations, the doctors found a precancerous growth on one vocal cord. This was scraped clean, leaving him more than a little hoarse for several days— and in considerable pain. But by the first rehearsal, Yul felt terrific, as he began to play the King again. The emotional impact of the original dialogue swept him away; by the time the rehearsal reached its crescendo, the walls shook with the power of his voice, and the other actors were dumbstruck to find themselves on stage beside a volcanic eruption. But the next day, Yul had no voice at all: just a deep, guttural growl, with what sounded like the gurgle of blood. The following day it was worse. He was unable to speak at all during the entire first week of rehearsals, and the second week was no better. His vocal cords were not healing at all.

The phone rang at my girlfriend's in LA on a Monday evening: Jacqueline was calling from Indianapolis on Yul's behalf. He could barely talk, and, because my voice was so much like his, the gurgling in his throat caused a sympathetic pain in my own. I had already told him I planned to visit him soon after he opened, when my job permitted. Now he sounded anxious for me to be there. He hadn't sounded that way for a long time.

I had settled in Southern California where I could spend time with my mother, who still lived alone. Having completed my computer training and finally resolved my immigration problems, I had just begun working for Bank of America, as a junior systems analyst in the Business Services computer department. Admittedly, I looked and behaved just a tad out of place in that corporate environment, and I learned that I have an extreme aversion to corporate gray—still, I was more proud of this accomplishment than anything I'd ever done in my life. I was twenty-nine years old, and this was my first steady job.

The next day I flew to Indianapolis, and the situation was very serious. Yul's voice had never recovered from the first rehearsal: he had mimed his way through three weeks of rehearsals, and now opening night was three nights away. He had just returned from Houston, where he had undergone a bizarre medical procedure, and now he was convinced that he would be all right on opening night: but only if he remained completely silent till then.

A word about the unusual treatment Yul had received.

Years before, Yul had met several astronauts at an official function in London, including Captain James McDivitt, commander of the Apollo 9 mission which had orbited the moon. At the end of a lengthy conversation, McDivitt jotted down a Houston phone number and offered it to Yul, "in case of some medical emergency." Now, casting about for any solution, he remembered the Houston referral, and had his secretary place the call. When she explained all the details of the situation, the fellow insisted she put Yul on the phone to listen to what he had to say, in Southern vernacular. "You can't rehearse the play anyway, so why don't you just get your ass on down here?" That same day he chartered a Learjet and flew to Houston with Jacqueline, where they were met by a limousine and driven in from the airport to NASA, then beyond NASA, to a residential neighborhood, and finally to a small suburban house inhabited by Tibetan monks.

There Yul was brought into the house and introduced to the principal healer. He was the caucasian fellow with the Southern accent. The others were all Tibetan or Nepalese. It was he who read Yul's eleven pulses, according to the tradition of medicine known only to men of this training. After the diagnostics, Yul was treated with extensive acupuncture all at once, from his toes to his eyebrows. Following that he lay down, while a dozen monks settled around him and began to chant. He was then struck unconscious by what he thought was a bolt of lightning. He awoke soon after, and was told he could leave.

The Tibetan name that the Southerner had adopted was Norbu Chen. He was originally from Kentucky, and one story Yul heard had it that after serving time for auto theft, he had spent a dozen years in Nepal learning this ancient science of medicine. By bribing the Chinese guards, he had even traveled into Tibet to discover its deepest mysteries. Upon his return to America, he had offered his services to NASA. It seems that the reading of the pulses was something they were very curious about, so for a time NASA reportedly helped to underwrite his foundation.

As Yul prepared to return to Indianapolis that afternoon, he was warned he must remain completely silent for seventy-two hours—right up to his opening night curtain. Then he would have his voice back.

Such was the situation as I arrived in Indianapolis.

We gave each other a big hug as I walked into the suite and, after almost two years, there was no doubt we were glad to see each other. Things had changed. To begin with, Yul could barely whisper, much less shout at the waiter or the maid and intimidate everyone in earshot. Something else had changed, which we could not help but notice as we embraced: I was taller than my father. Not because I had grown, but because Yul had become shorter as his disks collapsed and his vertebrae had started to fuse from his weight. Yul had lost three or more inches of height over a decade. Also, for the first time since childhood, I was actually standing up straight. It was both astonishing and eerie.

We sat, and I described the work I was doing for Bank of America, thanking him again for loaning me the living expenses I had needed during my training as a systems analyst. He nodded, trying hard to appear interested, but his eyes told me everything. Even though he didn't much like the adult I had become, he was aching to forgive his prodigal son. He still loved the memory of laddie, the boy I once had been: out of loyalty to that little boy, Yul was prepared to pretend he was interested in some computer programmer who worked for a bank. But he was lousy at pretending, and his eyes focused blankly in my direction.

"Dad, I've got an idea." He nodded.

"Jacqueline's explained that you're planning to mime your way through the dress rehearsal tonight, since you have to stay silent another day." Again, he nodded.

"Well, think about this for a moment. Instead of sending the dress rehearsal audience home—what if I stood with a microphone in the musician's pit, and lip-synced your voice?" It was the most presumptuous, audacious, outrageous idea he'd ever heard of, and it put an angry scowl across his face. But after a moment the scowl faded.

"We won't actually lie to them, Dad. The stage manager will make an announcement. The audience will be delighted: they'll certainly be happier than if they're sent home. Come on, Dad; it's easy. I know every intonation, from your first line to your deathbed scene. I spent my whole childhood rehearsing your speeches! I'll have the script in my hand. Listen to me, Dad: 'I am King as I was born to be, Siam to be ruled in my way. Not English way, not French way, not Chinese way. My way!'"

He was caught completely off-guard by how much I suddenly sounded like him. Then I leaned close to his ear and whispered. "C'mon Dad—you know the gaje. *They love being teased."*

And Yul began to smile.

That night we did it, exactly that way. The few hundred invited guests experienced an unprecedented experience in theater, and shared a unique moment for a father and a son. It was as close, perhaps, as he and I could ever be. For three hours Yul heard his own performance as the King coming from the voice that was his legacy. Twenty-five years after the original dress rehearsal, Yul and his son were creating the King together.

And, for one night, I was King of Siam.

13

The King Reborn

"Do you want to act, passionately?... To the ex-
clusion of all else?... You must be prepared to
sacrifice what most people call 'life.'"
—Ronald Harwood, *The Dresser*

The King and I opened on Broadway again in May 1977. Yul's
voice had recovered quickly in Indianapolis, just as the Tibetan
lama had promised. And the production earned good money
on the road. So plans for the Broadway production went ahead,
without much certainty about how the sophisticated New York
audiences would respond to the return of such an old show:
this would be the first attempt ever to revive a musical with
its original star. There was considerable skepticism about
whether the play or its star still had appeal in the disco era that
produced *Saturday Night Fever*. The hottest new musical on
Broadway came from a comic strip: *Annie*.

The New York Times review announced that this was a "Reminder of a Golden Age" for New York theater. And how did
Yul look and sound in the part, more than a quarter of a century
after his first opening night? The *Times* review began this way:

> Yul Brynner is a great actor—or at the very least a great
> acting presence—not because of what he does but because
> of what he is. He strides on a stage caught in the invisible
> spotlight of his personality. He gestures, gesticulates, and
> moves with the certainty of an automaton and the grace of
> a dancer.
>
> Often he is very still, his body seemingly carved out of
> time... He dominates... but also charms. He is a Genghis

215

Khan in a Savile Row suit and a Maserati . . . Mr. Brynner
grinning fire and snorting charm is as near to the original as
makes little difference.

The director of record was Yuriko, the lady who had danced
the role of Eliza in the original production; her daughter, Susan,
was now dancing the role she had created. Naturally, Yuriko
saw eye to eye with Yul on almost every aspect of the production.

For the first time in years Yul was again a big-time box office
star. But he was also achieving something no other star had
done: he appeared to have conquered time itself. How was it
possible? It was as if Yul had found the key to agelessness.
As one reporter put it: "Mr. Brynner, who says he is fifty-six
years old, but appears to be in a state of eternally lean, trim
fitness, said he felt more right for the part now than he did the
first time around." Therein lay the key and, like magic, it was
not obvious: the reason Yul seemed unchanged was that the
King had always been a sixty-year-old character. It was uncanny. Each night the theater was filled mostly with ladies from
the suburbs who had had a crush on Yul Brynner since 1951;
but now they often brought their grown daughters instead of
their husbands, to swoon along beside them. On Wednesday
matinees, the atmosphere could be positively lubricious.

Yul and Jacqueline rented a brownstone on the Upper East
Side that belonged to Henry Fonda and his wife Shirley. With
Mia, Melody and their nanny, it made for a warm, stable
household: by now the Brynners had been on the road nonstop
for almost three years, with only rare visits to their home in
Normandy. Indeed, there were times when Yul gladly would
have sold Criquebeuf: its upkeep was so expensive that Yul
had to spend fifty weeks on the road to pay for its maintenance,
just so that he could visit it for two weeks a year. He professed
to be content with the arrangement, but in fact he was trapped:
he realized he would have to spend the rest of his life playing
eight shows a week to pay for his castle. Later, the French
elected a socialist government, and the wealthy fled the franc.
Values tumbled on large properties, as a punitive tax upon the

very rich was anticipated, and Yul would have had to take a huge loss if he sold. Instead, he lived and worked three thousand miles from home, spending more than a hundred thousand dollars each year on a two-week vacation.

When he began preparing for *The King and I,* he bluntly warned Jacqueline that his schedule was going to be so demanding that he would have no more than sixty seconds a day to devote to his family. And while he enjoyed spending time with his daughters, he kept his word about the sixty seconds. His life revolved entirely around his dressing-room, just as it had in the early 1950s. That's where he held most of his meetings, took many of his meals, and met with all his girlfriends.

I was living in a shack on Topanga Beach. I had no work, no car, and no common sense. Returning to Malibu from Indianapolis a few days late, I had lost my job with Bank of America. Worse, I had lost respect for my own skills as a systems analyst: once again I had been exposed to all the excitement of my father's life, and my newborn efforts at a steady job suddenly seemed unbearably dull, unthinkably boring. At last I could live happily without alcohol; but could I live without excitement? I knew it was just what I needed, but I could not endure the thought, at the end of each day, that all that excitement was happening out there without me. So, instead of another office job, I became road manager for my favorite band. In fact, I became road manager for The Band. But that's another story altogether.

On the road with rock 'n' roll I resisted alcohol completely. Unfortunately, I started to develop another nasty habit that slapped me flat down to new depths: beware cocaine, the devil's dandruff. So I ended up beached in Malibu again, flat broke on the left edge of the American continent. Without a car, there was nothing to do but walk across the street to the nearest diner and ask for a job. I was serving a plate of waffles one morning when suddenly I recognized the place: sure enough, I was now the short-order chef in the same diner where Dad and I had eaten breakfast each morning, twenty years earlier: the Step Inn Café.

                            * * *

*"You've got to stop hoping to win your father's approval,
Rock,"* warned my mother. *"Yul has many qualities and virtues, and I'm sure he does care about you: it's just that he
doesn't have any approval to offer. His whole life has been
spent in the pursuit of power and domination. He cannot help
competing, even against you, and he cannot tolerate losing,
even with you. When you were eight years old I watched Yul
cheat at Monopoly, rather than let you beat him. So it's no
good hoping to win his approval. It's as if you were asking
him for peanut brittle: if he had any, he'd probably be happy
to give it to you. The man just doesn't happen to have any
peanut brittle to offer. No peanut brittle, and no approval."*

*A month later we had transformed that breakfast-counter into
the first sushi-bar in Malibu, called Something's Fishy Here,
and within weeks it was the hottest place on the Pacific Coast
Highway. Every star with a beach house dropped by on the
way home. I was hoping my father would be proud of me,
perhaps even touched that this was the same diner where we
used to share breakfast. But that was not how Yul felt at all.
When friends of mine went to New York, I arranged for them
to see* The King and I. *Afterward they visited my father backstage, along with some of Yul's wealthier friends. He asked
them how I was doing. They told him about the success of the
sushi-bar. Right away they could see Yul was embarrassed that
his son was involved with anything so lowly, especially in front
of his wealthy friends. Yul turned to them and said, "I have
another son who is a lawyer." Now he had invented an ima-
ginary son, to make up for his real son's failings, and there
was no guessing to how many people he had repeated this
fiction. There was no one around to challenge him, and no
limit to the fictions he would create just to flatter his vanity.
Still, this was a new one. Yul had no other son but me, and
he knew it; he also knew that I knew it, along with most of his
friends. But who would choose to pick a fight with this man?
Eventually, when I heard the whole story from my skeptical*

friends, I busted him for the lie on the phone. In his own way, Yul backed down and apologized.

One day a plump, bearded customer in dirty jeans and dark shades came up to me in the sushi-bar. He looked like a low-rent biker. ''Are you Rocky, Yul Brynner's kid?'' he asked, and when I nodded cautiously, he removed his shades. It was Steve McQueen.

In words I can barely remember Steve said that he'd always meant to stop by this roadside shack. Recently *The Magnificent Seven* had been shown on television, and a carpenter working on his house mentioned to him that I worked at this sushi-bar: that was why he was stopping by. Trying my best to ignore his appearance, I sat down with him at a table. He explained that by disguising himself as an ugly biker type he was free to move about publicly, the way ordinary folk do. I tried to picture Yul doing that. Then McQueen told me he'd been reviewing his life carefully for some months.

''Yul and I fell out over some stupid thing, a couple years after we made that movie.'' He paused. ''I don't remember. Maybe it was something in the press. Or the plans to make a sequel. We had an argument about The Deal. I'm sure he doesn't remember exactly either, it was such a trivial thing.'' McQueen was wrong; Yul remembered perfectly.

''Anyway, I stopped by so's to ask you to give him a message, next time you speak to him.'' He paused, but this was a different kind of pause. It was difficult for him to say what he had to say. And yet during the several seconds that he paused, it was obvious that something had happened, something had changed inside his soul.

''Ask Yul to forgive me. I was always grateful for what he did. He completely changed my career and my life. Then we had some stupid argument because I wouldn't appear in *Return of the Seven,* and I never saw him again. Well, I came here today to ask you to give Yul a message. Tell him I did wrong, and I'm sorry for it. I never stopped feeling bad about it, because there's no doubt, *The Magnificent Seven* was the film that made me a star. And I never did forget that, or forget him.''

I promised to give Yul the message, mentioning that Dad and I didn't talk much. I was going to say something about how unwell he looked, but then he might reasonably have asked what the hell I was doing working as a short-order cook. So I just told him that he'd been a real hero to me.

"I remember, Rock. You first suggested me to your father, because you were a fan of my TV show. I never forgot you either, all the time I was a star."

"But you're still a star," I objected. Steve McQueen didn't need me to tell him that. Then I was called back into the office to finish the accounts, and we said goodbye. A few months later, Steve McQueen was dead.

In New York, Yul was beginning the biggest bash of his life. Oh yes, he had known swift success before, from the start of his career, almost before he could speak English. He had also known prolonged failure in films—more than a decade without a good movie. But for all his bravado, Yul had never expected in his wildest dreams to re-experience the intoxication of superstardom: he had adjusted to being a middle-aged character actor, but now he had been reborn as a matinee idol. The self-righteousness he had stored up during the lean years fused with all his accumulated resentments. What began as intoxication became a binge of indulgence and a ceaseless Celebration of Self. Pity those who had crossed him over the years. In his daily schedule there would be no time left for subtleties: the exigencies of his routine demanded that every decision be reduced to simple black and white, and made swiftly and firmly: chung! Like Lawrence of Arabia, he had disavowed the civilized world, and would take no prisoners. Leaving carnage everywhere in his wake, my father gave new meaning to the words *monstre sacré*.

The new photograph with which they advertised *The King and I* showed a man whose ego had abandoned all limits of propriety. The character in that photograph had little to do with the "angel inhabiting a beast" that Oscar Hammerstein had found in the King; neither did it express "the search for God, through a higher sense of love," that Michael Chekhov defined as the essence of the theater. On sale in the lobby, that photograph was entitled "Curtain Call": because in the revival of *The King and I*, Yul turned the curtain call into an unabashed little three-act spectacle of its own. Yul made three appearances during the curtain calls: first scowling, then gracious, and finally throwing his arms up in the air, he invited the audience to share his shameless delight in the very existence of Yul Brynner. Yul had enough power over the producers to insist that every performance end with this spectacle, which audiences loved. Twenty-five years before, that is not how my father would have used his power.

Gratifying as it was to recapture stardom in his late fifties, eight shows a week was one hell of a price to pay. Five or ten years earlier, when he was being a European aristocrat, Yul would not have wanted such a rigorous routine at any price. But now he was a glutton for hard work, and if it meant money and adulation, he was prepared to do whatever it took.

And what did it take for Yul to *give his all* six nights a week, plus two matinees? To make the same damn play genuinely exciting and explosive again and again? It took everything he had to give. For the eight o'clock curtain, Yul arrived at his dressing-room before six P.M., having just eaten. The make-up, every bit as intricate as in 1951, took one full hour, plus there was body make-up to be sponged on, and, in his single most important ritual of the day, "receiving the numbers." An hour before curtain someone from the box office would come to his dressing-room to deliver the final ticket sales figure for the evening's performance, as well as a report on advance sales. He treated these numbers very solemnly. While finishing his make-up Yul was tracking sales trends, estimating demographics and projecting grosses. From the beginning, *The King and I* sold huge blocks of tickets to suburban theater groups, through a well-planned strategy of television commercials. This was not considered respectable for the legitimate theater at the time; but the "Bottom Line," Yul's growing fixation, was a compelling enough reason. That was probably the single biggest difference from the original production.

Each performance lasted three hours. In that time Yul created the King, again and again. He did keep it fresh, even when there were two shows a day, though the same could not always be said for everyone else onstage. It was the challenge that made Yul work harder. What drove him on, ticket sales apart, was his determination that, with every performance, something *real* had to happen to everyone present—something within them had to change. No audience ever left disappointed. Even having spent close to one hundred dollars for a pair of seats, every member of the audience went home knowing beyond a doubt that Yul had given it his all. The sheer physicality of his performance intensified their lives.

The curtain fell at eleven. Still in make-up, Yul greeted guests backstage in his plush two-room suite. This was his time of day to socialize with old friends, whom he usually invited there after the show, rather than having them to his hotel during the day.

Then, more often than not, Yul was ready to party. He still had a lot of steam to burn off, and a thirst for Scotch or fine wine. He was always game to return to the atmosphere he had known best since his teenage years: the nightclub. But this was New York 1977, and the In place was Studio 54..Never mind that he had just done a grueling three-hour show; at fifty-seven, Yul would hang out there until dawn with Bianca or Andy or Halston, or Liza. Nothing had ever rejuvenated him quite like this late, unforeseen success.

There was really only one problem: money. Like Dmitri Karamazov, he was never quite able to earn as fast as he could spend, what with the house in France, the rental in New York, and his own extravagant daily spending on limousines, VCRs, Gucci luggage, Piaget watches, chunky gold chains and chartered jets. Once again he was earning enough money to piss on.

And then there was his personal wardrobe. By the late 1970s, my father had settled into wearing one color: black. On the road he travelled with eighty-three pairs of hand-tailored trousers, and every single pair was black. He usually wore only a few pairs each week, but all eighty-three pairs had to be packed and hung and repacked again, to travel to the next town.

The play stayed on Broadway for a year and a half, selling out consistently almost until the end. At that point, it played for a couple of months in Los Angeles in early 1979, before shutting down in America. For the first time in his career, Yul had made plans to play the King—in England.

* * *

Since money and acclaim were so important to Yul, he couldn't help but regard his own son as a failure. By the age of thirty I had earned an MA in Philosophy, written and performed a one-man play in London and on Broadway, travelled as a street clown, and recovered from juvenile alcoholism. I had worked at a dozen different jobs, apart from computer programming: I'd driven trucks, cabs and buses and helped to start a few restaurants. All of this failed to impress my father. In Yul's eyes, nothing I did was big enough. Not even when Muhammad Ali hired *me* as his bodyguard. I expect that calls for an explanation.

During the early 1970s, before Red Hat the Clown became a complete lush, I travelled to Houston with my friend Harold Conrad, the legendary boxing promoter—a Swiss entrepreneur wanted to propose a bout in Zurich for "the People's Champion," and I was to translate. Ali and I hit it off right from the start. In those days I still wore flowing white robes, a burgundy Borsalino, and a large wooden earring. On the way to training one morning, while the entourage had gone to sell concessions, I stayed with the Champ as he paused for autographs. Before we knew what was happening, a large Texan redneck was shouting obscenities at Ali and swinging a fist. Ali faded back and frowned, and the Texan swung again—and again. Just one month earlier the United States Supreme Court had ruled that Muhammad Ali was a legitimate minister of his faith, and reinstated his boxing license. The Champ could risk losing his license again by raising his fist outside the ring; he bobbed back from another left jab.

I remembered a little trick Yul had taught me. With both hands I grabbed the redneck's fist, and bent his fingers back to his wrist till I heard them all crack: the big guy dropped to his knees with a howl, and Ali jogged off. I caught up with him a few seconds later, and he threw me a grin.

"Who'd a ever have thunk," said Muhammad Ali, "that the son of the Phar-aoh of Egypt would be protectin' a little black boy from Louisville!" And for the next few years, whenever Muhammad had a fight, I was invited along, to serve officially as the bodyguard to the People's Champion. I worked on half a dozen of Ali's fights, including his bouts with Ken Norton, Joe Bugner and Al "Blue" Lewis.

One day I phoned Yul while I was in Ali's hotel suite, and I put the Champ on the telephone so they could exchange greetings. Yul and I had rooted for Ali during the Rome Olympics. Ali complimented Yul for having a son who was "so fas'—an' so smart!" Ali glanced at me in my white hippie gowns and burgundy Borsalino. "Your son sure ain't as dumb as he looks," he said to Yul. I beamed at the dubious compliment. The Champ handed the phone back to me.

Yul was delighted. "It was destiny," my father said right away, "that someday the Champ and I would speak with each other." Apparently, Yul could see his son as little more than Destiny's method of putting him on the phone with Muhammad Ali.

What Yul was unable to see was that I was reliving, as precisely as I could, all the adventures of his own life. He had driven trucks and buses for Chekhov: I drove for Robbie Robertson and The Band. He had entertained in nightclubs with the Dimitrieviches, I played coffeehouses with Ramblin' Jack Elliott. He had been a circus clown, I was a street clown. He had studied Philosophy in Evanston, I studied it in Dublin; he had had his Broadway debut before he was twenty-five, so had I. He had used opium with Cocteau, so I had adapted Cocteau's notebook *Opium* and played Cocteau onstage. I had already ended my first marriage—to an actress in Hollywood.

It was almost as if I was trying to fast-forward through all the experiences of his life, so that I could then get on with my own. I was not trying to compete with my father—I was trying to *continue* him. From the day I was born, Yul had raised me to *feel* that way deep inside, as if I were not meant to have a soul of my own. "Man is born alone, lives alone, dies alone"; ah, but what if we could have been the first in the history of human souls to have broken *that* law together . . .

Yul meant no harm. He loved his son the way he loved himself—too much. And I had loyally spent the start of my life re-experiencing my father's, or as close to it as I could get. And what did I want from The Deal? A great slap on the back from Yul was not required: a quick nod of approval would have done nicely. He just didn't happen to have one on him. In fact, whenever my life most resembled his, he seemed to dislike me most. For example, when I drank the way he did, *nobody* liked the results; but, I had also learned, Yul hated the notion that his son was a non-drinker, a teetotaler—a spoilsport. Unless I was risking it all, Yul couldn't admire me. When I did, he was quick to condemn my recklessness. I had given him plenty of reasons over the years to be displeased, especially when I was young and drunk and confused, saying and doing things to him and to others which I could never entirely live down—and that he could never entirely forgive. He made it perfectly clear that I had failed him, not only as a son, but in every possible way: even as a financial investment.

What displeased him most was that if he could not admire his son, then he could not admire himself as a father. Since the birth of his first child, Yul ached to believe that his star-power would be hereditary: that he could pass to me the very *magic* that was Yul Brynner. He could not see that if I was to have any magic, I would have to invent my own, just like everybody else.

"Hi, Dad." I walked into his suite at the Bel Air Hotel, and we hugged. My father looked deep into my eyes, and said softly, "We cannot hurt one another any more."

We sat down and swapped jokes and stories. We made our way carefully around sensitive topics, deferential as hell, learning cautiously how to get along together. We made it clear to each other that we would refrain from any critical word or manner toward each other. In my presence, Yul was even polite toward his chauffeur, just this once.

Then a light bulb on the desk went out. He picked up the phone and asked for the manager of the hotel. When the manager came on the line Yul asked him, in his softest voice, to send an electrician, because a light bulb in his suite, his five hundred dollar-a-day suite, was kaput. Half an hour later a young man in a busboy's uniform appeared with a light bulb. Yul dismissed him immediately at the door, and called the manager again. This time his voice sounded like Mace.

"Now let me make this clear to you," Yul hissed softly. "I asked for an electrician. You sent me some kid with a bulb. So tell me, directly, right now: have you no respect for me whatsoever? . . . Thank you."

Moments later, a middle-aged fellow rang the doorbell. He was wearing an electrician's uniform and a wide leather belt full of tools. Yul watched with satisfaction as the electrician changed the bulb, hoping I'd appreciate the fact that he had never raised his voice. I did appreciate it, because at the age of thirty-three it still rattled me every time. He conveyed greetings to me from Liza, who had recently visited him backstage. We talked about trivial subjects for half an hour, and then I left. It was easy. We could probably get along together for the rest of our lives that way, so long as we never discussed a single thing that really mattered. Piece o' cake.

That night, his Monday night off, Yul took six of us to dinner, driving us himself. We waited twenty minutes outside the restaurant while Yul taught the parking attendant the CORRECT procedure for parking cars. "If I were as careless onstage as you are out here," he reprimanded the attendant, "where would we all be?" The bewildered surfer who parked cars part-time had no reply.

It was almost as if in the 1950s Yul had decided what the character of the King would be like, but by the 1970s it was the King who decided how Yul would behave. As a young man of thirty, he had imagined the King as vastly larger than himself; now the figure of Yul Brynner seemed larger than the Siamese barbarian, as if his old character had grown too tight, and he needed a psychological shoehorn to slip back inside the King's skin.

Yul played *The King and I* in Los Angeles for almost four months at the Pantages Theater—on the same stage where he had received his Academy Award for the King in 1957. That summer he, Jacqueline, Mia and Melody returned to Normandy, and Yul proceeded to London with the play. From there he commuted to his home by private plane for his day and a half off each week.

London was an even greater victory, for it was his first

conquest of the English theater—where thirty years earlier he had performed *Lute Song* and *Dark Eyes* to lukewarm audiences. The British were positively delirious: though predictably less demonstrative than American audiences, they were even more sympathetic to the plight of an authoritarian monarch whose time had passed.

More and more, the theme of the play became distorted by Yul's stardom. The King was a Mosaic figure, according to Oscar Hammerstein's plot, who can lead his people to rational enlightenment, but cannot renounce the beast within—his own passionate nature—to join them. Like Moses, he pays for that passionate nature, since it seems the King dies from a broken heart. The moral of the play, as Hammerstein wrote it, is that much really *is* wrong in Siam, and that is all dying with the King. But with the hoopla over Yul's curtain call, that moral was completely nullified, and even distorted, as if the audience were there to celebrate the values that the King represented. As his subjective and objective identification with the King grew more intense, Yul's own sense of infallibility began rubbing off on the King, as if the King, with all his emotional violence, was beyond reproach. The distinction between the nobility of the King's dreams and the brutality of his character began vanishing, to the tune of "Something Wonderful."

Yul welcomed and often *commanded* royal treatment. Every incident that erased the distinction between show business aristocracy and hereditary aristocracy delighted him to no end—especially in England. He had been presented to the Queen first in the 1950s; now, participating auspiciously in the Royal Variety Club fund-raiser, he was presented to Her Majesty a second time. By now, Yul was a true *believer* in monarchy.

His favorite anecdote about royalty concerned a moment that occurred in the lobby of Claridge's Hotel in London, where foreign dignitaries often stay. He had lunched there with Sam Spiegel, and was waiting for the doorman to summon his limousine. At the same time, he observed, the young King Constantine of Greece was waiting for his car, alongside King Hussein of Jordan and King Juan Carlos of Spain. They all waved Yul over to join them. As Yul told it, they waited together for their limos, and in the process he heard the concierge say to his assistant, ''Too bad this isn't a poker game—we're holding four kings!''

Such stories, which Yul could happily repeat three or four times a day to fresh listeners, were not meant to be tested for truthfulness. Whenever Yul related implausible stories like that, there was an unspoken understanding that they should not be challenged; otherwise, Yul might become angry. Nobody within earshot wanted that to happen. Yul rarely had to threaten people to get his way.

Since aristocracy is hereditary by nature, it saddened him that his son did not share in this presumption of royalty. It saddened him even more to realize that his son had no stomach for an established aristocracy based on breeding *or* merit, and regarded such beliefs as better suited to kennel shows than to human conduct. Of course, Yul did not suppose he had been *born* King, but felt he had achieved a sort of Divine Right within his personal world, by virtue of artistic excellence. Those who were masters of their occupation—the cream of the crop, the handful of Great Souls—formed an aristocracy of talent for whom special rules of human conduct applied. Yul believed that anyone who had earned the title of ''Superstar'' should be exempt from the responsibilities and restrictions of the average citizen: exceptional people must have exceptional latitude. Ultimately what his exceptionalism meant was that the Great are not obliged to be good. Genius exempts artists from all the rules—even the Golden Rule.

His identification with royalty was pounded in day after day, on stage and off. Approaching his sixtieth birthday in 1980, Yul had already performed the play for a total of *eight years* —more than 10 percent of his life. Not only was the schedule very hard, it was also unrelenting. There was no way to grab a day off for injury or illness. If he missed performances it would make the news, and ticket sales would start to drop. He had no understudy: what audience would stay to see his understudy? This underscored the fact that the audience was just there to see Yul Brynner.

But he was getting old. Most of his major physical problems were related to his back, which finally forced him to exercise his muscles. In his later years he had never taken up exercise: he did not jog, or swim laps, or do isometrics. He had moderated his ravenous appetite, and now he slept eight hours a night instead of the four or five he had lived on until he was forty. He had stopped smoking his beloved Gauloises at fifty; years later, asked if he ever thought about cigarettes he replied, "Every minute of the day." Yul also began to realize how much his public image was connected with cigarettes: over the decades almost all of his fan photos had featured a cigarette. Almost every character he played except the Pharaoh was a smoker. He had never been a casual smoker, and for years boasted frankly of his three to five pack a day habit.

The six days that he performed, each and every week, he drank no alcohol until after the performance, and then he drank only fine wine—very fine wine. Some nights of revelry he might drink a bottle or more of Bordeaux. But his one day off each week he developed a habit that poisoned his leisure. It was his special "reward" to go out for lunch and begin with two double dry martinis before lunch. This was often the first hard liquor he'd had in a week, and the impact was sudden, and subtle as a wrecking ball. For a time, it made him happy: he drank, he ate, he slept. But then came the bad part, since invariably he began his one free evening of the week with a mild hangover. That usually made him mean, or at least gruff. A cocktail or two before dinner helped, but usually by then his mood for the evening was shot, and the same for anyone near ground zero. Sometimes, honestly, he was just like a mean ol' bulldog who couldn't help barking at every sound, day and night. Just like the King of Siam.

To maintain the castle, which he could not sell, he was condemned to wander the earth, playing King. So, as his errant little kingdom shuttled about the Western world, he lived out the years of his life on the perpetual treadmill of eight shows a week. He loved his stardom, but he hated his life. There was nothing he could do to escape, and he resented everyone around him for the trap he was in. Once and for all, the bully he always was now overpowered the gentle artist he should have been.

But, like the boy at the Emperor's parade, I seemed to be the only one who noticed there was something wrong.

14

Monstre Sacré

> "Arrogant dragon will have cause to repent."
> —*I Ching*

In his early career Yul personified spontaneity, instinct, and the power of an animal. It was difficult to find a reference to him in the 1950s that did not compare him to some large member of the cat family. By the 1980s, the image that came most readily to mind was of a powerful locomotive, an automaton chugging relentlessly forward, dragging a massive burden, unstopping and unstoppable. The cold, deliberate monomania that kept him going became even more intense, his jaw more set in grim determination. The disregard and disrespect that typified his conduct toward everybody around him became more pronounced, and he lost all capacity to envision his behavior through the eyes of those who loved him.

In his peaceful moods, during the quiet hours at home, he was not all that different from the way he'd always been. He took special delight in his three daughters, for he was always refreshed by the company of children. I sometimes found it unbearably touching to watch Yul squat down with a six-year-old and play games—just as he had done with me. Apart from his daughters, with whom he was always caring and attentive, there were few who could evoke his gentle and most charming nature. When those moods spread across him, no one was more sunny and delightful. From time to time, when even he could see the preposterousness of his eccentricities—his insistence on a bulletproof limo, for example—he would smile his most endearing smile, throw his hands up in the air and exclaim irresistibly, "What can I say? I'm just a maniac!"

231

By the end of his career, Yul's biography in the Broadway *Playbill* was different from all others. Usually a brief, objective resumé of an actor's professional career, his was two pages of obsequious flattery and mythological invention:

> YUL BRYNNER. The name is as unique as the man himself. A consummate craftsman, he has triumphed in every phase of the entertainment world. Yul Brynner in *The King and I* proves conclusively that he is the most magnetic force on the stage today. His sheer presence rivets an audience and commands attention, as it has for over 50 years in the profession. Born in 1920 on Sakhalin Island . . . [*wrong*] . . . When he was 12 [*15*], he quit school to perform with a group of gypsies; he spent 5 years [*two*] working as an acrobat; he studied at the Sorbonne earning high honors in philosophy [*he never formally enrolled in college*] . . .

Et cetera. In his later career, Yul's press agents discovered there was never any danger of laying it on too thick. Humility, meekness, altruism, patience, obedience, self-sacrifice, forgiveness—these were not qualities Yul admired, or even pretended to admire. Yul was no hypocrite: the central teachings of Christianity, for example, held no attraction to Yul, and he never pretended differently. Having spent a lifetime imposing his will on the world about him, he had no patience with those who prayed, "*Thy* will be done." Or the Serenity Prayer of Alcoholics Anonymous: "God, grant me the Serenity to accept those things I cannot change, the Courage to change those things I can, and the Wisdom to know the difference." This was all Greek to Yul; he had no patience with serenity. Ego unbridled, Yul was willfulness run amok. His rationale was that *The King and I* was some sort of holy crusade that took care of all the moral obligations he had: if he just kept performing eight shows a week, he was justified in doing anything to anyone, anywhere. He now espoused social Darwinism with zeal, promulgating a dog-eat-dog view of the world with little or no empathy for the fallen: *only* the fittest survived, and so it must always remain.

Like John Henry with his hammer, it was not clear Yul could stop pounding away, even if he wanted to. The rawness of his

greed was frank and uninhibited. He kept careful record nightly
of every penny earned, even the cash taken in from T-shirt and
program sales at the concessions stands. That concessions
money was his own special little kitty, and he frequently complained about how dirty and smelly the public's money was.

By now, Yul's boasting took up 95 percent of each social
engagement over which he presided. The truth was, though,
there were fewer and fewer social engagements, as he lost sight
of the norms of behavior to which others adhered. He boasted
about breaking records, about his physical stamina, and, often,
about his son—whose life bore only a distant factual resemblance to mine. In one of his favorite anecdotes he described
how, in Indianapolis, we had played the King *together*; he
often spoke of it to mutual friends, boasting about the brilliant
job his son had done. But in all the years that passed, he never
mentioned it to me again. He was like a one-man football team,
playing all the positions, but he was also the team's noisiest
fan. Until now, it had always mattered to him that his conduct
be that of a gentleman, except with studio executives. Now he
really didn't care what people thought of him, as long as they
expressed admiration. And as he became more hateful to
strangers, he became more isolated—gradually, even paranoid.
He began to insist upon a bullet-proof limousine, just for peace
of mind, as well as several bodyguards *whenever* he was exposed to the public. Yul always explained that all this security
was because there was a crazy fellow whose girlfriend had a
hopeless crush on Yul, and this nut wanted to shoot him.

The greatest threat in Yul's life was not to his person. It was
to his dignity, and it became progressively more difficult to
keep him peaceable in public, if he felt his honor had been
challenged. Like Archie Bunker, he had grandiose pet peeves.
Perhaps his greatest contempt was reserved for Italian waiters,
and more than once I thought Yul really would break off some
unfortunate busboy's arm, as he often threatened to do. Usually, the people who fumbled around Yul were his greatest
fans, and the humiliation delivered that way by a star like Yul
was immeasurably cruel. I know: I experienced it myself when
I worked in restaurants, seating stars who behaved almost as
badly as my father.

I remember watching in horror, on New Year's Eve, 1975,

when a drunken girl, almost incoherent, stumbled up to Yul as we arrived at an informal cast party. Noticing his face for the first time, an expression of dumb recognition wiggled across her features. "Look, everybody," she announced with a slur, "it's Telly Savalas!"

Everyone laughed. And everyone nearby saw the scowl that crossed Yul's face. In a split second Yul brought his knee up hard into the girl's groin. He turned his back as she slumped to the floor. Minutes later we left.

Once, when the newspaperboy threw Yul's copy of the *Wall Street Journal* into a puddle for the third day running, Yul phoned the local office and threatened to expose the paper for the filthy rag it really was.

Put simply, in his later years, he would brook no opposition. None. He made it clear, daily, that he was prepared to unleash his full fury if anything displeased him, however trivial. It was this disproportion of reaction that made his rage such an effective tool for intimidation. A life-or-death situation might deserve such extreme emotion, but to suffer such a paroxysm because of an overdone steak was not just a display of willful authoritarianism: it was public demonstration of the fact that Yul was out of control. For some years I could imagine being awakened by the phone in the middle of the night: Yul had finally come up against some small-town sheriff who "ain't never heard of no King o' Si-yam."

I once heard it said that anger is a dubious prerogative for the very well balanced. Like greed or racism, hostility is a tendency to which we are all susceptible. Like every other mortal who kicks the curb in anger, Yul had his fair share of stubbed toes, and all too often his own brusque impatience caused the events which enraged him most. The sorriest saga of all was the story of the spare ribs.

During rehearsals for *Home Sweet Homer,* Yul took the director and leading lady to Trader Vic's for lunch one day during a short break in rehearsals. As they arrived he placed a huge order for pork spare ribs, and warned the waiter with a growl that they had to leave in half an hour. Obligingly, the waiter returned lickety-split with the orders of ribs, and other delicacies. Well, shortly before the Broadway opening, all three began suffering fevers and chills. They were diagnosed as having trichonosis, which put them all through a nightmare for several weeks. They may or may not have shared food at other times, but Yul decided to his own satisfaction that the sickness was the fault of Trader Vic's. He sued Hilton Hotels for a vast sum and, in a deposition, Yul even attested that he had been unable to perform connubial obligations because of Trader Vic's spare ribs. The Hilton lawyers had a heyday with that: I was driving along the Pacific Coast Highway when I heard CBS Radio report that Yul Brynner was blaming Hilton Hotels for his impotence. In the end, a settlement was reached secretly.

Yul rarely lost complete control of his temper: he did it just often enough to remind his entourage that he had a whim of iron. Usually his excessive demands were born of a good and necessary cause: only out of context did they seem excessive. The most famous example, published all over the world at one time or another, was the list of requirements that Yul's secretary sent weeks ahead to each hotel he was to stay at while performing.

He specified that his accommodations could not be on the same floor as conventioneers, nor within earshot of construction. Maids were instructed to be silent in the hallway every morning; the master bed had to have a single, king-size mattress; special blackout curtains had to be installed; the closets had to be supplied with wooden hangers, naturally; his dog be provided for; he required an outside Touch Tone phone line; and the kitchen had to be stocked with items from a supplied shopping list, including one case per week of Château Gruaud Larose '66. These demands seemed absurd to almost everyone. For Yul, however, this wasn't a question of a few stays here and there, but rather *the rest of his life,* in one hotel after another, trying to sleep late in the morning to perform each night. These were the same hardships on the road that Virginia had written her article about nearly thirty years earlier.

Yul also made demands of theaters, especially for his dressing-room, which was always to be painted chocolate brown. Since this was where he did most of his social entertaining, Yul wanted a comfortable, carpeted sitting room that didn't have filthy walls and a dirty sink to piss in—the traditional cliché for actors' dressing-rooms. It was no delusion of Yul's that even stars' dressing-rooms were usually a depressing combination of fluorescent lighting, graffiti and cockroaches. It seemed strange to theater managers that *only* Yul Brynner, of all the stars, complained about the dressing-rooms: to Yul it was incomprehensible that no one else made the effort. He sometimes ran into stars who had followed him into theaters and who thanked him for the improvement.

From his point of view, then, most of these apparent caprices were not unreasonable: but the diabolical grimness with which he made certain his demands were met was often so disproportionate to the job at hand as to make enemies of his fondest admirers. During the London production Yul generated such hostility with the cast that someone in the cast squeezed Superglue into the lock of his dressing-room door, and spread drawing-pins along the corridor down which he walked barefoot to the stage. Where complicated travel arrangements were involved, for example, he might plan for weeks. In the end the trip became more of a military maneuver. He might, for example, insist on chartering a Learjet to visit his daughters after he closed in one city and before he opened in another. His secretary would pore over airline schedules to coordinate the whole adventure, always with the involvement of the airports' VIP services, even to bring his limo on to the tarmac beside the plane.

There was a good reason for that: by the 1970s, Yul Brynner could no longer walk a city block. The pain in his spine and legs was so terrible it wasn't clear how he could perform at all, much less do the sweeping, ballroom polka with Mrs. Anna in "Shall We Dance?" Whenever his travel plans involved walking more than a few hundred feet—from the car to his gate at an airport, for example—Yul was obliged to travel by wheelchair. This was galling to him, especially when he arrived in a city to perform *The King and I*. Occasionally, a photographer even got a shot of this and published it, much to Yul's rage.

Yul had always been a man of action, not reflection; of imagination, not memory. The onrush of events never abated— the next performance, the next city, the next season—and *this* locomotive never even slowed for curves. He had, of course, many moments of triumph to recall, and a short list of wistful memories. But the sad truth was that, by their frequent retelling,

Yul's most precious memories had been fingered to shreds, and by now were no different from his more creative fictions. But apart from a handful of recollections and close friends, Yul felt about as sentimental toward past events and old acquaintances as a hit-and-run driver toward his roadkill.

It is often said that liars need good memories, but any time Yul was challenged on his facts, he regarded the effrontery as a challenge to his whole being, and quickly transformed a disagreement about details into a battle to the death. If a guest at the dinner table did not accept Yul's interpretation of some historical event, he would respond that upstairs in a filing cabinet he had the evidence that proved *scientifically,* for example, that the entire human race preferred leadership by an enlightened élite over democracy by 92.8 percent. But God forbid if that guest was not prepared to take his word for it, that was tantamount to calling Yul a liar—and it meant a long, rough evening ahead.

After more than a year in London, the play closed: Yul was unwilling to play a second summer at the Palladium if they didn't install air conditioning. Management, "the fuckin' parasites," refused to pay for it. So the mews house in Chelsea was packed up in two shipments, thousands of pounds each, one headed back to Normandy, and the other back to America—because Yul had decided to start *another* tour with *The King and I* across America immediately, making this his seventh consecutive year on the road (including *Home Sweet Homer*). He and Mitch Leigh had estimated that they would have a fresh audience in each American city every seven years. So, in the spring of 1981, with a hiatus of only a few months, he set out on the road again. It was exactly thirty years after the original premiere with Gertrude Lawrence.

For the first time, Yul and his then partner Mitch Leigh owned the company. As Yul explained it to me, they got a private bank loan for about half a million dollars with which to start the TV advertising of Yul as the King. With thirty-second spots selectively featured in local markets, starting with Washington, DC, money began rolling in, just as the start-up costs for the production came due. Having now made Mitch Leigh his partner Yul felt as if he was at last free from producers, "the financial bloodsuckers." But the truth was, he now had to contend with Yul Brynner as his own slave driver.

The cost of replacing the producer himself was potentially catastrophic for Yul: for every performance he ever missed, he would have to reimburse ticket-holders from his own pocket. So if he missed a week, for example, he would not only lose all his income, but would also have to pay the running cost of the production—the ''nut''—which was about two hundred thousand dollars per week. No wonder Yul personally reviewed the company payroll every week. The new arrangement compelled him to keep on performing, no matter how much pain he might suffer in his spine and legs. ''The show must go on'' had become a more merciless mandate.

As Yul and Jacqueline set out on the road again, their marriage finally came unglued. Much of his behavior had become unacceptable to her, and she had withdrawn more and more into herself. Jacqueline was prone to melancholy anyway, and after fourteen years at Yul's side—seven years of packing and unpacking all eighty-three pairs of his black trousers—it seemed as if all her *joie de vivre* had just plumb run out. Yul had warned her that he would have no time for her: he had not prepared her for his vicious cruelty and emotional violence with her these last years, as if trying to drive her off. After Yul had shut her out of his heart completely, it was only her devotion to him that determined how much suffering she would have to endure before she gave him up, or died. While sustaining the closest friendship with Jacqueline that I ever saw Yul share, he also resented his emotional dependence upon her. He could not understand her utter loyalty: she had been a mystery and intrigue to him from the day they met to the day they were divorced.

When my novel, *The Ballad of Habit and Accident,* was published, Yul was quite pleased: not for me, particularly, but he liked having a son who was hailed as ''a modern Dante'' by the *Wall Street Journal*: pleased enough to forgive the *Journal*'s newspaper boy. Of course, he never got around to reading the novel itself—just the reviews. I didn't expect him to read it: Yul had stopped reading books altogether some years before. I was given to understand that he really *wanted* to read it, but what with his busy schedule, he just wasn't going to have time. Not in this life.

From Washington the new production moved on—Valley Forge, Philadelphia, Buffalo, Boston, and then points west— eight shows a week, never missing a beat. Ticket sales generally broke records, though the recession of 1982 hurt the box office in some industrial cities. Like some vagabond tribe, the Kingdom of Siam scooted around the map of America. Yul was playing the King for the *fifth* time in Philadelphia, and in other cities. I visited him in Boston in the autumn of 1981, and saw this production for the first time. Yul was always a little more nervous than usual when I was out front: as he was first to point out, I had seen more of his performances from the audience than anyone else alive.

Once Yul owned the production, Mrs. Anna became a pale foil for the King: by the 1980s, she did not always appear in the TV commercial. Her job was to deliver all those famous tunes in a professional manner. Mitch Leigh had made one important musical contribution: he had persuaded the Rodgers and Hammerstein trustees to allow the orchestra to pick up the tempo of all the music considerably. Richard Rodgers had specified inviolable metronome values for every song, but the pace of life had accelerated since 1951 and, frankly, four verses of "Getting To Know You" at a slow tempo could reduce pulse rates to critical levels.

The production gave me a queasy feeling, as though something was *sliding*. The supporting cast had a certain overearnest quality that road companies have, but the audiences didn't care: they were always just grateful that Yul Brynner had chosen to play in their town. What was sliding in this production was the performance itself. The whole show was literally slipping downstage toward the footlights. The actors were delivering their dialogue to the audience instead of to each other. That is always a danger with musicals, in which the actors conventionally turn downstage to sing. Now they were all doing it, much of the time: even Yul, especially when he was having throat problems. So the cast were eroding the illusion of a "fourth wall" separating the actors from the public. Sometimes, a vaudeville-like interplay developed with the audience, especially as the King dictated a letter sending "President Ling-

kong'' elephants with which to win the Civil War. This was a
deliberate choice, sure to get laughs on the road, but it contributed to the general slide toward the footlights. Rather than
transport Philadelphians to Siam, this downstage mugging
seemed to consign Yul Brynner to Philadelphia. I don't mean
to exaggerate the effect of this, or to pretend it diminished the
audience's delight and gratitude. Doubtless the most startling
thing was not how much the musical had changed, but how
little. On stage, in the flesh, Yul was bringing great delight to
some 20,000 people a week, in their own hometowns. Under
the circumstances, any aesthetic criticism at all seemed churl-
ish.

As he travelled, he became progressively more isolated from
the cities he played. His method for surviving eight years
on the road had been to make the cities indistinguishable. From
the blackout curtains in the bedrooms to the chocolate brown
dressing rooms, his travelling environment remained largely
constant. He had hunkered down psychologically to an inflex-
ible routine that controlled him completely. Each afternoon at
5:00 P.M. exactly he ate his meal and left for the theater. The
bodyguards were in place for his stroll to the elevator, held for
his personal use. He arrived at the theater at six o'clock exactly,
to begin two hours of preparation.

With each visit, I noticed that the deference Yul expected,
even from his entourage, had increased. By now, the atmosphere of adulation exceeded saturation point—praise seemed
to condense around him and drip to the floor. Everyone had
learned the most important fact about Yul's appetite for admiration: it never, ever let up. Perpetual praise was not enough:
he needed to feel that the praise was growing ever greater,
week after week, from friends, audiences and strangers in the
street. In fact, Yul sometimes refused to make his final curtain
call if the audience failed to give him a *standing* ovation.

His weekly schedule on the road was as demanding as anyone
in the theater could endure: in just over forty-eight hours, between Friday and Sunday evening, the company gave *five* performances, each three hours long. That's because matinee sales
were better on Sundays than on Wednesdays.

In April 1983, after the tour had reached San Francisco, Yul
married one of the dancing girls from the London production

of *The King and I*; her name was Kathy Yam Choo, but she called herself Kathy Lee. She was eleven years younger than I, and I could not possibly have thought of her as a stepmother even if she had behaved like one; she had been in her early twenties when she became Yul's companion. The best man at their wedding was Mitch Leigh, with whom Yul had worked for almost a decade. I knew little about this young lady, except that Yul often boasted of her enthusiasm for sex.

So the company plowed across western America, as Yul played San Francisco and Salt Lake City for the fifth time. By September they were in Los Angeles. It was there he would give his four thousandth performance as the King, a record never equalled on the modern stage. A tribute, entitled *A Toast to the King,* was planned for the occasion—a gala soirée hosted by Dorothy Rodgers and Dorothy Hammerstein.

The day of his four thousandth performance, Yul learned he had inoperable lung cancer. Three hours later he performed the King's death scene as usual.

He had been a cigarette smoker at fifteen, back when he saw the fellow with the meerschaum pipe and decided to become a movie star. Every fan photo he'd ever autographed had featured a cigarette. When, as a boy, I told him about the dangers of smoking, he had waved my concerns away, warning me that he really didn't want to live to be an old man.

"Hey, Dad."

"Hey, laddie."

A long silence on the phone. I knew it was difficult for him to speak, so we confined ourselves to essentials.

"How do you feel, Dad?"

"I feel OK. The radiation therapy is very hard. It's actually burned out my salivary glands: so onstage I have to find ways of moistening my throat."

"How's your back?"

"Fine right now, the best it's been for years. It's behaving itself, so that my whole body can do battle with—you know, the other thing."

"For God's sake, Dad, aren't you taking the play off the road?"

"Well, yes, for a couple months. I haven't missed a show yet, even during the radiation therapy. But the insurance company isn't as sure as I am that radiation will work—together with the secret treatments from a doctor in Germany. So we're going to take a three month break, mainly to give ticket sales a chance to recover. When news got out that I have . . . this disease . . . it had a disastrous effect on the box office. In the first half of October, advance sales fell forty-one percent!"

"Well, Dad, people probably think you aren't going to want to go on performing right to . . . the end."

"Well, they're wrong. But we'll close the show at Christmas, to keep the payroll down. Then we'll start up a new tour again, as soon as the burning in my throat has eased off. From all the radiation, naturally."

"Dad, wouldn't you like some time for reflection, in your home, with family around?"

"There'll be plenty of opportunity for that, Rock. This isn't dying time yet. My new wife doesn't much like being in Normandy; she doesn't even speak French. And, of course, she knows that the house was part of another phase of my life."

"There have been so many phases, Dad. By the way, did you receive the letter my mother sent you?"

"Yes, I did. Thank her for the greeting, won't you? Explain how I have no time to reply, what with the performances and radiation treatment. I'm sure she'll understand. She never did remarry, did she? How long has it been since I last saw her?"

"Twenty-five years. No, she never remarried, Dad. She won't want to live much longer when the emphysema gets worse. She says she'd rather choose the moment than have the moment choose her, just like Charlie Wertenbaker said, remember?"

"I can't even imagine what you're talking about. Sometimes, Rock, it's as if you were on a different planet."

"Yes. Yes it is."

Just then, the stage manager made his ritual appearance at Yul's door. "Good evening, Mr. Brynner, may I call the half hour, please?"

"Yes, you may. Thank you." This was the only theater in the world where the stage manager had to ask permission to make the half-hour call. Soon Yul would limp painfully out to

the wings and take his place. Then for three hours he would
once again strut, stomp, snort, sing, dance, chuckle, command
and seduce, all for the four thousand and thirty-first time. By
now he had been playing the King for a total of twelve years.

At Thanksgiving the production closed down and Yul traveled
to Europe—first to a doctor in West Germany who had been
recommended by Edie Goetz, the elderly daughter of Louis B.
Mayer. This doctor was reputed to have discovered an extraordinary "vaccine" against the recurrence of tumors, based on
fresh carrot juice and other natural foods.

By January the doctors determined that radiation had effectively halted the spread of the cancer, and while the side effects
were often severe, Yul considered himself fortunate that che-
motherapy had not been deemed necessary. Within weeks, *The
King and I* was set to return to the road, starting in Baltimore.
Since the press had written extensively about his illness, Yul
decided to give a public party to announce that he had defeated
cancer. To make sure that the announcement was widely published, Yul invited his new friend Michael Jackson. Michael
had seen *The King and I* in Los Angeles, and become Yul's
most ardent fan. Yul returned the admiration, and visited Michael's estate in California. "I don't know why Michael feels
so strongly about me," Yul said to me offhandedly. "He seems
to think I am some kind of a god." Although Michael's schedule made it difficult, the young mega-star came to New York
for Yul's party at Studio 54. The national press obediently
reported that Michael Jackson had attended a party at which
Yul Brynner announced that he had conquered cancer, and was
going back on the road.

The following month the Hard Rock Café opened in New
York. I was its weekend manager. I had first introduced Yul
to the Hard Rock in London in the early 1970s: Not long after
my friend Isaac Tigrett created the Café with his partner, I was
manager. Now, at Isaac's prompting, I invited Yul to invest
in the New York venture: he pitched in about $25,000, and so
became partners with Isaac, Danny Aykroyd and others. In
March 1984, Yul flew from Baltimore to attend the opening
of New York's Hard Rock Café. He spent much of the evening

with Walter Cronkite, whom he had hardly seen in the thirty
years since they had worked together at CBS. He also spent
time with Danny Aykroyd, Eddie Murphy and some of the
other younger stars of the 1980s.

*As we sat there together at the heart of rock 'n' roll heaven,
I noticed Yul was staring at me. He smiled warmly when I
looked at him. "It looks to me," he said, "as though you've
finally found your place in the world, Rock." I stared back in
amazement: the Hard Rock was a fun place to be, but this was
not exactly what I'd been aiming at all my life. After the education I had had at his expense, in and out of school, Yul
wanted to believe this was the highest station I should aspire
to: rock 'n' roll maître d'. No, perhaps not. Perhaps he just
wanted me to feel that whatever I chose to do was good enough
for him. Like every parent, he wanted to have a simple answer
ready when friends asked about his son. Clearly, he preferred
to see me as the manager of a famous restaurant than the
author of a little-known novel.*

*The truth was that, in years gone by, my drunken madness
had left Yul few choices in dealing with me. When I was a boy
he had given me unlimited funds, not to mention the limo.
When I was a drunk, unlimited funding damn near killed me.
Yul was aware of my struggle for self-esteem, though he could
not entirely understand it; but at least he could see that self-
confidence required self-sufficiency. It's difficult to feel a whole
lot of self-respect when you aren't able to feed yourself. At the
start, for me, that meant busing tables and feeling proud of it.
By the time I was thirty, the routine was getting old. As the
son of the King, I inevitably had a powerful sense of failure
picking up my weekly paycheck as a short-order chef, made
out to Yul Brynner. My father could just dimly grasp what a
royal pain in the ass that was.*

*I should add that it had also become my habit to define
myself in terms of some larger entity, whether as bodyguard
to Muhammad Ali, or road manager for The Band, or Easy
Rock of the Hard Rock Café. It was not protection I was seeking
so much, perhaps, as the chance to recreate my sense of dependence. That dependence was exactly the tendency that al-*

most killed me. While Yul certainly did not want me to remain his satellite, neither was he pleased when I was independent enough to dissent from his emotional ruthlessness, or his élitist convictions. So, from the rubble of the great love between us, we had each built an invincible barricade. Is such unholy conflict between generations inevitable? Why do two people who are so resonant to each other punctuate a lifetime of mutual care to confront each other head-on over the very qualities they share?

I'll tell you the reason, won't cost ya a dime:

'Cause the young want more room, and the old want more time.

15

A Mortal God

"I make this in a warring absence."
—Dylan Thomas

With all the power he had left, Yul fought his cancer. It was a battle, for that is how he chose to see it. He used his considerable power of denial to interpret his temporary remission through radiation as the conquest of cancer. His imagination combined with his will-power to convince him that he would not succumb. "The Farewell Tour," which began in Baltimore in March 1984, was billed as the last year on the road, to be followed by a final four-month run on Broadway. At the age of sixty-three, and with inoperable lung cancer in remission, Yul went ahead with his partner and scheduled a further eighteen months of performance. By this time, Yul seriously considered giving fewer shows than eight per week, but "those parasitic bastards" at the unions made that just too expensive. So, terminal cancer barely changed his professional routine. After ten continuous years, it seemed easier to sustain the ritual of travel than break the pattern and return to his home. Suddenly to concede defeat and retire to Normandy in illness, alone with his young wife who spoke no French, isolated from the television shows he was used to, the medical attention he would require, and the few friends he still enjoyed seeing: that might prove even tougher than grinding out eight shows a week. He told one journalist, "Growing up in the Far East helped me. There was an idea that you go to bed not knowing if you'll have a tomorrow and you must be thankful for every tomorrow and make the most of it. It affects everything: how carefully you listen; how you taste things. I couldn't see myself going to bed and waiting to see what would happen with my illness. I preferred to play to two to three thousand people and standing ovations. The choice is quite simple.''

As often as possible, Yul arranged visits from his daughters Mia and Melody, as well as from Victoria in Paris. He was always gentlest at these times. He made a point of being soft-spoken when I visited with him in San Francisco, and again in Boston in September; of course, his lungs were still on fire from radiation. By now, his day was becoming so filled with medical rituals that, combined with six hours of make-up, performance and clean-up every day, there wasn't a whole lot of time for anything else. Make-up had become one of the hardest parts of the job for Yul: during the hour each night that he painstakingly reinvented the King's face while watching the evening news, he felt the full weariness and boredom of four thousand one hundred performances. It was also then that, surrounded by mirrors and bright lights, he was most aware of the changes taking place in his face and body. So it was in a melancholy moment while doing his make-up in Boston that Yul found my eyes in his mirror and said with a deep sigh, ''You know, Rock, the only time I'm ever happy now is on stage.''

While we were in Boston a wealthy friend of Yul's arranged for us to go sailing from Nantucket on his day off. Dad and I stood side by side for a precious few moments that could not last, wind and spray in our faces, just as we had stood on the decks of so many boats together over the years, from Connecticut to Acapulco, Cypress Gardens to Switzerland, singing ''Lazy River'': only once did we glance at each other, to make sure we were sharing the thought. A moment later we shared another: without a word, but beyond a doubt, we both realized that this was the last time we would ever be out on the water together.

Now all of Yul's intimate friends and associates were new-comers: everyone in his entourage was someone he had met in the last decade. His agent was a polished, elderly gentleman with a bedside manner and a chiropractic talent for manipulating egos. And by now Yul demanded that all the others in his immediate circle sound like skilled bootlickers: They were careful never to enrage him. His lawyer had only worked for him for a few years, but was nonetheless appointed co-executor of his will, together with Yul's young bride. These were the associates to whom Yul gave all his trust.

Yul was barely on speaking terms with Mitch Leigh, who had been best man at his wedding eighteen months earlier, and his partner for most of ten years. He relied upon his "team" for most contact with the outside world, even to find him an apartment to rent in New York. They found him a three-bedroom extravaganza in the Trump Tower, for eleven thousand dollars a month; although he was making well over a hundred thousand dollars a week, he was unhappy to be spending so much. Much of the time he felt tired and unwell, and the wallpaper really did not matter a lot to him at this point. He didn't much like spending time in this apartment, so we shared Christmas that year with my sisters at the Russian Tea Room, a few weeks before *The King and I* opened on Broadway for the last time.

The headline in the Sunday *New York Times* read "WHEN AN ACTOR IS TAKEN CAPTIVE BY A SINGLE ROLE." The article, published just before the Broadway opening, featured a full page cartoon of Yul as the King.

In 1884 the famous American actor James O'Neill [father of Eugene O'Neill], bought the rights to "The Count of Monte Cristo." The transaction merely formalized a sad reality: O'Neill owned the role and the role owned O'Neill . . . the part simultaneously liberated and enslaved O'Neill . . . it so fixed him in the public eye that he could never reclaim his reputation as a serious Shakespearean actor . . . Perhaps the greatest living example of this phenomenon is Yul Brynner. On December 26, 33 years after originating the role, Mr. Brynner returns . . . [He] has played on occasion to three generations of the same family—grandparents who saw the original production, parents who saw the revival in the late 1970's, and children.

. . . And there is a note of finality, of a circle come complete . . . Mr. Brynner has called it his farewell engagement, an unsettling double-entendre, given the actor's well-publicized treatment for cancer last year. Mr. Brynner says that he is in ''complete remission'' now as a result of radiation therapy, and he appears remarkably robust for a man in his mid-60's, muscular in the chest and arms, his voice deep and resonant.

Just before the play opened in New York, 60 *Minutes* interviewed Yul. Both Mike Wallace and producer Don Hewitt had worked with Yul in the late 1940s. At this stage of Yul's career, they were happy to give him another opportunity to tell the public that he had conquered cancer. But Yul also had an ulterior motive. During the interview, he declared that had he not conquered cancer, he would have made a TV commercial: ''I would have looked into the camera and said, 'The only reason I am dead now is because I was a heavy smoker. So to everyone watching I say, stop smoking now: you are taunting Fate.' '' If he died of cancer, he wanted that portion of the interview to be used for commercials for the American Cancer Society.

The official Broadway opening came on January 7, 1985, followed by a party three blocks from the theater, at the restaurant in which Yul was a partner, the Hard Rock Café. But that night, Yul had a very bad chest cold and almost no voice; at best, he sounded awful. It had been nine years since the night in Indianapolis when I had lip-synced the King, but this time I did not propose such a thing. He went on with the show, naturally, using the body mike more than usual, and skipping his soliloquy, ''A Puzzlement.'' I was still at the Hard Rock Café several nights a week, a worldweary presence strolling between the tables. That night, in honor of the premiere, sky-sweeping beacons lit the Manhattan skyline, and a trail of gold led from the theater to the restaurant. Mounted police guarded the path from the backstage door, just as Chris Forster had done back in 1951.

The reviews of the production were mixed, though the tributes to Yul were unrestrained. Frank Rich wrote in the *New York Times*:

> Yul Brynner's performance in *The King and I*—the longest running theatrical star turn of our time—can no longer be regarded as a feat of acting or even endurance. After 30-odd years of on-and-off barnstorming . . . Mr. Brynner is, quite simply, The King . . . Man and role have long since merged into a fixed image that is as much a part of our collective consciousness as the Statue of Liberty. One doesn't go to Mr. Brynner's "farewell engagement" at the Broadway to search for any fresh interpretive angles—heaven forbid! One goes to bow . . .
>
> The performance is ritualistic, all right, but the high stylization the actor brings to every regal stance, arrogant hoot and snarling declaration of "et cetera" has the timelessness of Kabuki, not the self-parody of camp.

But the review was hardly so generous toward the whole show.

> The production has declined steeply since its last, elegant outing in 1977. As perfunctorily staged by Mitch Leigh . . . staging and casting are throwbacks to the soupy, artificial operettas that Rodgers and Hammerstein had rebelled against . . . the lines are treated as inconveniences which must be disposed of as expeditiously as possible.

Yul couldn't have cared less: ticket sales for this limited engagement, which was due to end in May, were beating every show in town—even the hottest musical, *Cats*. And most critics agreed with the *New Yorker*: "Attendance is mandatory."

For the first time in many years I was able to spend several hours alone with my father every week. In his dressing-room during make-up, before he began concentrating for the performance, and before I began my evening at the Hard Rock. We were both very aware that we had not had much casual uninterrupted time alone, and likely would not have it again.

"Mom sends you her best wishes once again."

"Oh? How is Virginia?" He was applying the base make-up.

"She is very ill, Dad. She has pneumonia. After fifteen years of managing emphysema with exercise, it's all a little precarious, now." Two hours before curtain, he could not afford to consider this too deeply. *"Then why don't you go live with her?"*

"I proposed that some time ago, but she really doesn't want me in Santa Barbara caring for her: she'll end her own life before that happens. She was careful to write a Living Will so that she would not be kept alive artificially, by nasal feeding, for example. The doctors will often respect such wishes from older patients, regardless of the law."

"Yes, well, I've paid some of the most expensive lawyers in New York to take care of that."

"You have a detailed Living Will, Dad?"

"Naturally."

Relieved, I did not press further. *"Will you go back to Normandy in May?"*

"Certainly. There are movie scripts waiting for me, I must have a half-dozen projects back to back." But his voice expressed neither excitement nor conviction, and I thought, Oh, how tired this man is of the life he has made for himself. But that, too, was only part of the truth, for over the years, this was always his most melancholy time of day. Wasn't there anything that his only son could do to bring him a little joy? Apparently not. My third wife Susan had recently suffered a miscarriage, ending the hope that Yul might live to see a grandchild. Perhaps that might have made some difference in his life. Perhaps not.

"Dad, remember when I was seven years old, and I announced I would become a writer? We laughed about the book I would write about your life someday. That was the reason I always wanted to become a writer. Well, I still intend to write that book, Dad."

A short parade of memories marched across Yul's face and vanished. When he turned my way he half expected to see the little boy I had been, just as I searched his eyes for the father who once cared for me above all others. His eyes flickered briefly before his face sank back into a deadpan. The idea of *a book about his life might have posed a threat to his vanity, but Yul had always made it obvious that he really did not care what happened in his absence. "Sorry I won't get a chance to read it," he said nonchalantly.*

It's a tale as old as Telemachus, and as fresh as the Prodigal Son.

In April, Yul had to decide whether to run an extra six weeks with the play—until the end of June. Ticket sales were still strong, and he was offered significant financial incentives. He had known from the start that he would have this option, but waited until April to exercise it. He agreed to do it, and then regretted it immediately. Within twenty-four hours he began to suffer pain in his back unlike anything he'd ever known. Nothing would assuage it, and he began resorting to small doses of Percodan.

After a lifetime of watching my father do battle with pain of one kind or another, I knew this was a different dimension of suffering than anything he'd experienced: there was no rest from the sharpness of it, no way he could sit still and bear it. One evening when I arrived at his dressing-room an hour before curtain, Yul was on the telephone, nearly whimpering with pain, imploring his agent to find a way to cancel the final weeks of performance. But since Yul was his own producer, the cost of cancellation to him personally would have been monumental. Unless he bought back all the tickets they had sold, the thing could not be done.

Those weeks became an ongoing nightmare of pain and humiliation for him. He could barely walk from his dressing-room to the stage. His breathing became labored, and, from his back, the pain began extending to his lungs. He could not tell where it hurt him most: he could no longer sleep. Hardest of all was "Shall We Dance?" There were nights when Mary Beth Peil, playing Mrs. Anna, had virtually to carry him through the energetic polka as he moaned softly with pain. And he would stay in his dressing-room for more than an hour after the performance, until the last fan had left the stage door area. That was so that no one would see his bodyguards carrying him to his car. I could hardly believe what I was witnessing.

When I was a boy my father had taught me never to run from a fight; but he had also taught me never to fight a battle that could not be won. How much *money* could it be worth to endure so much pain, just to perform eight shows a week of a musical?

Finally, he actually missed several performances. It was a matter of some pride to him that he had never missed a performance, which was not quite true: he had missed a few in Chicago in 1954, and in Los Angeles the same year when his appendix was removed. But now the pain was so fierce he readily forgave himself for the half-dozen performances he couldn't do. "When I get to the theater, if I can't do the make-up, then I figure I can't do the performance," he told me. When rumors of his back pain appeared in the press, he posed for a cameraman doing a yoga hand-stand, which only aggravated his suffering. Those weeks of watching him endure his grotesque challenge dragged on for ever in the lives of everyone associated with Yul. This was not theater, it was a tragic masquerade of pain. I saw the play twice during those weeks, and found it unbearable. But looking across the rest of the audience, I saw only the faces of an enchanted and grateful audience that could not recognize his suffering.

In mid-June, the Tony awards for Broadway shows were given out. Because this was his third production of the same play, Yul was not eligible, but the committee honored him with a special Tony, which Mary Martin, Yul's first costar on Broadway, presented to him. After a long evening of winners who had thanked their families and their colleagues, Yul took the award with a smile and said, "I just want to thank Yul Brynner. He turned out OK after all."

A sign outside the box office read: "COME SEE YUL BRYNNER'S LAST SHOW! JUST $75, INCLUDING CHAMPAGNE WITH THE STARS AT STUDIO 54!"

The final performance had been ballyhooed for quite some time, but for his family and friends it was the conclusion of a protracted period of agony. There were few moments now when Yul was not preoccupied with pain, and they were short-lived: his suffering was more or less continuous, only lightly assuaged by painkillers and sleeping pills. That night, June 30, 1985,

Yul Brynner ended his career. It was his 4,633rd performance of *The King and I*. For much of the audience it was a transcendent night of theater history, followed by a quick glass of cheap champagne at a disco, where Yul appeared just long enough to wave. For those who knew the extent of Yul's agony, that night seemed as if it would be the end of his terrible torment.

It was not.

The next morning, after signing a new draft of his will, he left with his wife; he had just bought a fully furnished apartment overlooking the East River, but now he was anxious to visit his castle in France. Despite all the pain he was in, though, he actually made a short trip to Los Angeles first, to visit Edie Goetz, who had recommended a German cancer specialist. He gave Yul a revolutionary diet which would supposedly keep him, as well as Edie, cancer-free for years to come. He made the trip to see Edie, he told me, to fulfill a promise to her late husband, Bill, to whom Yul had pledged he would look after Edie. It was both touching and curious, because much of his life he had made no effort even to visit Edie across town.

But there was no rest from his pain, none at all. Trying to reach sleep, he was taking large doses of medication, and gradually that produced fearful hallucinations. To one family member who phoned him in Normandy Yul said frankly, "It feels as though I am already dead."

Six weeks after the play closed, Yul was back in New York. I went to visit him just before the doctors began treating him with morphine. His weight had dropped precipitously, and he could barely leave his bed. Now it was evident that the cancer was ravaging his body, probably destroying his spine, where most of his pain was concentrated—when he could even locate it. He could not escape the pain long enough to follow a news broadcast: his attention could not extend beyond the bed. The new apartment was unfamiliar, and his mood, that one afternoon, was of a desperate man, defeated by pain. From the moment I saw him, my greatest hope was that my father would die swiftly.

"I will see the doctors tomorrow, and they will give me morphine," he said slowly to himself. "My appointment is tomorrow morning at ten. That is just nineteen hours from now . . . I remember the last time I saw the doctor six weeks ago. I was so tough then, Rock! I was so strong, so brave about the pain. Ha! I had no idea the pain could grow so much greater. It's beat me all right. The pain has won, and I have lost. I couldn't even have imagined pain like that. Look at all the weight I've lost, laddie. The pain has just eaten me up with a spoon."

"There's no need for this much pain, Dad. It's not necessary. It should never have reached this stage."

"Tomorrow—tomorrow I will have morphine."

We sat quietly, though every few seconds he stirred with pain. It occurred to me that, in fact, this could well be the last time I would ever talk with my father, and so I clumsily interjected the things I wanted him to know most of all. That I loved him just the same as I had when I was a boy, because I had finally discovered that I really could love him without loving the things he did. I tried to help him reminisce about past triumphs, but his pain was too great a preoccupation.

"Dad, do you want to talk about your will?"

"Not particularly. I'm not that sick, laddie," Yul said weakly. "It's not dying time yet."

"That's why I brought it up now, to give you the opportunity to discuss it, so that the family might know what to expect. So that I might know what to expect."

"No, I don't, but I'll tell you this much: you will inherit my shares in the Hard Rock Café."

"That's wonderful, Dad. In fact I have good news for you about that investment. In eighteen months you've made more than one hundred thousand dollars profit on your original investment."

"Amazing," he said, eyes flickering with interest.

"That's more than it cost to raise me." I halfway meant it as a joke, but just then he was in too much pain to hear it.

* * *

The next day, Yul began receiving morphine for the pain in his back, as well as steroids to improve his appetite. He experienced immediate relief and invigoration, even though opiates increased the risk of a stroke. Before my next visit, Yul phoned and asked me to bring several quarts of ice cream from the Hard Rock Café. The morphine had actually cleared his head by removing the pain. Now he could converse, and watch television, and follow the boats navigating the East River below his window.

As we watched a barge execute the river's curves near the UN, we reminisced about the morning in 1953 when we had guided our new speedboat up the East River to the summer house in Connecticut. He did not ask about Virginia, and I did not mention that her health was failing as rapidly as his. But from his window Yul pointed down at 38th Street, where he and my mother had first lived together in 1941, over the dry-cleaner's. On Labor Day, September 2, I dropped by with more ice cream. Yul was chatting quietly in Russian to his cousin Irena, with whom he had grown up in Vladivostok. He was being maintained comfortably on progressive doses of morphine, and for several hours a day he was able and eager to talk with friends. He was so much better than he had been a fortnight earlier that everyone felt relieved. As I was leaving that day I mentioned that I had finally smoked my last cigarette.

"About time," Yul growled, as he kissed my cheek, and waved me off with a smile. Those were the last words I ever heard him speak.

Father,

It was night when the first stroke began sweeping over the left side of your body. You were able to talk when the ambulance picked you up, and when you were admitted to the hospit⸍. When your private nurse arrived and asked for an au⸍ you were in the middle of having a stroke.

Then you could no longer speak, and that ⸍ fell apart. Your entourage was utter⸍ Father: dependence had become⸍ scraggly group hoped bev⸍ again, until recoveri⸍

*important goal, but oh Lord it was not, not really. The simple
fact was that you were dying, not only from lung tumors, but
from the cancer that was found soon enough in your spine, as
well. Everyone wanted to believe the cancer was in remission.
Your cancer specialist, the "quarterback" of your medical
team, was in Europe. That meant that the only specialist who
could declare your condition terminal was unavailable. Until
he returned, you were to be treated as a stroke victim, instead
of a terminal cancer patient. And therein lay all the cruelty
and calamity. As you lay there, unable to speak from the stroke,
fighting pneumonia, with cancer wasting your body away, they
now exposed you to the worst pain of all you'd ever known—
infinitely worse than what you had suffered for months. Because
now, when you needed it most, they withdrew the only help
you had found for all your suffering: they took away your
morphine. That is the medical protocol for stroke. Cancer? Yul
Brynner had conquered cancer! Anyone who watched Sixty
Minutes knew that. As your suffering reached its most grotesque, the thrashing and moaning loud enough to be heard
down the hallway, your secretary winked reassuringly to me
and whispered in genuine awe, "He is a god."*

*Well, Dad, you spent most of your life proving that laws
which apply to ordinary mortals were not relevant to you. You
could fight harder, carry extra, sleep less, fly higher, eat more,
drink more, fuck more, and generally outdo every other son-
of-a-bitch that ever lived. You actually convinced the gullible
gajé that you had conquered the incurable. Remember, Dad?
You had people half-wondering if you were immortal. And each
night, while I struggled to sleep, you appeared before my eyes
as I stared aghast, helpless as Hamlet.*

*But there was no one to blame for your suffering. The
showgirl you married had studied the art of denial from the
world's greatest expert: yourself. She believed that you were
going to recover completely. You were so immense a presence
in her life that she just could not see you were dying. Two days
after you arrived in the hospital, when one doctor suggested
that all your suffering served no purpose, he was threatened
with litigation if he failed to take every heroic measure possible
to keep you breathing, at all costs. The neurologist was out of
town . . . doctors were afraid of a lawsuit, and your lackeys*

thought that you were an immortal god. So there was really no one to blame.

Nurses refer to pneumonia as "the old folks' friend," because it is a gentle death, by most reports. In your case, pneumonia set in quickly after the stroke, and you could have died less than forty-eight hours after you were admitted. Any heroic medical effort that could pull you through the stroke could only subject you to the much grimmer fate of dying from cancer, with no anesthetic. As tubes were inserted in your lungs to remove fluid, the presence of the tumors was duly noted. Still, Father, they would not let you die. To "control" the pneumonia, they withdrew the morphine. As a teenager you always found opium when you needed it, down by the docks. Now, on your deathbed, your highly paid medical team withdrew that same relief. For days, Father, your desperate, speechless, bellowing breath could be heard in the hall, as you suffered morphine withdrawal on top of the stroke and terminal cancer. That was the most awful sound I have ever known. Because I share your voice, I could feel your agony in my own throat; especially when they began performing a series of spinal taps.

Oh Dad, why wouldn't they just leave that bruised old body alone, to do what every mortal body does? This fight could not be won. Dying is exactly the right thing to do when you have done everything else. But under the circumstances, the doctors felt compelled to find out what was in your spine, and so they drained off spinal fluid. That was how they learned you had meningitis, on top of your cancer, pneumonia and stroke. They double-checked it with another spinal tap, until at last they found the metastases they were looking for. In the meantime, each tap meant a new fury of pain, followed by days of migraine. But of course, you could not speak.

You always thought you'd get through Hell in a hurry. All through your life you told me you expected to die young and burn in Hell. That was not just some barroom vanity. Doctors are professionally committed to keeping their clients alive; so are torturers. Your neurologist offered little comfort. "Can you assure me," I asked him, "that my father is not suffering?"

"I can assure you that if he were to recover," the doctor

replied, "he would not remember what he has experienced."
    It was not the same thing.

Week upon week this horror show, this charade of care, unfolded in slow motion. Yul was moved to a "more comfortable
room." The story of his dying days was not long kept secret:
anyone at the supermarket could glance at the cover of a cheap
magazine to learn of his "heroic struggle." The trash tabloids
pay hospital employees to report on the decay and demise of
the rich and famous. A stranger actually burst into the hospital
room with a camera to photograph Yul Brynner on his deathbed;
round-the-clock bodyguards were brought back on duty. Those
are the perks that come with standing ovations.

    He faded in and out of consciousness, experiencing islands
of lucidity. Sometimes he squeezed my hand while I talked to
him. Mostly he lay silent, with either Irena or the nurse sitting
quietly by his side. Then, suddenly, with his only useful hand,
he'd snap his fingers to get someone's attention. Day after day
he lay there, a speechless, suffering old Lear, and I his powerless Fool. He was rarely left in peace. "Stroke patients should
be surrounded by normal activity"—that was often repeated
by his bedside, because it made the cancer easier to overlook.
And so they turned on the TV. Sartre could hardly have
dreamed up a nightmare of such banality: as Yul lay dying the
TV played game shows, soap operas and ball games, and senseless chitchat prevailed. Only Irena could see what was happening, but she, too, could not understand the senseless
suffering that was being forced upon him. Week upon week
she sat by his side whispering in Russian, the language of their
childhood, for hours each day. The surrounding madness and
the helplessness of the situation made Irena ill for months after.
One afternoon, as a pennant game played on TV, Irena turned
to me and asked, "Are we in Disney World?"

*Finally your anguish was so great that, with your one good
hand, you tore the heart monitors off your chest, tried to pull
the intravenous needle out of your arm, and swung your fist
at the I-V bottle beside your bed. It was the only way you could*

express your wish to be disconnected from the machines that were keeping you alive. There was nothing that I could do to spring you from the trap you had made for yourself. Everything was exactly the way you had arranged it. My greatest regret is that I did not murder you swiftly, Father, there upon your deathbed.

Instead, I sat beside you and reflected upon the path you had forged with your life. I remembered the people and places that had meant the most to you, and I hummed "Okonchen Poots." And sometimes, in the very voice you gave me, I softly sang the words: "Up a lazy river by the old mill run, That lazy, lazy river in the noonday sun . . ."

Now it was October, a month since he had been admitted. Mercifully, he was no longer conscious. Hurricane Gloria struck New York, and Yul lived on: this King had already survived Halley's Comet. His wife was there regularly, and Victoria spent hours caring for him each day, along with Mia and Melody, who spent all the time they could with him. And others kept vigil near the room: his secretary, his agent, his lawyer, his accountant, his chauffeur and his bodyguards. Yul had not known any of them for more than a few years. His business partner of a dozen years was not even welcome at the hospital.

I started visiting less often, for now Yul was said to be "sleeping" twenty-four hours a day. At his bedside there continued to be some optimistic talk, but the medical staff was at last gingerly insisting to his young wife that Yul might not recover.

I held your hand as you died, Father. By then you were mercifully peaceful. Victoria was there, and your wife. After the nurse thought you had passed away, you suddenly took one last breath, teasing the gaje one last time. It was the first hour of the morning, October 10, 1985. Later, as I drove home, CBS radio began its news broadcast with "Shall We Dance?"

and the announcement that the prolonged battle had ended, and the King was dead.

Oh Father, that was no damn way for you to die.

Epilogue

> "I'd been told of all the things you're meant to feel.
> Sudden freedom, growing up, the end of depend-
> ence, the step into the sunlight when no-one is
> taller than you . . ."
> —John Mortimer, *A Voyage Round My Father*

Within hours the body that had swaggered across six continents was placed in a kiln and reduced to fine ash. Yul's powerful hands, from which my own were fashioned, had forever ceased to exist. My eyes were no longer like his, nor my lips, nor my voice, for now I am all that remains of our resemblance. The ashes were given to his brave young widow, and on the next day lamas from Nepal and Tibet came to his apartment and prayed from the *Tibetan Book of the Dead* with a handful of "friends and acquaintances." Frank Sinatra was not there, neither was Elizabeth Taylor, nor Bob Mitchum, nor Kirk Douglas, nor Michael Jackson, nor a single one of Yul's profes- sional peers: just agents, lawyers, studio executives and pro- ducers. Even my school friend Harry Dalton, who had worked for Yul for ten years, was too busy to fly in and I never did see him again; last I heard, though, he was still wearing those Gucci shoes. Liza, however, who has always been my closest ally, was at my house and by my side a few hours after Yul died.

In the middle of the night I awoke to the sound of my father's voice speaking directly at me from across the room. I had been in a deep sleep, with a bad chest cold, and I awoke very

*suddenly. It had only been a few weeks, and I was just coming
to terms with his death.*

*Yet this was no dream: it was the specter of the old King
himself, facing me, as he warned against taunting Fate.*

*"Dad?" I whispered. Then I understood. I had fallen asleep
with the television on. It was Yul's anti-smoking commercial
that had awakened me.*

*The cold sweat subsided after a few minutes, but it was hours
before I fell asleep again.*

For many generations, the Brynners have been practicing Chris-
tians: first Calvinist, then Russian Orthodox, the church in
which Yul was christened. But it seemed somewhat unusual
when Yul's widow and his lawyer—the co-executors of his
estate—held a Christian memorial service in Yul's hometown.
The event was curious for at least two reasons: first, because
neither of them is Christian; second, because neither Yul's
Catholic daughters nor his Christian son was ever even informed. The memorial service for our father was held without
us. A year later, by chance, I heard that my father's ashes,
flesh of my flesh, had been dispersed some time thereafter.
Three months after his death, a professional memorial was held
in a Broadway theater instead of a church, although most of
the speakers were television personalities. David Hartman,
Mike Wallace and Betty Furness spoke; each had interviewed
him. Mary Martin was also there, and director Sidney Lumet.
But I really don't know what was said, because I did not attend
the Broadway memorial.

One afternoon I picked up the *New York Daily News*, and there
I finally read my father's will, which the executors had refused
to show to the family first. That is when I discovered the whole
sorry truth with which Yul had concluded his extravagant life:
he had disinherited his own children. To the maximum extent
usually allowed by the courts, he had written everyone out of
his will and left his entire estate to the young dancing girl he
had married twenty-nine months earlier. He left each of his
kids one week's pay. Soon the national press and then the

international press reprinted this sordid news item. Yul had not bequeathed one single item to any of his own descendants. During his lifetime he had earned close to twenty million dollars. *People* magazine reported that Yul had made five million dollars just from *The King and I*. He had carefully bestowed paintings upon his lawyer and his agent, but left not even a memento for his own children. Shortly after Yul died, Yul's widow began selling off his property at an alarming rate: cameras, paintings, VCRs—et cetera, et cetera, and so forth. Most of my father's friends didn't realize she was selling property which she might have shared with his children. It was the kind of story you only heard about in other people's families.

Even beyond death, Yul had demonstrated that he could dispose of *any* sentimental bonding, and withhold his love for anyone at whim. The fact is that five years after his death, Yul's children have never been offered a single souvenir of his existence: not even photo albums of our own childhood. It is as if every last reminder of Yul's long life had been lost at sea. It seems I will never again play the guitar on which my father taught me, or hold the Academy Award that he had placed triumphantly in my hands, or treasure one of his many wristwatches. That's how Yul left things. In his sixty-five years, at one time or another, Yul cut himself off emotionally from his father, mother, sister, three wives, thousands of friends and associates, hundreds of mistresses, and now his children. Not surprising, really.

While it might seem more gracious to overlook the whole dismal subject, it is in fact the way Yul himself chose to end his long and tangled tale. Besides, it is hardly a family secret: as I said, I myself learned about it all from the *Daily News*.

Yul's conduct could have been remedied, had his executors been able to impose more generous or wiser counsel. But Yul alone is responsible for the mess he left behind. While he was in England in 1981 he arranged a special scholarship for a gifted student he saw on the news: but in his will he made no provision to help his seventy-year-old cousin Irena, who had cared for him from crib to deathbed. These facts remain. The principal legacy Yul Brynner left for his descendants was one of sorry bewilderment.

* * *

I left the Hard Rock Café, and enrolled at Columbia University to earn a doctorate in American history. It was several months before my mother reminded me that in the early Fifties she used to walk me to the playground on Riverside Drive, across the Columbia campus, about a million lifetimes ago. Many of my childhood friends and acquaintances had become second generation superstars—Liza, Pete and Jane Fonda, Carrie Fisher, Michael Douglas, Jamie Lee Curtis. Although I enjoyed acting, I always felt that I had other cats to whip, as the French say. So I chose not to exercise whatever acting genes I might have inherited.

In the next few months I discovered one thing I had inherited from Yul: his rage. With my temper set on a hair trigger, at the slightest provocation I erupted like Ol' Faithful, with hot vapor, alienating many acquaintances and a couple of fair-weather friends. At every inconvenience I bellowed and barked and hollered and ranted. Of course with all that thud and blunder, I sounded more like my old man than ever. That made me even more furious: all it took to remind me of my father's disaffection to his family was the sound of my own voice raised in anger at some stupid, clumsy slob waiting on tables—before reflecting that I too was once a stupid, clumsy slob waiting on tables. That only made me angrier; everything made me angrier. Finally I retreated from the world and, alone upon a mountain, I set out to understand a man who was determined to be great, without bothering to be good. After a few years I began to write this book, for which I had been preparing for all my life:

Most of all, I felt compelled to understand the legacy that had been handed down from our parish, Jules. Like my father, I acquired a code of masculine behavior that has produced a century of domestic grief, a legacy of emotional violence. Never once did a Brynner strike his wife a physical blow, and yet every cold-blooded severance produced psychological mayhem within the family. Abandoning women had come to seem like the *manly* thing to do. Repeatedly, the Brynner men have turned their backs on their families, and the anguish of each abandonment has resonated down the years. *This* was the power Jules handed down, by the example he set, to his son Boris

Yulievich and to his grandson Yul: the power to cut and run. Our saga began in the 1860s, when a Swiss teenager named Jules walked away from his family, never again to live in his motherland. He boarded a pirate ship, sailed to the Orient, and built a family in Japan, as well as a business empire. Jules disposed of that family forever, and resettled in Russia with his Mongolian princess, Natalia.

At about the same age, his son Boris abandoned Marousia and her children, just to marry Katya. That trauma hardened Yul's heart, reverberating through the rest of his life—and my own. Yul grew up in a world where it was a valuable strength to be unsentimental. The gypsies taught him that the world of the *gaje* is a cabaret filled with easy marks. Then Chekhov taught him to invent his characters through creative imagination instead of factual memory. Yul did just that, with his own character as well.

We each see the world through the lenses we grind: soon disdain toward all other people became Yul's second nature, and cynicism one of his wardrobeful of characteristics, along with naïveté, bravado, seductiveness and aggression. But once Yul became a world-famous star, humanity came to mean to him a hateful mass of pens and pencils and bald-jokes poked in his face, pleading for autographs. This was no paranoid delusion: for more than thirty years, strangers usually behaved very badly in his presence.

Virginia never remarried. She lived alone for almost three decades. Her life was busy and full: between Alcoholics Anonymous, Vedanta and the physical exercise that she needed in order to survive with emphysema, she kept herself that way. At home she maintained a continuous monologue with her cat, Tigger. That helped most to ward off the bursts of lonely grief that could sweep her away in a flash—and sometimes did for a few hours at a time—before she took control again.

After her bout with pneumonia, Virginia had taken care to write a thorough and explicit Living Will, detailing the medical procedures she would find abhorrent if doctors tried to sustain her life in the event of any terminal condition. Living on less than fifteen thousand dollars a year, she sought legal counsel

from national organizations and from one very special book,
Derek Humphry's *Let Me Die Before I Wake, Hemlock's Guide
to Self-Deliverance for the Dying*. For a year and a half she
struggled with the final stages of emphysema. Sixty-six years
old, she was obliged to wake up every four hours of the night
to pedal a stationary bicycle, like treading water, just to stay
alive another day. Frail and failing, Virginia was powerless,
and yet she remained completely in control of her circumstances.

Her death became imminent as soon as Yul died. Intense
emotion was the greatest peril to her breathing. I was not able
to warn her when Yul's will was reported in the press. That
almost killed her. She refused to be placed on a respirator,
because she knew she would not have the legal right to be
disconnected. Most of all, she fought to maintain authority
over the end of her life, sometimes quoting Charlie Wertenbaker: "I'd rather choose the moment than have the moment
choose me." Whether or not she needed urgent medical help,
she refused to be admitted to a hospital. Finally, she decided
that her next emergency would be the last.

I visited my mother for the last time a month after Yul died.
Remaining calm and matter of fact to ensure her breathing, we
reflected upon her life and the changes she had made in the
lives of others, especially through AA. Since she wanted most
of all to see her son laughing and happy, she rented a video-
cassette: we spent our last evening together watching *Beverly
Hills Cop*. The next morning we remained nonchalant, even
as we said goodbye for ever. Her health stabilized for three
more months, as she balanced cortisone against its side effects,
and visited her friends—she had a wealth of friends. Then in
the spring she began her preparations.

Virginia scheduled everything she would do, hour by hour,
during the last month of her life. She gave most of her belongings away to friends in AA and to other charitable groups.
She packed up her kitchen utensils. She organized her own
cremation, and paid cash in advance for the distribution of her
ashes at sea. She made all the arrangements for her own memorial, a simple service at the Vedanta temple. When we spoke
she never once hinted to me when she planned to die. She
wanted to make sure that neither I nor her friends would be

burdened. So she had her car serviced. She even filed her tax returns early that year. Having lived frugally for twenty years, and managed her investments cautiously, she had nearly doubled her capital.

On the last day of her life, Virginia laundered all her linen and packed it up for Goodwill. She threw out all the food that might spoil in her kitchen, and wrote detailed instructions explaining all the arrangements she had made. Her note ended:

> I'm sorry, Rock dear, you've had such a bitch of a year—but there is just no way I can go on—I can't get any better, only worse—more and more fighting for breath, and I am exhausted . . . You have played the hand you were dealt and played it beautifully . . . I love you, Mom.

She had given such thought to everything that her passing became almost a ritual of purification, like a tea ceremony. On the day she had appointed the vet came to her house and put her beloved old cat, Tigger, to sleep. And that night, with a well-chosen handful of pills, Virginia put herself to sleep. Less than six months after Yul's death, Virginia ended her life on Good Friday, 1986.

Well, Dad, time for the final curtain. You traveled such a long way from Vladivostok—how much more mileage could you have wished for? You made it pretty clear that, if you had had a few more years, you would have continued exactly the same way: playing eight shows a week. No, you had a full and passionate life, all right. About the only thing you lacked was contentment. We watched the same damn thing happen to a number of older fellows: those powerful men who swaggered through life, boasting how their wives couldn't tame them. Then, middle-aged and exhausted, they invariably threw up their hands and submitted completely to the domination of some younger lady. Who, after all, is more powerful: Napoleon with his army, or Josephine with PMS? But what was it exactly that had so exhausted these men? Was it really the women? Or was it not, perhaps, the swagger?

You lost the plot, Dad. In all your wanderings, with all your

*wives and concubines, you gradually lost sight of the goals
that had been the very engine of your early success, when
idealism, not greed, was the bonfire burning in your soul, when
you demanded of yourself the same standards of honesty and
consideration that you expected from others. That was the Yul
Brynner whom Marianne Moore saluted with her poem. But it
was not your idealism that the world admired, it was your
broad shoulders and basso voice. And, in the end, it was not
the romanticism of your masculinity so much as its explosive
violence that the public rewarded most. As your identification
with the authoritarian monarch grew more intense, the King
who had been your creature became your pitiless master. By
then, your whole entourage lived on eggshells, tiptoeing around
your fragile ego. And Dad, sometimes I'd swear you had yourself doing the same thing: once or twice while we were alone
your voice dropped to a whisper, as if to be sure Yul Brynner
didn't hear us. At the same time, it seemed that the whole world
was collaborating to confirm your delusions of grandeur. Oh
yes, even great men can suffer delusions of grandeur.*

*Power corrupts, and sunlight is the best disinfectant. When
power serves no higher purpose than self-gratification, then,
sure as God made green apples, power corrupts. The castle
began to collapse upon itself when you turned inward to the
dungeon of your soul, where that dragon of an ego dwelled,
bellowing for human sacrifices. With all that power, you could
not control your own willfulness. In that respect you were
neither unique nor unforgivable: though larger than life, you
remained entirely human, all too human.*

*There are many lessons in this parable of power, but only
one moral to the story: the talent for disposing of people is no
power at all, but rather, a failure of devotion. Every time you
lopped someone off your family tree, you became more insen-
sitive and self-involved. With each lapse of loyalty, with every
forsaken friendship, with all your threats of violence, and with
one damn bow after another as King, the dehumanization of
Yul Brynner advanced almost imperceptibly, in the name of
Art. It would be easy to suppose that the death you died was
the price you paid for the life you led. Too easy.*

*Well, how did I do, Dad? Was I honest? Did I tell the truth
mainly, like Mark Twain? Or did I distort the whole story out*

of bitterness or ambition, like Mark Antony? There I go again, like every father's son, still looking for peanut brittle. In truth, my loyalty to you has never dimmed, even when I was the only one shouting that the Emperor had no clothes. Any of the bootlickers in your entourage could have written a puff piece; I have honored you with the truth. Anything less would have done you no honor at all. I was neither Goneril nor Cordelia, but merely your Fool. Or, strip away the theatrics and I was just a little boy, and you were a loving father, until everything went awry. That's OK, Dad, now everything is OK.

I have searched my very soul to make sense of it all, now that I am the last of the Brynner men. Hereafter, with this chronicle complete, I am free to transcend the anger and pain, and simply celebrate the triumphs of your lifetime. Aloft, there is only love.

Adieu, old man.